PROFILES IN AMERICAN JUDAISM

Profiles in American Judaism

THE REFORM, CONSERVATIVE, ORTHODOX, AND RECONSTRUCTIONIST TRADITIONS IN HISTORICAL PERSPECTIVE

MARC LEE RAPHAEL

1817

Harper & Row, Publishers, San Francisco

Cambridge, Hagerstown, New York, Philadelphia, Washington
London, Mexico City, São Paulo, Singapore, Sydney

FIRST HARPER & ROW PAPERBACK EDITION PUBLISHED IN 1988

Library of Congress Cataloging in Publication Data

Raphael, Marc Lee.
  PROFILES IN AMERICAN JUDAISM.
  Bibliography: p.
  Includes index.
  1. Reform Judaism—United States—History. 2. Conservative Judaism—United States—History. 3. Orthodox Judaism—United States—History. I. Title.
BM197.R33 1984   296.8′3′0973   84-47734
ISBN 0-06-066801-6 (cloth)
ISBN 0-06-066802-4 (paperback)

88 89 90 91 92 HC 10 9 8 7 6 5 4 3 2 1

For Stanley F. Chyet

Contents

Preface

We begin our discussion of Judaism in North America with Reform Judaism, for its adherents first organized a union of congregations (1873), a rabbinical seminary (1875) and a conference of rabbis (1889). We turn next to Conservative Judaism, a branch of Judaism which emerged, largely in response to Reform, before carving out its own identity in the second and third decades of the twentieth century. Its rabbinical seminary began early (1886; reorganized in 1902), while its synagogue union (1913) and rabbinical association (1918) came later. Orthodox Judaism existed before either Reform or Conservative Judaism, and we trace its development from the eighteenth century, long before Reform Judaism appeared. But Orthodox's institutionalization, and vigorous assertion that observance, not just affiliation, is required, is a development of the twentieth century. The union of congregations (1898) and of rabbis (1902), as well as the creation of a seminary (1886; reorganized in 1915), put Orthodox Judaism in a position to build an organizational foundation and to respond to an increasingly Americanized Orthodox constituency. Subsequently, rival Orthodox institutions would compete for the allegiance of sectarian Jews who sought not to compromise with North American styles and values. We conclude with Reconstructionist Judaism, which only in the most recent decades became a fourth branch of North American Judaism with its own panoply of institutions.

John Loudon conceived the idea for this book, and Jacob Neusner provided me with the opportunity to write it. The chapters on Reform Judaism grew out of a seminar I offered at Brown University in 1981 and two lengthy conversations with Michael A. Meyer; they were improved by the careful reading and questioning of Anthony D. Holz. The chapters on Conservative Judaism emerged from a seminar I led at The Ohio State University, and owe much to the careful reading of David Spritzer and Jeremy Cohen. The section on Orthodox Judaism developed, too, from an OSU seminar, as well as from numerous conversations with Harold S.

Himmelfarb and Jeffrey S. Gurock. The latter patiently guided me to many sources I would otherwise have overlooked. My discussion of Reconstructionism was influenced by a lengthy conversation with David A. Teutsch. To all of these friends, and to Sharon LeBell, Kathy Reigstad, Dorian Gossy, and Linda Purrington, whose skillful editing greatly improved these pages, as well as to Clara Goldslager, whose interlibrary loan expertise made it possible to bring the manuscript to completion, I am very grateful.

My interest in American religious history received its first encouragement from Moses Rischin, then at UCLA, and subsequent stimulation from Stephan Thernstrom, also at UCLA. My decision to pursue the Jewish historical experience resulted from courses with Michael A. Meyer at The Hebrew Union College. All of these directions narrowed under the tutelage of Stanley F. Chyet, who, over the eighteen years of our friendship, has constantly supported, criticized, stimulated, and, most of all, enriched my understanding of the American Jewish historical experience. With abundant affection, I dedicate this book to him.

June 1984

PART I

REFORM JUDAISM

---

1. History, Ideology, and Institutions: 1810–1885

Reform Judaism, as a movement, had a rather clear beginning and historical context: early nineteenth-century Germany. But the early reformers, not surprisingly, vigorously argued that Reform tendencies had long been part of Judaism and that the movement of the nineteenth century merely developed these tendencies to their logical conclusion. And despite the apologetic zeal and exaggerations of these early reformers, with the dispassionate scholarship of a hundred and fifty years behind us we may safely argue that many of the characteristics we associate with Reform Judaism in North America have direct connections or, at least, affinities with developments in premodern Judaism and that the early reformers wove together many of these precedents.

It is surely an anachronism to conclude, as did one reformer in 1910, that "modern Reform was adumbrated at the early dawn of Judaism" and that the Talmud was "the trunk from which sprouted . . . Reform." Nor is it more correct to conclude, as did one Reform rabbi, that "Phariseeism must accordingly be vouchsafed a place among the Jewish reform movements." Yet interpretations of biblical laws, in the spirit of Reform Judaism, occurred by the earliest century of this era. Deuteronomy 15:1–2 states that "everyone who holds a pledge shall remit the pledge of anyone indebted to him." Thus the Pentateuch clearly states that the advent of the seventh year in the septennial cycle carries with it remission of all debts. But to encourage loans to the needy, to whom money might not otherwise be lent, Hillel accommodated the law to the conditions of everyday life by introducing a certificate, the *prosbul* (derived from the Greek *pros boule,* "before the council"), in which the creditor deposited a note with the court stating that a debt owed to him might be collected at any time the creditor chose. This *takkanah,* or decree, which Hillel ordained to enable the people to supply small loans even in the sabbatical year, typified the type of reforms of the ancient rabbis as well as the modern reformers, reforms where the spirit of the law, rather than the letter, dominated, and where the law was accommodated to historical conditions.[1]

The German reformers, as I shall note later, frequently were criticized by their more traditional brethren for their tendency to acculturate—that is, to adopt the external forms of their environment—in institutions and ideology. For example, when Israel Jacobson established the first Reform synagogue in connection with his school in Seesen, Westphalia (1810), his model was a Christian church. The reformers often responded by pointing out to their critics that such imitation occurred consistently in the medieval Christian and Moslem world, despite the verse in Leviticus 18:3 ("You shall not do as they do in Egypt . . . nor shall you do as they do in the land of Canaan . . . you shall not conform to their institutions").

Indeed, Abraham Maimonides, the son of the distinguished medieval Jewish philosopher Moses Maimonides, specifically excluded Moslems from this biblical injunction, and then proceeded to reform the worship by boldly recommending that a number of Sufi practices—including prostration, sitting erect, facing the entire congregation in the same direction (rather than along the four walls facing each other) during the entire worship service—be incorporated into Jewish worship. Synagogues in Moslem Spain were built in the style of mosques, and to adorn their synagogue walls the Jews employed verses from the Bible, written in elegant Spanish characters, in imitation of their Moslem neighbors who adorned their mosques with verses from the *Koran*. The best example was the synagogue of Samuel ha-Levi Abulafia, minister of Pedro the Cruel, built in the Toledo Jewish quarter in the mid-fourteenth century. Synagogues in Christian Europe were no less imitative, especially of churches and monastic refectories; the Worms synagogue, for example, imitated the cathedral of Worms. Whether in Spain and North Africa, or in Germany, after lengthy periods of such acculturation, such explicitly non-Jewish styles became known among Jews as "traditionally Jewish."[2]

A somewhat similar polemical argument, frequently used by traditional Jews against reformers, was that they made their reforms or changes out of an excessive concern for *Mah yomru ha-goyim,* "what will the non-Jews say?" Their argument was that—in contrast to themselves, traditional Jews who supposedly ignored outside opinion and only asked whether or not something was or was not "Jewish"—reformers were Jews bent primarily on following gentile public opinion in order to facilitate their eventual assimilation.

The reformers responded that concern for non-Jewish opinion and sensibilities had always been integral to Judaism. Maimonides himself, for example, the paradigm of Jewish observance, stated that it was not necessary (or even desirable) that Jewish worship have, in some parts of the liturgy, the silent reading of prayers followed by the public reading of those same prayers by the leader of the service (as today in traditional synagogues), but merely the public reading. Why? Because, since the congregants tend to walk about and chat during the repetition of the prayers, non-Jews who peek in and observe the lack of decorum might mock the Jews in public! So, the reformers would conclude after such examples, imitation of and concern for the opinions of non-Jews had always characterized normative Judaism.[3]

The most immediate symbol of Reform Judaism, just prior to its emergence as a movement, was the German-Jewish philosopher Moses Mendelssohn (1729–1786). Although enlightened, westernized Jewry traces its intellectual origin to this philosopher, this attribution is ironic. It is true that Mendelssohn worked toward changing those aspects of contemporary Jewish life that he felt prevented the individual Jew from gaining general acceptance as a Jew within the larger society (the same goal as Reform Judaism had a generation later). However, he believed that Judaism consisted of a special set of laws given to the Jews, through a supernatural revelation, at one place and one time. Thus while he provided German Jews with a program for cultural emancipation, he urged them to remain (like himself) completely observant of the scriptural laws, for he saw nothing to reform in Judaism. But as Jews increasingly found the ceremonial legislation anachronistic, burdensome, and without meaning, and developed a notion of progressive revelation, Mendelssohn became increasingly remembered for his efforts to liberate Jews and Judaism from its narrow intellectual confines.

In addition to his liberating efforts, Mendelssohn was applauded by the early reformers for his one specific reform. In 1772 the Schwerin Jewish community asked him, "Must Jews bury their dead on the same day they die?" (Traditionally Judaism said yes, but the Duke of Mecklenburg-Schwerin had issued an edict requiring his subjects to postpone burials for at least three days.) Mendelssohn sided with the civil authorities, who feared the burial of a seemingly dead but actually living person, and said "not necessarily." He broke with Jewish custom on this occasion not only on the basis of Talmudic arguments he brought to the discussion, but also on practical grounds as well (need time to notify relatives). And the reformers, who sought either type of support (if not both) for their changes, eagerly quoted Mendelssohn's process of reasoning. Precedents in the Judaic past, and the exigencies of living in the modern world, were the tools of the reformers' agenda.[4]

The precedents for Reform that surfaced here and there in the centuries before 1800 were but one factor in the emergence and development of Reform Judaism as a self-conscious movement. In addition, the absorption by German Jewry of the moral, intellectual, and esthetic values of the outside world; the estrangement from Judaism of significant numbers of Jews (conversion); and the role of the government in the process of Reform all played important parts in the rise and growth of the new form of Judaism.

Reform Judaism was solidly rooted in the optimistic faith of the eighteenth-century Englightenment. The Enlightenment, and its German expression (the *Aufklärung*), emphasized a firm belief in human progress and the ability of reason to promote such progress. Reason could bring men and women together by demonstrating that behind the different religious expressions there was a common faith—the religion of humanity. This religion distrusted irrational doctrines and repressive institutions, superstitions, and unreasonable authority. It was enough to worship a personal and good God, to believe he created a world that is getting better, to accept an ethical system whose precepts were as self-evident as the postulates of reason, and to make a clean sweep of those prejudices long darkening the emergence of a culture of universal reason.

Concomitantly, the Enlightenment placed an emphasis on polished manners, decorum, solemnity, and reverence in worship. It not only sought to expunge belief in devils, omens, ghosts, and much more that it viewed as irrational among the orthodox, but contemporary esthetic values also dictated a style of worship, dress, and behavior filled with dignity, order, brevity, and taste. Reform Judaism sought, in its earliest stages as well as when it crossed the ocean to America, to bring the externals of Judaism, the doctrines and creed of its faith, and the Jewish style of worship as well into closer harmony with the ideas and values of the *Aufklärung.* The Jews were now modernized in their habits and tastes, and they wanted their Judaism to fit them as modern people; they wanted to assimilate Judaism to the modern Jew.[5]

Many German Jews, inhaling the first breaths of the Enlightenment and Emancipation but painfully aware that their religion placed on them many *de facto*, and, in most places, still *de jure* disabilities, especially in career opportunities, chose the path of conversion. Others followed the same path not for political or professional advancement but because they found the Judaism of their ancestors—the only Judaism available in the 1790s and early 1800s—anachronistic, unenlightened, and unappealing. For these Jews, conversion to Protestantism represented the effort to find a faith that they believed was free of the mass of prejudices and ceremonies attached to traditional Judaism. Reform Judaism offered Jews seeking to remain Jewish but simultaneously enthusiastically wrapped up in the Enlightenment an expression of Judaism that abolished much of the Mosaic legislation that many German Jews found meaningless and utterly outdated and that they viewed as separating themselves from their environment. It offered, in the vocabulary of the times, an "enlightened" religion which sought to stem the tide of conversion to Christianity by Jews estranged from what they perceived as the obsolete rituals of Judaism and frustrated by the discriminatory practices of their society.[6]

The role of the Prussian government in the early history of Reform was significant too. Frederick William III, for example, like his father, viewed with ambivalence the proliferation of new sects within Protestantism, for their emergence demonstrated not only the vitality of the faith but also the possibilities of anarchy or chaos. As for the Jews, the government was equally ambivalent: on the one hand, it very much wanted to see the Jews assimilate, and an enlightened denomination might encourage this. On the other hand, it did not want to promote sectarianism of any kind nor see Judaism vital and vibrant—and Reform Judaism might provide this very attractiveness to a new generation of Jews and their children. So the Prussian government closed the Berlin Reform Jewish temple and forbade all changes and innovations in the ritual and liturgy. And later in the century the Prussian, Austrian, and Hungarian governments stopped Reform services. Yet at other times these very same governments felt that any form of Judaism that might wean Jews away from the traditions of their ancestors and improve their image in the eyes of enlightened Christians ought to be supported. In sum, a history of Reform Judaism in Europe is inseparable from the often active role of government authorities.[7]

The first Reform Jewish synagogue ("Jacob's Temple") was established by a layman, Israel Jacobson (1768–1828), a prominent financier and philanthropist, in Seesen, Westphalia, in 1810, and the leaders of Reform Judaism for a whole generation were to be business or professional men. Eyewitness accounts of the 17 July dedication, and Jacobson's dedication address itself, delivered in Protestant clerical garb, clearly enunciated the motivations of this first reformer: (1) to eliminate rituals, customs, and prayers that he considered unenlightened, unintelligible, and unesthetic; (2) to arrange the manner of worship to fit contemporary standards of beauty, dignity, and taste; (3) to demonstrate to Protestants and Catholics in attendance that Judaism was as progressive, modern, and enlightened an expression of the common religion of humanity as any other faith; and (4) to bring back wayward Jews into the religious community of acculturated Israelites. A worship service that included a German sermon, prayers in the vernacular, an organ, a choir led by a Christian, and a closing hymn by the Protestant writer Christian Gellert ("How great is the Almighty's Christian goodness") brought Judaism into concert with the universalism and rationalism of the Enlightenment.

Jacobson moved to Berlin in 1814, and he soon established Reform services in his home. Shortly thereafter, private services in the home of the wealthy banker, Jacob Herz Beer, especially for those Jews to whom the Hebrew of the traditional services meant nothing, were even more popular. These services, as in Seesen and later in Hamburg, were characterized by several changes in the traditional worship experience, including an organ (traditional Jewish worship had no musical instruments on Sabbaths and holidays), an abbreviated liturgy, vernacular German prayers as well as scriptural readings and sermons, mixed seating, choral singing, the alteration of some unacceptable references in the liturgy (substituting *redemption* for a personal messiah or *redeemer*), a greater emphasis on slow unison congregational reading, newer melodies, and an edifying and dignified address. In sum, when Jacobson spoke of "true religiosity," "pure reason," and "progressive enlightenment," in contrast to "thoughtless proper recitation" and ceremonies "offensive to reason," he stressed a philosophical rationalism and style of worship in harmony with contemporary esthetic values. These services continued until Frederick William III forbade them on 9 December 1815. A month later, reconfirming his edict, he explained that the synagogue, not a home, was the proper place for worship services and that sectarianism could not be tolerated.[8]

In Hamburg, about the same time, Jewish laymen were also adapting Judaism in an attempt to convince their co-religionists that the ancient customs and traditions need not remain unresponsive to modernity. The Hamburg Temple Association or Society (1817), a synagogue (the Hamburg Temple, 1818), and the first Reform prayer book (the Hamburg Temple *Prayer Book,* 1819), emerged in a rush; the latter featured German prayers, transliterations, the omission of words and phrases felt alien to the Enlightenment's spirit, the Sephardic pronunciation rather than the "harsh and guttural" traditional Ashkenazi, and was combined with a choir, organ, and vernacular sermon. Despite fierce rabbinical opposition from traditionalists, especially over the changes in the prayer book, much of what constituted Hamburg Reform—decorum, unison prayer, modern music, and an edifying weekly sermon—soon became commonplace in all expressions of Western Judaism, not just in the Reform congregations that spread throughout Germany in the 1830s and 1840s.[9]

This desire to reform traditional practices in the light of contemporary esthetic norms, and to be alert to non-Jewish sensibilities, echoes through-out North American Reform Judaism. Rabbi Joseph Krauskopf (1858–1923) of Philadelphia painted the following portrait of traditional synagogue worship, and indicated as well, in the following quote from an 1888 essay, the sensitivity to *mah yomru ha-goyim,* "What will the non-Jews say?"

> During the reading of the weekly portion from the [Torah] Scrolls, the women, who were inclosed behind the latticed galleries, apart from the men, being considered unworthy of worshiping near their fathers and husbands and broth-ers, gossiped freely; the men conversed and often carried on business transac-tions undisturbed; the children ran in and out; the uninitiated Christian stranger shook his head in misgiving when told that this constituted the Jewish mode of worshiping God.[10]

The struggle to establish Reform Judaism in Germany was to be re-peated in the "New World" with much success in a relatively short time. The earliest attempt at reformation occurred in Charleston, South Carolina, the cultural and commercial center of North America in the 1820s and the young nation's second largest Jewish community. The liberal spirit of the land, the absence of a vigorous and traditional Jewry to oppose reforms, and the desire, once again, to articulate a Jewish ritual in the idiom of the times for those who found the ancient ways no longer theirs—all combined to spur the first Reform Judaism movement in North America.

On 21 November 1824, a group of members of old Beth Elohim met to formulate a petition to the leaders of the synagogue. The resulting "Me-morial," sent to the president on 23 December, was returned on 10 Janu-ary 1825 with a letter noting that since it was contrary to the constitution of the congregation it was not debatable. One week later the petitioners established a Reformed Society of Israelites, drew up a constitution (signed by forty-three men) a month later, and set about to carry out the details of the petition. These included a weekly sermon in English, En-glish prayers, a commentary on the weekly scriptural portion, and a more solemn service.

The petition explicitly continued the pattern of Reform that had emerged already in Europe. When the petitioners mentioned a "reformation which had been recently adopted by our brethren in Holland, Germany, and Prussia," they had in mind the founding, and liturgical reforms, of Amster-dam's Adat Yeshurun (1796), Westphalia's Seesen Temple (1810), Berlin's Beer Temple (1815), and the Hamburg Temple (1818). As stepchildren of the European Enlightenment, many Charleston Jews had concluded that Juda-ism was, as the petitioners expressed it, without "decency . . . beauty . . . dignity . . . intelligibility . . . reason . . . enlightenment . . . [and]

understanding," and that it must offer a "more rational means of worshipping the true God."

The petition was also a response to the North American Protestant environment. The context of the Charleston petition was the eager expectancy, unbridled enthusiasm, restless ferment, and freewheeling frontier spirit of the period. "We are all a little wild here with numberless projects of social reform," Emerson wrote to Carlyle in 1840. The North American environment—with its absence of tradition and separation of church and state, the absolute sovereignty of the congregation, the heady freedom of the new land with its absence of social controls and its sense of individualism, nonconformity, and pregnant possibility—encouraged a spirit of experimentation. Successive waves of revivals and open rebellions against the Protestant ecclesiastical establishment by Shakers, Transcendentalists, Mormons, Unitarians, Millerites, Spiritualists, and the like left many people torn by a sense of anxiety and disunity.

Not only the challenges to traditional theological formulations that shook the churches, but the attraction of enlightened Protestant simplicity, brevity, dignity, and decorum, and especially the local upheavals in Charleston churches, provided the impetus for the petition. The Second Independent Church of Charleston broke off from the First Independent Church in 1817 over a doctrinal dispute, and the former church's minister, himself a Unitarian, had cordial relations with Charleston Jewry. Such upheavals gave the petitioners courage to present their demands, a sense of the justice of their demands, and the firm belief that they were, as their leader Isaac Harby stated, "enlightened descendants" of ancient Israel.[11]

The Reformed Society itself had but a brief existence, yet its influence was significant, for by the late 1830s Beth Elohim had itself moved in the direction of reformation. In 1836 the congregation hired a German-trained Polish Jew, Gustav Poznanski (1809–1879), to serve as its leader, and despite his traditional demeanor he offered no objections when some members of the synagogue requested both the letter and spirit of German Reform Judaism. The congregation voted to use the organ (albeit on alternate weeks), to eliminate some of the prayers not considered central to the service by the early reformers, and to have Poznanski deliver sermons in English—as the Charleston petitioners had demanded a decade earlier. Although it is an exaggeration to describe Beth Elohim as a Reform congregation, it did represent the first U.S. Jewish synagogue to take a few steps in the direction of Reform Judaism.[12]

Reform *vereinen* (societies), and then congregations, spread throughout the East and Midwest in the two decades following Beth Elohim's commitment to Reform Judaism. They included Baltimore's Har Sinai (1842), New

York's Emanuel (1845), Albany's Anshe Emeth (1850), Cincinnati's Bene Yeshurun (1845) and Bene Israel (1855), Philadelphia's Keneseth Israel (1856), and Chicago's Sinai (1861).

The extent of "reform" in each of these congregations varied, and it is not always clear at what point, prior to the emergence of a formal union of Reform congregations in 1873, to label a synagogue no longer traditional. At Baltimore's Har Sinai, created by members who resigned from the Baltimore Hebrew Congregation and formed the Har Sinai Verein in 1842, men and women did not sit together during worship, men wore head covering, and the dietary laws were observed, but the use of an organ and the ordering of prayer books from the Hamburg Temple seems to have given it the designation of the first self-declared Reform congregation by historians. But when? Even by 1855, when the radical reformer David Einhorn (1809–1879) became the rabbi, Har Sinai clearly had not become a "Reform" temple: the second day of festivals was celebrated through 1856, the ladies' gallery remained until 1858, and Einhorn himself retained *kippah* (head covering), *tallit* (shawl), and strict Sabbath observance throughout his rabbinate.[13]

New York's Emanuel, too, began as a *verein* and the synagogue emerged with only minimal changes in the traditional service: separate seating, monetary offerings at the reading of the Torah, and a standard liturgy remained. But with an organ and German hymns in the late 1840s and family pews, abbreviated prayers, elimination of second-day festival services, and English sermons in the mid-1850s, Emanuel too moved steadily, if slowly, in the direction of Reform. Cincinnati's Bene Israel, chartered in 1828, was, according to David Philipson, "strictly orthodox" until 1855, but even the "reforms" introduced in that year, and "attended with difficulty," were merely to improve decorum, while Bene Yeshurun, established in the same city in 1840, remained committed to the "wholly law of Germany"— that is, strict traditionalism—until at least the mid-1850s. Chicago's Sinai is a bit easier to date, for its 1861 platform, representing "theses" that its "rabbi," Bernhard Felsenthal (1822–1908), had articulated three years earlier, explicitly repudiated most traditional beliefs and practices. But perhaps Sinai ought to be dated to 1858, the year that most of its founders resigned from Anshe Maarav and formed the Jüdishe Reformverein (Jewish Reform Society) with Felsenthal. Felsenthal himself argued that "on this day [20 June 1858] the first foundation stones were laid for the Sinai Congregation; we are perfectly justified when we say that 20 June 1858 was the real birth day of Sinai Congregation."[14]

What features did the earliest congregations we call "Reform"— Charleston's Beth Elohim, Baltimore's Har Sinai, New York's Emanuel, Albany's Anshe Emeth, Cincinnati's Bene Yeshurun—have in common?

All five installed an organ and a mixed choir; all introduced confirmation ceremonies for boys and girls; all abolished the second day of festivals and substituted the triennial Torah reading cycle for the traditional one-year format; and all made changes in the liturgy, including eliminating some prayers and adding, in the vernacular, others. While in many other areas (family pews, wearing of hats during worship) varying positions were staked out, these several areas define the common features of Reform Judaism in the middle decades of the century.

With the growth of these Reform Jewish congregations in the mid-nineteenth century, congregations largely peopled by German Jewish immigrants already sympathetic to Reform, U.S. Jews sought guidance from the intellectual leadership developing in Germany. German-trained rabbis, many of them students of Abraham Geiger (1810–1874), the spiritual and theological leader of European Reform Judaism (and thus, in a sense, of North American Reform Judaism too), at the Hochschule für die Wissenschaft des Judentums (Seminary for Judaic Knowledge), began to look to America for employment, and congregations began to take a serious interest in rabbis, especially those with secular education and the promise of quickly learning to lecture fluently in English. In this way a German-trained professional leadership emerged to give both spiritual support and ideological development to nascent North American Reform Judaism.

Max Lilienthal (1815–1882), a native of Bavaria, was the first person with both a rabbinic and a university degree to settle in the United States. He arrived in New York City late in 1845, after abandoning a well-publicized project of reorganizing the Jewish educational system in Riga, Russia, and his appearance excited the German Jews of New York. Within a few weeks all three German congregations that had invited him to lecture (Anshe Chesed, Shaarey Hashamayim, and Rodeph Shalom) joined in electing him their rabbi; this union, however, lasted only two years before "pettiness and immaturity" brought its dissolution.

At the suggestion of Isaac Mayer Wise (1819–1900) in 1855, Lilienthal was elected rabbi of Cincinnati's Bene Israel, a traditional congregation, and served there until his death twenty-seven years later. A vigorous proponent of Reform Judaism, he quickly introduced moderate reforms at Bene Israel, culminating in his refusal, within days of his arrival, to officiate at Tishe B'Av (Ninth of Av) services, and the subsequent withdrawal of many Orthodox members. He argued that to fast and lament, as Jews had done for centuries, on this day of the anniversary of the destruction of the Jerusalem Temple by the Romans, was improper, for it ought instead to be a day of joy. The Romans, he argued, actually did the Jewish people a service, ushering in the Diaspora and the possibility of Judaism's world mission! Fiercely antinationalist too, Lilienthal rejected any Jewish return to Palestine: "here is our home; here our fatherland." Lilienthal introduced Wise's *Minhag America (American Ritual,* a revised prayer book in Hebrew, German, and English), the Reform prayer book; led the move to remove head covering during worship; and frequently preached in Cincinnati's churches the "truth which is at the foundation of every religion: . . . this doctrine of universal unsectarian love." He also assisted Isaac Mayer Wise in establishing both the Union of American Hebrew Congregations and the Hebrew Union College, and served as a member of the faculty at the latter institution. In addition, Lilienthal founded, and served as the first president of, the original association of U.S. rabbis, the Rabbinical Literary Association (1879). And he vigorously fought for the independence of religion from the state, courageously opposing the reading of the Bible in Cincinnati's public schools (1869) and traveling frequently to other states to lend his support to similar efforts.[15]

Isaac Mayer Wise, born on the Bohemian-Saxon-Bavarian border and briefly a rabbi in the Bohemian provincial town of Radnitz, came to the United States in 1846. Unlike Lilienthal, he lacked reputation and credentials. Aggressive and ambitious, however, he quickly became the leader of Albany's Beth El congregation. Whether or not he moved immediately in the direction of Reform is uncertain. Writing his autobiography *(Reminiscences)* in 1874–1875, he gave the impression that he wasted no time in "getting rid of all the medieval rubbish" and promptly instituted a number of reforms (a choir of men and women, elimination of many traditional prayers, especially those with references to a personal Messiah). But in a letter written at the time he served in Albany he noted that "the Sabbath was observed as strictly in the *Bethel* congregation . . . as in [very traditional] Wilna and Brody." Most likely, Wise introduced a few modest changes in music and decorum, and worked harder on mastering English, history, philosophy, and general Americana than at reforming traditional Beth El.[16]

By Rosh Hashana of 1850, however, Wise and the congregation's president came to blows (literally, and on the pulpit) and Wise and his supporters left Beth El and organized Albany's first Reform synagogue, Anshe Emeth, by the time of Yom Kippur. Little hard evidence suggests that this was a split of reformers versus traditionalists, but rather a struggle between lay and rabbinic authority as well as between two stubborn (and petty) people.

Anshe Emeth probably introduced modest reforms, including an organ and family pews, but in 1853 Wise was viewed as sufficiently moderate, if not traditional, to be hired as rabbi by Cincinnati's quite traditional Bene Yeshurun congregation. There, too, he seems to have introduced, at least initially, only the most modest of innovations, and even later, Wise noted, "reforms [took] place quietly." When the peripatetic journalist I. J. Benjamin visited Bene Yeshurun in 1860, he found men and women still seated separately and the *Siddur,* or traditional prayer book, still in use, despite the fact that three years earlier Wise and two colleagues had published *Minhag America.* [17]

Despite his moderation, Wise was clearly steering his congregation in the direction of Reform with late Friday evening services (initiated in the late 1860s) and other features that, especially by the 1870s and 1880s, became synonymous with Reform Judaism. Well before he died, Bene Yeshurun, or as most people called it, Plum Street Temple, was probably the most well-known Jewish congregation in the United States.

Wise's position in Cincinnati provided him with the geographical and institutional base, as well as financial support, to build Reform Judaism into the dominant expression of U.S. Judaism. He traveled up and down the roads and rivers to scores of cities, founding congregations and dedicating new synagogues, lecturing, and spreading the message of Reform Judaism wherever there were German Jews and their children. For nearly half a century he wrote, edited, and published the English language weekly, the *Israelite* (renamed the *American Israelite* in 1874), and the German language weekly, *Die Deborah.* He used the *Israelite* continually to call for a union of Jewish congregations, a U.S. rabbinical seminary, and a permanent rabbinical organization, as well as to give moral and spiritual support (and press) to Reform congregations all over the land.

Bernhard Felsenthal arrived in America in 1854 from Bavaria. In 1858, dissatisfied members of Kehillath Anshe Maarav in Chicago began meeting with Felsenthal as the Jüdisher Reformverein, and in that same year his *27 Theses,* and the following year his *Kol Kore Bamidbar (A Voice Crying in the Wilderness),* both articulated a well-developed ideology of Reform. Ordained by both Samuel Adler (1809–1891) and David Einhorn, in 1861 and 1863 respectively, Felsenthal and the *verein* formed Chicago's Sinai congregation in 1861, and Felsenthal served as its rabbi through 1864. From 1864 to 1887 he served Chicago's Zion Temple, and stood out as the staunchest "Western" supporter of Reform Judaism.

Felsenthal's *Kol Kore Bamidbar,* subtitled *Über Jüdishe Reform,* was a widely read statement of U.S. Judaism and, together with his other writings, made him a prominent spokesman for this rapidly developing religious expression. He articulated a vision of Reform's mission ("the distant future in which the whole of mankind will unite in one single grand temple of God"), of sorting out the eternal ("divine teachings [that] gladden the heart, enlighten the mind, and ennoble the spirit") from the external forms (the "dead weight of ceremonies which have lost all meaning"), "the spirit, not the letter." He also emphasized repeatedly the "absolute freedom of faith and of conscience for all"—a growing conviction among the leaders of Reform—and used this freedom to announce a bold vision of a self-governing Jewish state in Palestine. Based on "Jeffersonian principles of democracy," to be sure, it would be the "only means of bringing radical salvation to my suffering brethren." Felsenthal's commitment to Zionism would not be shared by most of his Reform colleagues for more than another half-century.[18]

David Einhorn, a battle-scarred veteran of controversies with the traditionalists during his rabbinate in Birkenfeld, Hoppstädten, Mecklenburg-Schwerin, and Budapest, led the radical wing of nineteenth-century North American Reform after he came to the United States and Baltimore's Har Sinai congregation in 1855 with a fully developed Reform ideology. In his inaugural sermon, September 29, 1855, he vowed to "emancipate Judaism" from "lifeless customs" and "mere outward forms" that "corrupt the inner life" and replace them with the "essence of the divine law"—the "religious and moral truth as expressed . . . in the decalogue of Sinai."

Einhorn fought verbal battles in America, as in Germany before, but in the New World they were primarily with moderate reformers, especially Isaac Mayer Wise, rather than with traditionalists. He and Wise carried on this deep antipathy in their respective newspapers: Wise in the *Israelite* and Einhorn in *Sinai,* a German language monthly he began in 1856 and continued through seven volumes. Einhorn also published a prayer book, *Olat Tamid (A Perpetual Offering),* in 1858, a book whose abbreviated services, German translations, many original prayers, and crucial deletions not only made it much more radical than Wise's *Minhag America* but also probably gave it more enduring value. Widely used, its liturgical arrangement and prayers were eventually incorporated into the standard Reform liturgy, the *Union Prayer Book.*

Einhorn, who had denounced slavery in a proslavery state, fled for his life to Philadelphia in April 1861. He served that city's Keneseth Israel congregation from 1861–1866 when he moved on to New York's German-speaking Adath Yeshurun—which, when it merged with Anshe Chesed in 1874, became known as Temple Beth El. He was a co-organizer of the Philadelphia Conference of 1869 and articulated impressive defenses of its Reform principles in German sermons and English writings through the 1870s. Primarily through his son-in-law and disciple, Kaufmann Kohler (1843–1926), Einhorn also deeply influenced the Pittsburgh Platform of 1885 and hence a generation or more of Reform Judaism.[19]

Not all the German-trained rabbis leaning toward or committed to

Reform emigrated, of course, and those who remained in Germany led the movement into its second stage of development. From a dominant concern with laity-initiated externals (revisions in the worship service), philosophers, theologians, historians, and rabbis—dominated by Abraham Geiger's universalist, scientific, progressive interpretation—now began to articulate an ideology for Reform Judaism. This movement took place in unpublished sermons and published essays at three rabbinical conferences (Brunswick, 1844; Frankfort, 1845; and Breslau, 1846), and at the synods of Leipzig (1869) and Augsburg (1871). The central themes that emerged, in discussions and eventually (1871) in the first platform, were (1) the dynamic, evolving, changing nature of Judaism ("progressive revelation" and "historical evolution"), (2) the need to "regenerate many of its ceremonies," (3) the necessity of subjecting Judaism to "earnest scientific research," and (4) the obligation of Jews ("messianic task"), in the words of Samuel Holdheim (1800–1860), to fulfill their mission "to make the pure knowledge of God and the pure law of morality of Judaism the common possession and blessing of all the people of the earth."[20]

In North America by 1880, German-trained rabbis imbued with such an ideology combined with the rapidly Americanizing German Jewish immigrants to clearly make Reform the dominant version of North American Judaism. By that time thirty-four Reform congregations had united in the Union of American Hebrew Congregations (1873), and the Hebrew Union College had been established (1875) to train Reform rabbis in the United States.

With numerous congregations, a union, and a rabbinical seminary to train rabbis for the congregations, Reform Judaism had begun to secure a place in U.S. society. Yet all was not well, and Barnett Elzas summed up what many have noted:

> [In 1885] Judaism was in a parlous state. The scientific spirit of the day was manifest in all the affairs of life. . . . Indifference to all things Jewish prevailed everywhere. Ethical Culture, Christian Science, Spiritualism . . . were winning an ever increasing number of adherents from within the ranks of Judaism.

As often happens, religious leaders respond in such times with doctrinal or credal statements of their faith. So, despite the warning by a rabbi of New York's Emanuel that "every fixed creed of to-day will be a dwarf to-morrow [and] every synodical edict of yesterday is to-day a deformity," nineteen rabbis gathered in Pittsburgh in November 1885 and hammered out an eight-point platform that one of the participants called the "Jewish

Declaration of Independence" ("independence" from rabbinic authority) and another considered "the most succinct expression of the theology of the reform movement that had ever been published in the world."[21]

Its antecedents in the ideological positions of German Reform (and, to a lesser extent, first, the Philadelphia [Reform] Rabbinical Conference of November 1869, where Einhorn's proposed set of religious principles was adopted with little change, and, second, the Cincinnati [Reform] Rabbinical Conference of June 1871, where Wise's resolution to establish a Reform rabbinical seminary and a union of congregations was affirmed) are everywhere evident. Yet the Pittsburgh Platform also accurately reflected late nineteenth-century North American Reform rabbinic thinking as well as the general expression of Reform in North America for decades to follow. The platform is quite properly designated as "classical" Reform Judaism.[22]

The Pittsburgh Platform states that Judaism is an evolutionary and progressive faith which changes in every age according to the "postulates of reason." Although constantly developing, it possesses an essential core of "moral laws" and a "God-idea," that is, ethical monotheism. Ecumenical in spirit, the platform views Judaism as one religion among many religions, sees no contradiction between religion and such "scientific" theories as Darwinism, and, as U.S. Protestants were doing, calls for a strong commitment to eradicate social injustices. The platform explicitly rejects all customs and ceremonies that do not "elevate," emphasizes that Reform Judaism is a religious confession and not a peoplehood or nation, articulates the notion of a mission, and rejects, in addition to ceremonies that "obstruct . . . modern spiritual elevation," beliefs that are not compatible with "modern civilization." Filled with a naive optimism about the inevitability of progress and, implicitly, the late nineteenth century as the age of the consummation of historical truth, the Reform rabbis in Pittsburgh, with their vigorous rejection of ritual, radically separated themselves from the rapidly increasing number of traditional Jews streaming into North America. In the decades ahead, or for more than three-quarters of a century, this attitude toward the tradition would dominate Reform Judaism and would enable its followers, in the words of David Einhorn, to leave "behind [them their] old home, the temple, and its sacrificial cult, the pomp of the sacerdotal services; [give] up the symbolism of the age for preparation for [their] larger historic duty; [march] forth to found everywhere temples of a truer worship and a deeper knowledge of God and to lead by [their] self-sacrificing devotion all mankind to the spiritual altar of atonement."[23]

The Union of American Hebrew Congregations

Isaac Mayer Wise's efforts to form an organization of congregations began with communications he sent all over the East and Midwest in 1848 from Albany and culminated in 1872 and 1873. In 1872 the president of Wise's Cincinnati congregation, Moritz Loth (1832–1913), a prosperous merchant, pushed the other Cincinnati congregations to issue a call to western, southern, and northwestern congregations "with a view to form a union of congregations." The conspicuous absence of the eastern congregations was an explicit rejection of David Einhorn and his "radical Reform" colleagues, such as Samuel Adler and Kaufmann Kohler.

Loth's goals were to establish and financially support a seminary to train U.S. Reform rabbis, to publish educational texts for children, and (the shadow of Einhorn was ever-present) to commit the congregations in the union to hire only moderate Reform rabbis. Loth's committee issued the invitation in March 1873, and in July, in Cincinnati, thirty-four western and southern congregations formally alligned themselves into the first association of American synagogues committed to religious goals: the Union of American Hebrew Congregations (UAHC). In addition to choosing Loth as its first president and having as its "primary object" establishing a Hebrew Theological Institute, the UAHC affirmed congregational autonomy from the start by agreeing not to "interfere in any manner whatsoever with the affairs and management of any congregation." This decision, already an established policy of Reform Judaism, continued to guarantee the maximum individual freedom for each synagogue and, therefore, to keep Reform congregations extremely diverse. What all these synagogues had in common was an affirmation of the right of each one of them to express its Judaism in any form it wished, or, as their joint constitution expressed it, there would be no "interfering in any manner whatsoever with the affairs and management of any congregations."[24]

Although the eastern Reform congregations had not been invited to join the UAHC, they had already formed a union of their own in 1859. The Board of Delegates of American Israelites, modeled after the Board of Deputies of British Jews, expended its collective energies not on Judaism but on the philanthropic, civil libertarian, and political defense needs of American Jewry. By 1878 it amalgamated with the UAHC and deeply influenced the UAHC in two ways: the greatly expanded UAHC took on the secular tasks of the board ("the civil and religious rights of Israelites") and moved steadily to the religious left—if not all the way to radical Reform, at least a giant step away from Loth's early attempt to impose moderate ritual or observance levels on rabbis and congregations. The enlarged UAHC—of over seventy-five congregations by 1879 and a council or governing body that met every other year after 1879—hoping to appeal to all Jewish congregations, sought to be as inclusive as possible.[25]

Hebrew Union College

Wise's determination to establish a rabbinic seminary had been as steady as his goal of a union. By 1854 he began calling for such a school; in an editorial he wrote, "We must have an educational establishment of a higher order to train up men who will be able to defend our cause, to expound our law, to inspire our friends, to silence our enemies, and to convert our opponents." He actually opened Zion College in Cincinnati on 26 November 1855—and closed it one year later. In 1873 an Indiana Jewish leader pledged $10,000 toward a seminary on the condition it would be established within three years; in 1876 the UAHC pledged to raise $60,000 for the school; and in October 1875 the Hebrew Union College (HUC) opened, despite mostly uncollected pledges, in the cellar of Bene Yeshurun congregation, with Isaac Mayer Wise as the first president. While it did not fulfill Wise's initial goal of being the only seminary serving all U.S. Jews, it surely prospered, and its first class (David Philipson, Henry Berkowitz, Israel Aaron, and Joseph Krauskopf) was graduated in 1883. The HUC remained the only successful rabbinical seminary in North America for many years, and even after Conservative and Orthodox seminaries emerged, it continued to be the only rabbinical school, with the exception of the Jewish Institute of Religion in New York (founded in 1922), training rabbis for Reform Jewish congregations.[26]

2. History, Ideology, and Institutions: 1885–1937

One of the rabbis at the Pittsburgh conference (Wise) had, for some time, dominated Reform Judaism in North America, while several others (Emil G. Hirsch, Kaufmann Kohler, Joseph Krauskopf, David Philipson) would strongly influence the generation of Reform Jews who inherited the Pittsburgh creedal statement. They and their colleagues, largely following in the footsteps of the German reformers, would articulate a vision of Judaism that gave detailed life to the doctrines of 1885.

We can grasp the depth of this vision, and the ideology of classical Reform, through a detailed look at the writings and sermons of Rabbi Jacob Voorsanger—rabbi of the largest and wealthiest congregation in the West (more than 500 families were affiliated with San Francisco's Temple Emanu-El in 1902). Voorsanger was also professor of Semitic languages and literatures at the University of California at Berkeley from the inception of the chair in 1894 until his death in 1908 and chaplain and annual lecturer in Old Testament in the department of bionomics at Stanford University. He founded and edited San Francisco's Jewish weekly newspaper, *Emanu El,* translated the books of Obadiah and Jonah in the 1917 Jewish Publication Society edition of the Holy Scriptures, and wrote several books. And he was on the boards of directors of many religious, philanthropic, and civic organizations.[1]

A descendant of several generations of German rabbis, Voorsanger was born in Amsterdam, Holland, in 1852. He came to the United States after completing his rabbinical education at the Amsterdam Jewish Theological Seminary in 1872. Voorsanger occupied the pulpit of Bene Israel Congregation in Philadelphia from 1873 to 1876, resigning when the congregation could no longer afford him. He "officiated on trial" as *hazzan* (cantor) and preacher in Congregation Adas Israel, Washington, D.C., in 1876, was elected, and remained there for one year. From Washington he went to Providence (1877–1878) and then to Houston (1878–1886), and in 1886 he accepted a call to San Francisco's Emanu-El as Elkan Cohn's assistant, became his successor in 1889, and remained Emanu-El's rabbi until his death in 1908.[2]

Voorsanger wrote for the *American Israelite* and for San Francisco's *Jewish Progress* under the pseudonym of Koppel von Vloomburg, edited the New Orleans *Jewish South* (1881–1883), and edited as well as wrote many features for the Cincinnati *Sabbath Visitor* (1883–1886). The latter was a rather large weekly for Reform Jewish religious schools and the "instruction of young Israel at large" and contained the first draft of Voorsanger's *Moses Mendelssohn, Life and Works*. He edited the *Jewish Progress* from 1893 to 1895, founded the *Emanu El* in 1895, and remained editor of the latter until his death. Voorsanger's "Weekly Chats" and published lectures, his European and national news coverage, and particularly his ability to convince the finest Jewish scholars in America to write articles for the newspaper, all combined to make *Emanu El,* during Voorsanger's lifetime, one of the most articulate weeklies in North American Jewish life.[3]

Voorsanger, unlike the great majority of his generation of Jewish preachers in the United States, did not shy away from political and other controversial issues. Following the vogue in other Reform synagogues, Voorsanger substituted the lecture for the sermon and attacked with frenzy, from the pulpit and in his writings, Zionism, open immigration, Orthodoxy, ritual, the Philippine War, imperialism, legalism, socialism, materialism, Edward Bellamy, Rabbi Emil G. Hirsch, the Democratic Party, and his local non-Reform colleagues. His sermons, or better, lectures, like those of Hirsch and Kohler, were intensely intellectual, consisting of elaborate exposition of scholarly themes delivered as a university professor might present a lecture to a class.[4]

Voorsanger's interpretation of Reform Judaism virtually rested on the Pittsburgh Platform; he agreed with Kohler that the 1885 declaration proclaimed "what Judaism is and what Reform Judaism means and aims at." On this well-constructed scaffolding Voorsanger put both feet forward.

> We hold that the modern discoveries of scientific researches in the domains of nature and history are not antagonistic to the doctrines of Judaism, the Bible reflecting the primitive ideas of its own age and at times clothing its conception of Divine Providence and justice dealing with man in miraculous narratives.[5]

The last decades of the nineteenth century witnessed the wholehearted acceptance of the Darwinian theory of evolution by progressive North American theologians, both Christian and Jewish. Isaac Mayer Wise, in public lectures on science and faith, agreed that "Whatever philosophy and science have overcome, is dead" and that "SCIENCE [and] PHILOSO-PHY [are] the eternal banner bearer[s] of eternal truth." Emil G. Hirsch (1851–1923) of Chicago's Sinai congregation felt that "The rhythm of Judaism's own progress beats an even measure with the thought of evolutionary theory." Voorsanger was influenced, according to his own words, by nineteenth-century critical biblical scholarship and by Darwin's studies in evolutionary philosophy; he strongly rejected any notion of supernatural revelation and magnificently adjusted Jewish theology to the accepted scientific theories of his day. "No man," he argued, "with a logical mind, finds any difficulty in accepting the law of evolution as a competent expression of the divine order of things." Understanding revelation, he wrote, means "removing from it all elements of supernaturalism," and he described Judaism as "divinely evolved" rather than divinely revealed. What then constituted the content of revelation? Revelation was the "natural process" through which thoughts of the divine were generated in people. Revelation in no way attested to the reality of the supernatural but merely to "conceptions of the eternal" and the "power of God in man." Examples of revelation, which appeared frequently in Voorsanger's sermons, included the "progress of the ages," the "march of mankind" toward monotheism, and the "operations of nature." Miracles, in particular, were "the voice of God." Whether "poetic representations of the slow-going processes of change," or, as he more frequently thought of them, "brilliant metaphors," he agreed with his Reform colleagues that miracles certainly were not "breaks in the natural order of the world."[6]

Miracles, Voorsanger felt, stimulated thoughts about God, and such thoughts had an evolutionary development paralleling the "gradual progress of the world's mentality." Man's thoughts of God grew to the extent that man revealed a capacity to understand; "as his intelligence grew so grew his God." Sinaitic revelation was "the last stage of an interminable series of mental struggles" among Israelite minds, and the understanding of this "human agency" clearly depended on human intelligence rather than God's "outpouring." Sinai then only became possible, Voorsanger explained, when our minds were ready, and it was the "purest form of human consciousness of God." Revelation too, clearly perceived, was the saga of the "growth of the human consciousness of God." To drive this concept deep into the minds of his contemporaries, Voorsanger—as did the Pittsburgh Platform itself—would speak only of the "Sinaitic evolution" (never of Sinaitic revelation) and of "progressive revelation." By the latter he meant a gradual but continuous growth in the Jewish understanding of the Deity from animism to a concept of a "pure Deity." The God of the people, obviously, remained the same, but the "Jewish mentality" was progressive. Thus the gradual perfection of human life revealed how much God grew in man's mind, for "as man grew so grew his God."[7] As the Pittsburgh Platform states, "We recognize in the Bible the record of the consecration of the Jewish people to its mission as priest of the One God."

Perhaps the most important doctrine in Voorsanger's conception of Judaism was his view of the mission of Israel, for here lay the basic justification for the preservation of Judaism in the Diaspora. Voorsanger, as did his colleagues almost without exception, could negate Jewish nationalism while affirming the need for what he called "complete assimilation" (except religious) into the North American fabric. Judaism was a "world-embracing system" and its mission, the spreading and the inculcation of "eternal truth," was "perpetual." This eternal truth, for Voorsanger and other late nineteenth- and early twentieth-century rabbis, was ethical monotheism (the "prophetic mission" and "universal prophetic Judaism"), of which the Jews were the "teachers." Leon Harrison (1886–1928), Voorsanger's colleague at Temple Israel in St. Louis, applauded the "mission" of the "Wandering Jews": The "historic mission of enlightening men's souls, of teaching them the Truth [ethical monotheism] . . . that bring[s] them together and make[s] them all a single human family." Monotheism's mission, Voorsanger felt secure in stating, was successful in overthrowing idols, and "Reform Judaism will continue to prove victorious in rooting up the remains of pagan influence."[8] As the Pittsburgh Platform states, "We recognize in Judaism a progressive religion, ever striving to be in accord with the postulates of reason."

Voorsanger's age was an either/or age: either rational religion *or* irreligion. He labelled both unethical and irrational religion *paganism*. The term was used not so much for the belief in a multiplicity of gods but for "irrational worship" and "unbecoming practise." To speak of God in human terms or even to define him was unbecoming: "the Bible contains not a single definition of God," and thus "in Judaism, God need not be defined." Voorsanger also agreed with most Reform thinkers that it was also irrational to suggest that God was in any way finite or limited, like His creation. And to pray, because God either demanded or willed it, rather than for human benefit, was "irrational superstition." Finally, to conceive of a God that rewarded and punished humanity for human behavior was anthropomorphic and "erring." In short, Voorsanger and his Reform colleagues argued as follows: (1) religion must be rational; (2) Judaism's historic genius was its "rationality" (ethical monotheism); and (3) reason was winning the struggle against paganism as the world moved toward "the growth of the brotherhood of man and the triumph of human goodness," the triumph of morality over materialism, and the time when, in Isaac Mayer Wise's famous phrase, "the pantheon of gods will bite the dust before Jahveh." *Emanu El* succinctly formulated this credo in announcing that it represented a "progressive, rational Judaism."[9]

Reform Judaism, Voorsanger insisted, most fully grasped the mission of Israel and was responsible for most distinctly presenting the theory of moral evolution. This presentation of the mission of Reform had been "adjusted," it was true, "in the light of its North American environment," but still remained true to "prophetic universalism and progress." This religious rationalization of evolution carried with it the uncritical assumption of the corollary belief in progress. Moreover, progress was at work in the religious and moral realms as well as in nature. Progress, Voorsanger confidently asserted, was real, and evolution provided cosmic sanction for trust in the ultimate triumph of good. And since the human mind was "eternally progressing upon the pathway of truth," Reform Judaism's mission was to "finish the story of perfection."[10]

Of this progress Voorsanger seems never to have had any doubt. The accommodation of liberal religion to the leading scientific philosophy of the nineteenth century—Darwin's theory of evolution—emphasized the ethical aspects of Judaism and linked moral and religious improvement to the current optimistic belief in progress. Voorsanger and his colleagues accepted the evolutionary hypothesis as a dogma, and strove mightily to bring Judaism into accord with it—thus reconciling religion to science (rather than religion and science). Joseph Krauskopf noted that "the world moves, and moves upward and onward. Mankind hates less, persecutes less, enslaves less, kills less today than it did in former times. Men are closer to each other, more helpful, tolerant than they have ever been before." Voorsanger's friend Rabbi David Philipson (1862–1949) claimed that the essence of Reform Judaism rested in the fact that "Judaism . . . passed through various stages of growth and development" to reach today's highest plane. Voorsanger himself quickly and effectively adapted traditional beliefs to the evolutionary theories, concluding that nothing in a strict formulation of the doctrine of evolution required him to abandon his creationism, and shifting his attention away from origins to formulating a world view fastened securely in the present and, less firmly, in the future. In their optimistic odes to the present, Krauskopf, Philipson, Hirsch, Wise, Kohler, and Voorsanger were joined not only by other Reform rabbis but also by Protestant clergy. The mood of the times produced a climate of "manifest destiny," which implied for most citizens that the United States would not only solve its most pressing social problems but would also dominate the future destinies of humanity. Reflecting the dominant Pollyanna mood of his North

America in his religious version of evolution, Voorsanger extolled contemporary progress: "I am witnessing the triumphant vindication of man's moral destiny."[11]

This concept of Judaism, viewed by Voorsanger as the principal legacy of the nineteenth to the twentieth century, was articulated with considerable concern for non-Jewish approval. Voorsanger hoped that a large number of Christians would be attracted to the synagogue by the "ideal of a pure religion," that the non-Jewish world would applaud a Judaism "neither secular nor partisan," and that a "universal ritual" would be so broad that the Christian could "join in adoration of the same God." The goal of such a concept of Judaism would be that the non-Jew "look on the Jew as a creature after his own image and likeness."[12] The Pittsburgh Platform announced that

> Today we accept as binding only the moral laws and maintain only such ceremonies as elevate and sanctify our lives, but reject all such as are not adapted to the views and habits of modern civilization. We hold that all such Mosaic and Rabbinical laws as regulate diet, priestly purity and dress originated in ages and under the influence of ideas altogether foreign to our present mental and spiritual state. They fail to impress the modern Jew with a spirit of priestly holiness; their observance in our days is apt rather to obstruct than to further modern spiritual elevation.

The mass migration of East European Jews to the United States, during the last two decades of the nineteenth century, provided a particularly strong influence on the thought of Reform rabbis. The former's traditionalism, or at least what the rabbis imagined to be their religion, continually agitated reformers, while the tendency of these newcomers to congregate in large numbers in eastern cities proved equally alarming. Additionally, Reform Jews' grasp of other contemporary issues, especially Zionism, was to be affected by their relationship to Jewish Orthodoxy.

Voorsanger—as did Wise, Philipson, Krauskopf, Kohler, Hirsch, and others—interchanged four terms in describing the Judaism of the immigrants: *orientalism, Talmudism, rabbinism,* and *Kabbalism.* Rejecting the messianic "Return to Zion," whether in its religious or political form, as a *"reductio ad absurdum* scheme," and viewing the North American existence of the Jews as the "most highly developed state of Judaism," Voorsanger looked on himself as an "American Israelite." His religious expression was attuned to that of the West, while traditional Judaism was a heritage from the East.[13]

One such heritage was Yiddish, the mother tongue of the immigrants; nearly all the Reform rabbis of Voorsanger's generation despised it. Yiddish was for them a "jargon" that "created a spirit of antagonism to American institutions." When Voorsanger noted that the *London Jewish World* wrote approvingly of the "revival in Yiddish" as a "literary tongue," he was angered. There is, he argued, "no greater drawback to the progress of the Jew in England and America than the clinging to the almost unintelligible German tongue."[14]

Traditional, "minute, soulless practises of ritual" were not only from the East but "meaningless, Oriental rites." These "dead branches on our tree of life" chained Jews to the ghetto, prevented the mind from exploring the influences of modern civilization, and made "Americans uncomfortable amidst Jews." David Philipson agreed, noting that "Judaism is broader than any forms, ceremonies, customs . . . and when they are no longer expressive of the needs of its worshipers they must pass away; they are not necessary for the preservation of the faith." Adolph Moses (1840–1902), of Louisville's Adath Israel, yearned for the "speedy abolition of time-honored and immemorial forms and ceremonies," for they were "mere dead-weight, clogging the spiritual progress of the soul." Rituals of the "Orientals and semi-orientals," Voorsanger preached, with a reference to the customs of both Orthodox and Conservative Judaism, were "senseless" and "irrational" and must be discarded. Reason, he argued, must be paramount and must be the yardstick by which rituals are measured. "Irrational, senseless Orientalisms" included such traditional rituals as tieing the strings of a mourner's shroud, throwing three spadefuls of earth on the interred remains, covering the heads of worshippers in the synagogue, kissing the mantle of the Torah scrolls, and even believing that God annually reviewed one's behavior on Yom Kippur.[15]

Rabbinism and Talmudism were usually reserved by Voorsanger to depict those that defended orientalisms, especially non-Reform Jewish teachers and traditional rabbis. Their most serious fault was the opposition they demonstrated to "modern progress," to "critical investigation," and to the "spirit of the times." They insisted on "laying their *Tephillim* [phylacteries] and kissing their doorposts" while claiming that "progress"—the favorite word of clergy at the turn of the century—was a delusion. Thus those traditional leaders represented "retrogressive forces." And one of their number, "a doddering idiot, of course," even had the audacity to "exhort his people not to send their children to the public schools."[16]

The "spirit of the times," for Voorsanger and other Reform rabbis, clearly called for assimilation—that is, eradicating all vestiges of orthodoxy and peoplehood—and Reform Judaism was the "instrument of assimilation." Traditional rabbis were "inimical" to such a spirit; therefore their "religion, their philosophy and their interpretations of questions of life are not ours." These same leaders "attempt to arrest the victorious march of progress" toward the assimilation of the Jew to his "dear native land" by making distinctions in public between Jew and non-Jew. It was rabbinism, too, whose pertinacity kept the Jews separate and secluded "when the time for segregation had long passed." Rabbinism kept the Jew in "darkness and seclusion," refusing to actualize prophetic universalism and "tear out the title page between the Old and New Testament."[17]

Kabbalism, although properly the subject of Jewish mysticism, was reserved by Voorsanger for his most hostile thoughts on the religion and the religious leaders of the East European Jews. Kabbalism was the "garbage of science," the distillation of "all the aberrations that disfigure our literary and intellectual history." It included Jews that mumbled their prayers, concerned themselves with clean pots and pans and this food or that, failed to take their heads out of their Talmuds, sought out *"ghetti"* for their residences, and insisted on what Voorsanger perceived as "rigid, unbending, intolerant legalism." Kabbalism represented the "embodiment of a dead tradition" or "excrescences," and thus "modern Jews" had "experienced a revulsion of feeling toward it." True Judaism, as Voorsanger understood it, was a Judaism "cleansed from the foreign coating that mysticism, isolation and the infusion of geographical ideas gave it." It was, in sum, freedom from a "galling yoke."[18]

In order to escape the yoke of Kabbalism, the East European Jewish immigrants would have to be moved out of their "reeking pestholes—the ghetti." The specific terms Voorsanger used for this program were *distribution* and *colonization*—terms also used by the Union of American Hebrew Congregations to give financial support to these efforts—but the removal of the immigrants from the crowded centers of orientalism was part of a large program called by Voorsanger "Occidentalization." A Judaism for North American Jews would have to be occidentalized—cleansed of its oriental features. Voorsanger continually urged such a program of cleansing.

The nineteenth century, which witnessed the emergence of Reform Judaism, also gave birth to the occidentalization of the Jew. Reform Judaism, which for Voorsanger was nothing less than a revolution against orientalism, restored to the Jew his "birthright" and "an honorable place beside his fellow critizens." It took him out of the ghetto, opened his mind to the influences of modern civilization and the language of his neighbors, and broke through the "trammels of legalism." North American Reform Judaism provided the fulfillment of the revolution against "rigid, irreconcilable, retrogressive Ghetto Judaism." There were, Voorsanger made clear, "but two issues in North American Judaism, Orientalism or Occidentalism, Reform or Orthodoxy, modern Judaism or Rabbinism."[19]

By the end of the nineteenth century, the occidentalized North American Reform Jewish community was "confronted by an invasion from the East" that threatened to "undo the work of two generations of American Jews." In the third issue of *Emanu El,* Voorsanger sounded the alarm by noting that he had warned the Occidental Lodge of B'nai B'rith: "A wave of orientalism has struck the country!" The 250,000 Jews in the United States of 1880 were joined by more than 1 million Jews during the next two decades. Voorsanger claimed that 700,000 had settled in New York City, 60,000 in Philadelphia and 60,000 in Chicago. These Jewish immigrants "herd together and refuse to scatter," and will soon create "not merely a New York Ghetto, but a Chicago Ghetto, a Boston Ghetto, a Ghetto in every city in the Union," including San Francisco. This posed a threat to both "Occidental spirit and culture" by opposing assimilation as well as by hostility to the "instrument" of assimilation: Reform Judaism.[20]

Fears of East European Jewish traditionalism, "visibility," as well as the hope of a rapid assimilation and Americanization, were major influences in shaping Voorsanger's and the Reform Jewish attitude toward distribution and colonization. But the compelling reasons were more subtle still; they revealed not so much the needs of the new arrivals as the needs of the spokesmen for these plans. Voorsanger urged not only that concentration of the immigrants should be utterly discouraged but also that "they should be made to understand that their distribution over the full length and width of the country would be salutary for themselves and less provocative of social and economic problems to their co-religionists." When Voorsanger spoke of the "settlements of Russian Jews scattered throughout the wide Northwest solving the Jewish 'question,' " the "question" he referred to was the possibility of the non-Jewish population failing to distinguish the assimilated North American "Israelites" from the "Yiddish-mumblers." With James Russell Lowell writing of "wretched street vendors" and "sly traders" and William Z. Ripley claiming that "an unalterable characteristic of this peculiar people" is to congregate in cities, the stereotype of the Jew was not one fitting the Yankee ideal of tough, stoic, pioneer breed. And not every San Franciscan non-Jew would separate, as the Brahmins curiously did, their Americanized Reform Jewish friends from the "morally degenerate" East Europeans. Distribution, colonization, and Occidentalization— that is, joining a Reform temple, were the most viable solutions to this dilemma.[21]

Voorsanger yearned for the "ultimate homogeneity" and unification of the Jews into "one great nationality" of English-speaking, public school-attending Jews. In a Thanksgiving sermon he dreamed aloud of a "million homogeneous American Jews" leaving the "seething and sickening centers of Slavic Jewish immigration" behind and assimilating. They would all then sing, with one heart, "God bless the flag with its increasing and refulgent stars, now and forever."[22] As the Pittsburgh Platform noted,

> We consider ourselves no longer a nation but a religious community, and therefore expect neither a return to Palestine, nor a sacrificial worship under the administration of the sons of Aaron, nor the restoration of any of the laws concerning the Jewish state.

The Reform movement, an outgrowth of the universalistic hopes of the Enlightenment and especially of the hope that the differences between people would disappear, possessed an attitude bound to become anti-Zionist. The new nationalisms of Europe, including the Jewish version, appeared retrogressive to most Reform leaders, for they denied, apparently, the universalistic vision. Thus antinationalism came naturally to the rabbis at Pittsburgh, even though the North American Reform notion (expressed in the platform) that the Jews no longer constituted a nation was not developed in opposition to Zionism. Indeed, the idea came eleven years before Herzl published *The Jewish State*. Zionism and Zionist activities were "Oriental aberrations" in Voorsanger's mind. His philosophy, reflecting explicitly the position of Reform Judaism as framed in the Pittsburgh Platform, tended toward a broad universalism; it saw in Judaism a prophetic call for humanity to strive toward a higher moral order. For Voorsanger, the Jewish people was a "spiritual concept rather than a physical reality." Israel's mission, he wrote in 1898, "is a spiritual one; its political aspirations are dead forever." The Jew was the bearer of a mission, and to exercise this mission to greatest advantage the Jews' dispersion among the Gentiles was a *conditio sine qua non*. Nationalism, especially in the form of Zionism, was for him a double contradiction: it violated the spirit of the universal mission of the Jew, which could only be achieved in the Diaspora (especially America), and it concretized a spiritual idea into political reality —a far cry from the supranational prophetic urgings of the Bible.[23]

Isaac Mayer Wise, Voorsanger's close friend and colleague, had developed this position quite clearly in the decade prior to the emergence of Theodore Herzl into world prominence. The charge that in North America Zionism was a creation of and supported only by "recent immigrants" from Eastern Europe appeared in Wise's writings as early as 1885. He continued to denounce this "Russian-Polish hobby," primarily as a threat to the North American allegiance of the German Jews, for the remainder of his life. These Zionists turned the "mission of Israel" away from its "universal and sanctified ground" to the "narrow and political." They are "phantastic dupes of a thoughtless utopia," and their movement was particularly upsetting to Americanized Jews striving to convince their fellow North Americans of their loyalty and patriotism, for it "confirms the assertion of our enemies that the Jews are foreigners in the countries in which they are at home."[24]

At a time when Americanization programs were trying to divest the immigrants of their culture and customs and to mold them into the prevalent stereotype of Anglo-Saxon Americanism, Reform Judaism felt that Zionism could only weaken the Jew's claim to United States citizenship and expose all Jews to charges of disloyalty, because, as Voorsanger put it, "Zionism persists in the segregation of Israel from mankind." Its nationalistic implications were a reflection on North American citizenship, and a Jew must have no attachment that would in a "special way distinguish [him] from his neighbors."[25]

Zionism, Voorsanger argued, demanded that the Jews of North America deny that "America is our Jerusalem." While he attacked the movement as "false, mischievous, and dangerous" as well as hypocritical, insincere, and irrational ("it is not merely folly; it is a crime"), he reserved his most scathing indictment for its challenge to the Americanization of the Jew. Americanization obviously excluded nationalism and a "separate political future for the Jews." Yet Zionism called for a political loyalty "above the starry folds of our venerated flag" and a "fanaticism that would immediately deny the claims of nation and flag." It maintained, Voorsanger argued, the "impossible doctrine" that the Jew cannot become domesticated in countries such as North America. This fear of a new nationalism agitated Voorsanger, for he viewed its emergence as harmful to the North American Jews and to Reform Judaism. He felt it would immediately raise the question of "double loyalty" or "intertwined sentiment"—something Americans could not understand. Hence it was a "dangerous doctrine," for it assumed the incapacity of Jews to "assimilate with their Gentile neighbors" and embrace North America. Instead, in the words of Emil G. Hirsch but with the conviction of Voorsanger, he felt that "my political dream is spelled . . . not by the star of Zion . . . but by the forty-six stars of Columbia."[26]

Zionism was also the "most extravagant perversion of the old prophetic ideals." It stated, as Voorsanger understood it, that the Jew had no home, and "American Jews deny this"; it announced that "the Jew hath no business amongst Aryans," and North American Jews did not believe it; and it denied the "wisdom that Sinai and Zion are to radiate throughout all the avenues which civilized man follows" and thus prevented Jews from becoming "homogeneous elements of all other nations." Voorsanger, as many of his colleagues in the Reform rabbinate, anticipated a new world of justice and freedom in which Jews would enjoy equal rights and privileges with all other citizens wherever they lived; Zionism declared that Jews would be strangers everywhere until they could reclaim their own homeland. Zionism repudiated "the prophetic ideals" of spreading the "Torah [to] millions, tens of millions of followers, who are not Jews," for the prophetic summons to Israel was a message of salvation to all the world. To return to the "tribal conditions of 5,000 years ago" was to admit that Israel "are strangers and sojourners before God and man." To assure his non-Jewish friends that this was merely "a dream," he told an Independence Day gathering in 1904 that "the Jews of America . . . are not in sympathy with Zionism. Even the rank and file of the various Zionist societies . . . have no patience with the Zionist platform." Reform Jews, therefore, were on a par with their fellow North Americans, differing only in religious faith. Other North Americans went to a house of worship on Sunday; the Jew on Friday, Saturday, or as we shall soon see, on Sunday.[27]

Voorsanger's conception of Jewish history, no less than his understanding of Reform Judaism, supported his anti-Zionist position. The history of ancient Israel and of the Second Jewish Commonwealth, he and Wise too argued, was essentially concerned with monotheism, not with political policy. The Jews of antiquity were busy with "prophetical policy" and with developing, maintaining, and preserving the "great truths that constitute the moral element in civilization"; they were "never politicians or economists." The prophetic function of the Jews would only be fulfilled in Western Europe, Russia, and North America.[28]

Jacob Voorsanger, like many of his colleagues in the reform rabbinate, was skillfully able to adjust Jewish theology to the accepted scientific theories of his day and the social configuration of his United States. The Americanization of Judaism by Reform Jews demanded greater emphasis on the developments in United States society than on the theological resources of Judaism. Voorsanger negated Jewish nationalism as a catalyst for Jewish life, choosing instead to understand the mission of Judaism as seeking full integration, save in religion, into North American society. With reason as his vigilant companion, he continually tested the fabric of contemporary Jewish life and never lost his optimistic faith. The result was the general rejection of all that stood between Judaism and the non-Jewish world. By surrendering its national aspects, Judaism would parallel Christianity as a religious sect pure and simple, so that Jews, like their neighbors, would be patriotic North Americans differing from their fellow citizens only in religion. Steering clear of all exclusiveness, couching his vision of Reform Judaism in an all-embracing universalism, and denouncing most Jewish customs and practices, Voorsanger brought the message of the Pittsburgh

Platform to large numbers of San Francisco Jews for almost a quarter of a century.

Voorsanger, Wise, Einhorn, Kohler, Krauskopf, Hirsch, and others were at the center of a controversy that agitated Reform Judaism for nearly a quarter-century and that had its catalyst in the declaration of 1885. Much earlier, in 1861, when David Einhorn became the rabbi of Philadelphia's Keneseth Israel, the minutes of the congregation reported that "Dr. Einhorn is very dissatisfied with the attendance in the synagogue and would expect more visitors to listen to his instructions." In subsequent decades, too, attendance remained a problem in synagogues almost everywhere, especially as economic pressures made Saturday morning worship a dilemma.[29]

Despite shorter services, an organ and choir, contemporary hymns, an English liturgy and lecture, and decorum and order, North American Jews in significant numbers stayed away from synagogues on Sabbath mornings. Furthermore, the Sabbath was being ignored by Jews not only as a day of spiritual rest but also as a day of physical rest. With North American society observing Sunday as the official day of rest, most Jews (Reform or otherwise), as most others, labored on Saturday. To both these dilemmas some Reform Jews sought a solution: replacing the traditional Saturday service, which occurred on a North American working day, with a Sunday morning service, or supplementing Saturday services with Sunday worship.

On the Sabbath issue, the rabbis who gathered in Pittsburgh in 1885 opened the way for the debates of the next two decades with their statement that

> It cannot be denied that there is a vast number of working men and others who, from some cause or other, are not able to attend the services on the sacred day of rest; be it Resolved, that there is nothing in the spirit of Judaism or its laws to prevent the introduction of Sunday services in localities where the necessity for such services appears, or is felt.

These rabbis were not the first, however, to make such suggestions, for German reformers, nearly a half-century earlier, had proposed the same innovations. At the Breslau Conference, for example, Samuel Holdheim argued that "the religious purpose of the Sabbath can be realized on some other day," in order to "save the Sabbath for Judaism, and to save Judaism through the Sabbath." And in North America, Einhorn had already quietly instituted regular Sunday services (worship, singing, lecture) at Baltimore's Har Sinai in the early 1870s, while Kaufmann Kohler, in a well-publicized 1888 lecture, claimed he too had conducted them for nearly two decades.[30]

But the first serious public discussion of a remedy for flagging attendance tied to the Sunday services statement of Pittsburgh emerged in the short-lived (1887–1897) Rochester *Jewish Tidings*. During 1888 this Anglo-Jewish weekly began to suggest a Sunday Sabbath, and then to publish its responses to negative reactions that appeared in other newspapers. Although the *Jewish Tidings* could identify only three Reform congregations with Sunday services (Chicago's Sinai, Baltimore's Har Sinai, and Philadelphia's Keneseth Israel), the paper's vigorous campaign for supplemental Sunday worship and (to a lesser extent) a Sunday Sabbath reached its peak in the early 1890s. Claiming to have the largest circulation among North American Jewish publications, the *Tidings* would regularly publish the results of its query of leading Jews on the Sunday service question. Typical was the response of Louis Marshall (1856–1929), the prominent Syracuse Jewish attorney:

> While I am firmly convinced that the observation [sic] of the historical Sabbath is one of the fundamental requirements of the Jewish faith, I know of no good reason why supplementary religious services on Sunday should not be encouraged. The most orthodox should not object to them, whether their purpose is to instruct the adherents to Judaism in religious history, morality or ethics, or to enable them to worship the Almighty; for services of a purely devotional character have been held by them on each day of the week from time immemorial. On the other hand, Sunday services, if properly conducted, would attract many who find it now impossible to attend to their spiritual wants on any other day. Something must be done to interest the present generation, in the history and traditions as well as in the religious doctrines of the Jewish people, if it is deemed of importance to perpetuate something more than a name, and a memory.[31]

By the late 1890s, supplementary Sunday services even emerged as a topic of discussion among the traditional East European Jewish immigrants who, in large numbers, labored six days a week just to maintain themselves in their impoverished circumstances. The most heated debate over the Sunday Sabbath issue followed a letter written by Judge Mayer Sulzberger (1843–1923) and published in the New York *Jewish Chronicle* in 1897. Sulzberger, a strong supporter of the emerging Jewish Theological Seminary (a rabbinical school to train rabbis for non-Reform congregations) and later president of the American Jewish Committee, directed his suggestion for a "Shabath Sheni" (a second Sabbath) to the "orthodox, Russian Jews" who, on the whole, emphatically denounced it. The reformers, of course, quoted Sulzberger endlessly in their polemical writings.[32]

The discussions of a Saturday and/or Sunday Sabbath reached their peak between 1902 and 1905 when they dominated the annual conventions of Reform rabbis. The debates focused on the issue of time, and the proponents of change argued primarily on three grounds: the North American economic and social environment presents Jews with a serious problem on Saturday, and since Sunday is the North American day of rest, why not add worship to the day of inactivity? They said that (1) the Sabbath is essentially an idea, a spiritual concept, and it remains an exalted notion whether acknowledged on Sunday or Saturday, and (2) a Sunday Sabbath would greatly increase attendance. Such arguments stimulated a significant number of Reform congregations to experiment with Sunday services early in the twentieth century. Most, however, rather quickly terminated such services.[33]

The reasons most frequently expressed for either not worshipping on Sunday or for ceasing such an experiment were (1) a Sunday Sabbath opens up the danger of conversion by such a drastic imitation of Christianity; (2) the traditional Sabbath day (Saturday) is not only a divine commandment but of great significance in its historical meaning and continuity; (3) late Friday evening services (about 8 P.M.) are beginning to bring Reform Jews back to the synagogue for worship. Less frequently heard in these discussions, but ultimately more convincing, was the realization by some far-sighted rabbis that the future growth of Reform Judaism would depend on the children of the hundreds of thousands of East European Jewish immigrants flocking to the United States, and the only way to win their affiliation would be to maintain the traditional Sabbath. Largely for this very practical reason of survival, the Reform rabbinical conferences only recommended encouraging Sunday *weekday* services, using the daily, not the Sabbath liturgy, and thus treated Sunday as they did Monday through Thursday. Weekday services were always encouraged within Reform Judaism, and there could be no more objection to a weekday liturgy on Sunday than any other time. By the end of the first decade of the twentieth century, although a number of congregations maintained services on Sunday as well as Saturday, rare was the Reform synagogue in which the Jewish Sabbath was celebrated on Sunday.

The Sunday Sabbath controversy was but one aspect of a larger trend within late nineteenth- and early twentieth-century Reform Judaism known as "Radical" Reform. Emil G. Hirsch, one of its spokesmen, and one of only two rabbis who refused to place a Torah in his congregation's ark, once sounded its clarion call: "I [am] the Minister of a Radical Reform congregation [Chicago Sinai]; . . . now the younger men have come; they speak English and dare follow the bold example of Einhorn, dare be aggressive." Radical Reform's background included the intellectual difficulties provoked by scientific discoveries, such as Darwinian theory; religious scholarship, especially in the areas of Bible and the origin, or comparative study, of religion; and profound shifts in moral and religious attitudes, particularly those resulting from the impact of positivistic naturalism and the thorough-going challenges to supernaturalism. This new intellectual climate not only created Radical Reform but produced radical solutions outside the established Christian churches as diverse groups revolted against the common understanding of Christian faith.[34]

A strong influence on most of the Radical reformers within Judaism was humanistic theism, liberal theology, radical religion, or what the French positivist Auguste Comte (1798–1857) called the "religion of humanity." One of the most important spokesmen for radical Christianity in North America was Octavius Brooks Frothingham (1822–1895), a popular preacher in New York City's Lyric Hall in the 1860s and 1870s and the author of *Religion of Humanity* (1872), but radical theology emerged in nearly every Protestant denomination in the late nineteenth century. Many theologians and ministers wrote and preached a universalist and humanist faith, an empirical and scientific naturalism, and there were a number of Reform rabbis, especially Radicals, whose discussions with and reading of their Christian counterparts propelled and sustained their own daring.[35]

The religion of humanity found permanent institutional expression in the Society for Ethical Culture established by Felix Adler (1851–1933) in New York City in 1876. Adler, the son of Rabbi Samuel Adler of New York's Emanuel, came to the United States with his father in 1857, taught Sunday school at Emanuel while attending and graduating from Columbia College, and returned to Germany to study briefly at the liberal rabbinical seminary in Berlin (the Hochschule für die Wissenschaft des Judentums) and to earn his doctorate (at age twenty-one) from the University of Heidelberg. Adler returned to the United States to teach briefly at Cornell University, but left Ithaca and his conservative Christian opponents to found the Society for Ethical Culture, an organization in which people of diverse religious backgrounds, who shared similar views about humanity's ethical responsibilities, might find a community. Only one other Radical reformer rejected his heritage as did Adler, who saw Judaism as a "stumbling block in the path of unification of the moral forces of man," but some of these men carried Judaism to a further extreme than simply a Sabbath on Sunday.[36]

Solomon Schindler (1842–1915) became "Reader, Teacher and Preacher," or rabbi, of Boston's traditional Adath Israel in 1874 and labored, for two decades, to introduce Reform Judaism to New England. He initiated not only family pews, English prayers, a choir, organ, and the Sunday Sabbath, but enthusiastically strove to eradicate the barriers that separated Christian and Jew. Schindler welcomed non-Jews to the synagogue so enthusiastically and openly that a Unitarian minister noted that "more than half [of the 1,000 worshippers were] Christian." Rejecting several of the tenets of the Pittsburgh Platform, including the existence of a personal God, while celebrating Social Darwinism, Schindler articulated his version of the religion of humanity: a faith of North Americans in which there would be a reconciliation of Christianity and Judaism, and a "religion of the future" that "will be neither specifically Jewish nor Christian." When, in order to effect this reconciliation, he encouraged marriages between liberal Jews and liberal Christians, the congregation had heard enough; in September 1893 Adath Israel and Rabbi Schindler parted ways.[37]

Early in the twentieth century Pittsburgh had a Radical reformer in J. Leonard Levy (1865–1917), who was an associate of another Radical reformer, Joseph Krauskopf of Philadelphia, from 1893 to 1901. Krauskopf, a member of the Hebrew Union College's first graduating class and himself in the tradition of David Einhorn, whose pulpit he occupied for three and a half decades, used his *Service Ritual* (1888) and its thirty different Sunday morning liturgies during the years Levy assisted him. This prayer book is entirely in English, except for one Hebrew sentence in each service to give it a "distinctively Jewish tone," and includes not only universal hymns by James Russell Lowell, John Greenleaf Whittier, and Joseph Krauskopf, but original prayers addressed to "Father of all" and filled with words that avoid sectarianism and exalt the religion of humanity.[38]

Rabbi Levy left Philadelphia and went to Rodef Shalom in 1901. He initiated Sunday services, not only to have a large forum for his lectures six months of the year but to "afford a meeting-place in which members of every religious denomination have been welcome." Like the other Radical reformers, his sources of inspiration were primarily non-Jewish authors and historic personages, about whom he lectured annually. Typical was his series of nine Sunday lectures on "Heroes and Models" in 1904–1905; in addition to one Jew, Isaac Mayer Wise, Levy chose Carlyle, Emerson, Tennyson, Parker, Ruskin, Tolstoy, and Lincoln as "prophets." Jesus of Nazareth was also a favorite topic of Levy and his like-minded colleagues, especially before large Christian audiences at synagogues, and Levy's thoughts in a 1905 sermon were typical of the rabbinical apostles of a religion of humanity: "We cheerfully respect and honor our brother, the Jewish teacher of Nazareth, as one of the glorious lights shed upon a darkened world. . . . I believe that such an attitude may tend to influence vast numbers in their endeavor to find a rational religion."[39]

Most interesting of all the Reform rabbis who at one time or another saw themselves or were seen as Radical was Charles Fleischer (1871–1942), the successor (1894–1911) to Rabbi Schindler at Boston's Adath Israel, soon to be Temple Adath Israel and then simply Temple Israel, and subsequently the founder and leader (1912–1918) of the nonsectarian "Sunday Commons."

Fleischer made Sunday services permanent in 1906; regularly exchanged pulpits with Unitarian and Trinitarian ministers; excited New England Protestants with his fusion of Judaism, liberal Christianity, and the Transcendentalism of Theodore Parker and Emerson; and introduced his congregants to the "religion of humanity" and the "religion of democracy." Fleischer steadily moved away from even Radical Reform: by 1905 he was writing that churches and synagogues were outmoded, by 1908 he insisted that Jews accept Jesus as the greatest of all prophets, in 1909 he announced that he preferred Emerson to Moses and also urged Jews to intermarry, and in 1911 he finally left Judaism (and Temple Israel) to "encourag[e] assimilation," to move "beyond sectarianism," and to establish a nonsectarian religious congregation. As Fleischer's Radical Reform melted into a "religion" of progress and American democracy, we see the fullest impact of religious liberalism on North American Judaism.[40]

The radical spirit of the Pittsburgh Platform was not simply confined to the small number of Reform rabbis who may be explicitly labeled Radical reformers but, at times, influenced the entire Reform rabbinate. In 1892 the Central Conference of American Rabbis (CCAR), only three years old and including in its ranks nearly every rabbi serving UAHC congregants, dropped circumcision (and any other "initiatory rite, ceremony or observance whatever") as a requirement for conversion to Judaism and approved cremation (traditionally prohibited). In 1897 the CCAR affirmed Isaac Mayer Wise's view that all the Jewish legal codes, on which the traditional foundations of Judaism rested, were merely "religious literature" and, in response to the emergence of an infant but vigorous Zionist movement, rejected (again) any attempt to establish a Jewish state. The Reform rabbinate also consented to circumcisions by surgeons, rather than by ritually qualified *mohels,* and eliminated the traditional *get* (divorce decree) and *ketubah* (marriage license). Even after the startling Balfour Declaration (1917) guaranteed British support for a Jewish homeland in Palestine, the CCAR rejected the notion that Palestine "should be considered *the homeland* of the Jews."[41]

Radical Reform, even at its peak, was not a dominant expression in Reform Judaism, and as the years passed its impact steadily diminished. "Mainline," or as some preferred to call it, "classical" Reform, characterized UAHC congregations, and this was largely a program of worship, education, and activity embodying the Pittsburgh Platform.

In the area of worship, with the publication of the *Union Prayer Book* by the CCAR in 1894 (see Chapter 3), worship services became overwhelmingly standardized. The *Union Prayer Book* immediately went to the fore, as did the popularity of late Friday evening services, even in the Midwest and South, where Wise's *Minhag America* had dominated. By 1905, a decade after the *Union Prayer Book* appeared, 62,000 copies had been issued and they were being opened in 183 congregations. In its revised editions—as heavily rationalistic as the first edition and the Pittsburgh Platform—it was virtually unanimously adopted by UAHC congregations.[42]

Cantors *(hazzanim)* were rare in Reform congregations, as was more than a minimal amount of unison singing (opening and closing hymns, a few responses), but congregations prided themselves on their professional choirs. Encouraging quality—without distinction as to religious affiliation—these choirs accumulated rich repertoires of (mostly English and mostly Protestant) hymns that led visitors to comment on not only the passivity of worshippers but also the stirring performances in the choir loft.

The Reform rabbi, in the decades after 1885, functioned largely in four spheres: administrative executive, counselor, teacher, and preacher. As an executive of leisure activities, he supervised the increasing number of cultural and recreational events taking place in the temples, including club and fraternal meetings; congregational dinners, dances, and parties; concerts; lectures; debates; readings; theatricals; Boy Scout and Girl Scout exhibits; and even gymnastics. As a minister, he heard congregants tell him of family tensions, career problems, marital tensions, and their understanding of daily events affecting the Jews. And as an educator, he supervised the religious school, taught the confirmation class, offered adult education courses, participated actively in community organizations seeking civic reform, and (more likely than not) lectured widely on Judaism in the religious and secular institutions (Christian ministerial organizations, general service clubs, churches, and schools) of his community. Baltimore's William Rosenau left a record of his duties during one typical year: in addition to teaching Bible classes and supervising the religious school, he delivered fifty-six sermons, gave twenty lectures, officiated at thirty-four marriages and thirty-five funerals, and made 637 visits with his wife and 1,122 by himself![43]

But more than anything else, the Reform rabbi prepared sermons (or lectures) for Sabbath eve, Sabbath morn, and holidays. Judging from the stenographically reproduced sermons of a score or more of these men, the sermon probably occupied more of the worship time than did the liturgy, and surely served as the focal point—for both rabbi and congregant—of the service. One rabbi, in fact, bemoaned this in the early 1920s:

> We are now in danger of making the worship of such minor importance as to reduce it to a mere routine. The people feel this and show it by the prevailing discourtesy of tardiness which lands them in their seats just in time for the sermon and often prompts their withdrawal immediately after its delivery.[44]

There is little indication, however, until well into the 1960s, that the Reform rabbinate began to respond to this situation.

At the 1934 convention of the Central Conference of American Rabbis, with the fiftieth anniversary of the Pittsburgh Platform approaching, some rabbis offered a resolution calling for a restatement of the principles of North American Reform Judaism. The resolution noted the "many ideological and material changes in Jewish and general life," and called for a "symposium re-evaluating the platform." This "re-evaluation," in the form of a symposium, did take place the following year, and to better understand its impact we ought to briefly explore the "changes in Jewish and general life" that had been occurring in the several decades prior to 1935, and on the eve of the reevaluation.[45]

The most basic change was demographic. In the thirty-five years prior to the United States' entrance into World War I, more than two million Jews from eastern Europe came to North America. Unlike the German Jews who populated Reform congregations in the nineteenth century, these Jews had no awareness of Reform Judaism prior to their arrival in the United States. Despite the breakdown of their familiar world occurring in eastern Europe late in the nineteenth century, these Jews were overwhelmingly "traditional." Their lives had been filled with precisely those customs, ceremonies, and rituals that the rabbis at Pittsburgh argued "obstruct rather than further modern spiritual elevation." And while neither they, nor their children, remained as observant as were their parents and grandparents in Europe, they were extremely reluctant to join synagogues where *tref* (nonkosher) foods were served, rabbis and congregants rejected *tallit* (prayer shawl) and *yarmulkas* (head coverings), Hebrew was hardly present in the liturgy, choirs (rather than cantors or congregants) sang English hymns (rather than Hebrew melodies), support for the political goals of Zionism was absent (and, frequently, every last trace of national allegiance to Palestine in the Jewish heritage was to be discarded), and the total worship experience—with its solemnity, decorum, and formality—was unfamiliar.[46]

Well before 1935, the leaders of Reform congregations realized that congregational growth would depend on the children of the immigrants, for of the several million Jews in the United States, the large majority were now of East European background. There was little chance of a common ground between the immigrants and Reform synagogues, but as the immigrants' children began to Americanize they frequently visited Reform congregations. Rabbi Martin Meyer (1878–1923), San Francisco's Emanu-El's rabbi, admitted in 1911 that "Frankly, the future of the Jew in American will be in the hands of the Russian-descended contingent . . . because of the preponderance of numbers." And another Reform leader, Cleveland's

Rabbi Barnett Brickner (1892–1958), noted in 1924 that "the masses of children of European Jewry [are] in a position to receive a message of reform." Bernard J. Bamberger (1904–1980), for many years rabbi of New York's Shaaray Tefilah, recalled that when he was a boy, his rabbi, William Rosenau (1865–1943), of Baltimore's Ohev Shalom, urged him to prepare for entrance to the Hebrew Union College by attending Orthodox services "so as to familiarize [myself] with the traditional liturgy." As the years passed, the second generation became more comfortable with an expression of Judaism much different from that of their parents and grandparents, and this was made possible by a gradual absorption into Reform of aspects of traditional patterns of Jewish expression. These included weekday afternoon study of Hebrew culminating in a Bar Mitzvah (a study of Reform Jews in 1930 found nearly half had no instruction in Hebrew), the introduction of numerous ceremonials in the worship service (marching with the Torah scrolls, chanting the *kiddush* (sanctification of the Sabbath wine), breaking a glass at a wedding, and much more), and an interest in minor (or ignored) festivals such as *Sukkot, Simchat Torah,* and *Shavuot.*[47]

Greatly aiding this process of integrating more tradition into Reform Judaism was the demographic change in the Reform rabbinate. A new generation of rabbis, themselves children of East European immigrants, helped bridge the gap between North American Reform and immigrant sensibilities. Rabbi Samuel H. Goldenson (1878–1962) noted, in a speech to the CCAR in 1924, that "today Reform Judaism in America at last is fast losing its German character, and the reason is that the new leaders are either American born or from eastern Europe."[48]

Moreover, the Hebrew Union College student body was changing demographically. A 1930 survey of the campus population revealed most rabbinic students to be second-generation East European Jews—strongly in favor of increased ceremonialism and sympathetic to Zionism. The HUC faculty too was undergoing change; Robert I. Kahn (1910–   ), rabbi of Houston's Temple Emanu-El, recalled that "when I came to Cincinnati [1927], most members of the faculty . . . were non- to anti-Zionist. By the time of [my] ordination [1935], most . . . were pro-Zionist." And the Reform laity was undergoing similar changes: a survey of forty-three Reform congregations in eleven large cities, conducted from 1928 through 1930, demonstrated that nearly 40 percent of the temple members now had East European parentage, and 19 percent of UAHC families were enrolled in a Zionist organization. As early as 1937, the UAHC convention in New Orleans made a plea to include in Reform services "traditional symbols, ceremonies and customs . . . the singing . . . of the *kiddush* [and] traditional Jewish Hymns by the congregation." It also resolved, in the face of events that have put "a large portion of Jewry . . . desperately in need of a friendly shelter," to put on record a strong pro-Zionist statement, culminating with the hope that "all Jews, irrespective of ideological differences, [will] unite in the activities leading to the establishment of a Jewish homeland in Palestine."[49]

The second, and fundamental, change was a combination of the growing commitment to Zionism within the Reform rabbinate and the awareness, by the mid-1930s, of the necessity to provide a haven of refuge for beleaguered German Jewry. Although he himself believed that "Reform Judaism is not bound up with anti-Zionism," Hyman Enelow (1877–1934), in his 1929 presidential address to the CCAR, admitted that "there is no denying that as a whole Reform Judaism has been opposed to [Zionism] and our Conference, representing Reform Judaism, has been opposed to it." Isaac Mayer Wise, a fervent anti-Zionist, unloaded a blistering attack on political Zionism following the first Zionist Congress (1897). Henry Berkowitz (1857–1924), a member of the Hebrew Union College's first graduating class, explained to his colleagues in 1899 that "I am not a Zionist[;] Zionism is sentimental and . . . chimerical." Adolph Moses of Louisville's Adath Israel, describing Zionism as "madness, folly, treason, and blasphemy," insisted that "we no longer are a nation within a nation; we no longer hope nor wish to be restored to Canaan; we are here to stay forever." The UAHC, at its 1898 convention, agreed with Berkowitz:

> We are unalterably opposed to political Zionism. The Jews are not a nation but a religious community. . . . America is our Zion. . . . The mission of Judaism is spiritual, not political. Its aim is not to establish a state, but to spread the truths of religion and humanity throughout the world.

Kaufmann Kohler, a militant anti-Zionist who served as president of the HUC for nearly two decades (1903–1921), dismissed pro-Zionist Caspar Levias from the faculty in 1905 and hired Max Margolis, "no Zionist." A decade later he canceled the scheduled appearance of an outspoken Zionist, Horace Kallen, invited by the student body. But whereas for years views such as those of Wise and Kohler dominated the rabbinate, and Reform rabbis had responded negatively to both the messianic hope for the reestablishment of the Jewish nation in Palestine and the more practical efforts of active Zionists, a gradual change had occurred.[50]

By the 1920s strong student support for Zionism emerged at the HUC; by 1928, in fact, the college was even prepared to award an honorary degree of Doctor of Hebrew Letters to Chaim Weizmann, the president of the World Zionist Organization. By 1923, Reform laymen, through the UAHC, endorsed the principle of Jewish settlement, and reconstruction, of Palestine. In fact, by the 1920s and even earlier, some of the leaders of the Zionist movement in the United States were Reform rabbis, including Judah Magnes, Louis Newman, Abba Hillel Silver, and Stephen S. Wise.[52]

Judah Magnes (1877–1948) served as the secretary—its chief executive officer and most influential spokesman—of the American Zionist Federation (1905–1908) during several years of his rabbinate at New York's Emanuel (1906–1910), and, after moving to Palestine in 1922, served as the Hebrew University's first chancellor (1925–1935) and first president (1935–1948).

Louis Newman (1893–1972), leader of New York's Temple Rodef Sholom for more than forty years, was a fierce nationalist who may have been the first Reform rabbi to endorse Vladimir Jabotinsky's militant Revisionism and who certainly was a vigorous opponent of Reform's anti-Zionist position as early as the 1920s. His denunciation of this position was merciless, as in this sermon he delivered at the 1927 commencement of Stephen S. Wise's Jewish Institute of Religion (JIR) in New York: "The most flagrant blunder of Reform Judaism is its opposition to Zionism. If it continues to be 'dead against' Zionism it will soon be entirely dead." Abba Hillel Silver (1893–1963), rabbi of Cleveland's Tifereth Israel (The Temple) from 1917 until his death, founded and presided over the Herzl Zion Club, a Hebrew-speaking group in New York, while still a child, and subsequently provided eloquent and vigorous leadership to North American Zionism for over half a century. He presented the case for a homeland for the Jews in Palestine before the General Assembly of the United Nations (1947). Year after year, beginning in the 1920s, Silver pounded away relentlessly at both the CCAR and UAHC positions on Zionism, and was the obvious choice to present the pro-Zionism position in the CCAR's 1935 symposium. Stephen S. Wise (1874–1949) was one of the leading American Zionists from the time of the First Zionist Congress (1897), and served both as vice-president (1918–1920) and president (1936–1938) of the Zionist Organization of America while the rabbi of New York's Free Synagogue from 1907 until his death. Although Wise was probably the most well-known North American rabbi at the peak of his career, he was much less involved in the CCAR than was Silver. Nevertheless, he was responsible for the radical decision of the CCAR to include (despite stormy opposition) "Hatikvah" (the Jewish national anthem) in the organization's *Union Hymnal*. And he had a powerful impact on a generation of Reform rabbis, especially through the JIR (Jewish Institute of Religion), which he founded and which eventually merged with the HUC.[52]

Despite men such as Magnes, Newman, Silver, and Wise in its midst, by no means was the CCAR or the UAHC even close to unanimous support of political Zionism on the eve of the Pittsburgh Platform's fiftieth anniversary. As late as 1935 the CCAR could only pass a "neutrality resolution" on the subject, while the UAHC did not support the 1935 resolution or the CCAR's 1943 resolution ("no essential incompatibility between Reform Judaism and Zionism") until 1946. And its leadership, three weeks after the birth of the Jewish state, greeted the event with the notice that "the Executive Board of the Union of American Hebrew Congregations takes no stand on the problems of political Zionism, nor does it intend to cancel or to minimize this attitude." There can be no doubt of the fact that among the Reform Jewish laity the preponderant majority of the leadership was anti-Zionist. Nevertheless, the general rise of anti-Semitism in the United States —the dissemination of the *Protocols of the Elders of Zion* by Henry Ford and the virulent radio addresses of Father Coughlin—undercut Jewish confidence in the United States as Zion, while the Great Depression caused many as well to reconsider the messianic mystique of the U.S. And the worsening of the situation in Nazi Germany shook the Jewish confidence in the achievements of Emancipation. All these developments convinced large numbers of Reform rabbis, on the one hand, to reconsider particularistic aspects of Judaism, and on the other, that despite their reservations about a Jewish state, the times required a strong statement on the economic, cultural, and spiritual building up of Palestine and its potential as a place of rescue for a growing stream of refugees.[53]

These developments of the decades since the Pittsburgh Platform—as well, perhaps, as the growing impact of Conservative and Reconstructionist Judaism (especially Mordecai M. Kaplan's influential *Judaism as a Civilization*)—led to the desire on the part of many rabbis to "reform" Reform ideology. At its 1935 convention, the CCAR "re-evaluation of reform" revolved around a variety of topics such as God, the Torah, and Israel, a symposium at which articulate spokesmen—some affirming the adequacy of the 1885 principles and others demanding changes—presented position papers and fielded responses. There is little indication in the presentations that change was inevitable, but the vigorous discussions after each lecture indicated that those rabbis who still felt that Reform Judaism was a religion, and a religion only, were a decided minority of the North American Reform rabbinate.

Samuel S. Cohon (1888–1959), Felix A. Levy (1884–1963), Samuel Schulman (1864–1955), and Abba Hillel Silver presented the most vigorous attacks on the Pittsburgh Platform and the need for change. Cohon, a professor of Jewish theology at the Hebrew Union College, spoke of the Platform's "infelicities, growing out of the dominant rationalism of post-Kantian thought and over-confident liberalism" and urged his colleagues to consider a new platform that would reject at least two of the Pittsburgh Platform's eight planks and acknowledge a personal, living God and the "thousands of historical and psychological ties unit[ing] the Jews into a peculiar people." Felix Levy, the scholarly rabbi of Chicago's Emanuel, also spoke of "historic continuity," scored the earlier generation of Reform rabbis for "neglect[ing] and despis[ing]" Jewish "particularism," and emphasized the role of the Torah in Jewish uniqueness. Schulman, the rabbi emeritus of New York's Emanuel, argued that the ceremonial law was "indispensable," and Silver argued that "nation, . . . land, and language were always vital and indispensable concepts in Jewish life," and that, contrary to the 1885 declaration, they were "indissolubly associated . . . with religion." With the fervor that these men brought to their presentations, and the cries of affirmation they received afterward, it perhaps came as little surprise to many of the rabbis to learn, when they assembled one year later, that a special Commission to Redraft the Principles of Judaism, chaired by Cohon, had been appointed, had met, and had ready a draft of a "Guiding Principles of Reform Judaism."[54]

The draft of the "Guiding Principles," after vigorous debate, was not approved, but the handwriting was on the wall. Rejecting a motion to dismiss the commission and dispense with its report, the CCAR endorsed instead a proposal to produce a platform, and instructed the commission to revise its draft. It did both, and when the Reform rabbis gathered in Columbus, Ohio, in June 1937, the "Guiding Principles" presented by the Commission, with only minor changes, were approved. But the approval, which signaled a strong statement about Reform's need to accommodate its East European constituency and to respond to Zionism, did not come easily.[55]

First, the commission had considered (and rejected) two additional sets of principles, drafted by others, during the course of the year. One of them, the "Statement of Principles for the Guidance of the Modern Jew," was the work of Rabbi Schulman, who headed the commission before his resignation. What the commission finally submitted, according to Cohon, was "the point of view of the average man of the Conference." By this he meant a balance between a strongly "nationalistic interpretation" of Judaism and a purely religious or "denominational" interpretation. In this, he and the commission were remarkably successful.[56]

Second, the commission had to listen to a number of attacks at the conference itself. Some members of the CCAR singled out individual plans for criticism; others preferred one of the two platforms rejected by the commission; and others, in what many concluded was the opposition's best hope, moved and supported a motion that would express abundant gratitude to the commission but would reject any platform. In fact, this strategy nearly worked: an 81–81 vote on the motion ended a morning session, and only after lunch did the rabbis learn that the president, Felix Levy, broke the tie by casting his vote against the motion to dismiss, with thanks, the commission. After the lunch break, the opposition again moved to not adopt the platform, and again suffered a narrow defeat (48–50); they then lost a move to postpone action for one year (42–46); and, finally, lost a motion to have the commission further consider the matter (43–46).

Third, the platform itself, or more specifically, each of its planks, had to be debated, and then approved or rejected, *seriatim*. The crucial vote, on the entire document, was by no means a foregone conclusion, for despite the strategies of the pro-Zionist rabbis, a sizable number of men were prepared to reject it for nothing more than its statement on Zionism and their difficulty in explaining it to their congregants or justifying it to themselves. Nevertheless, after the plank on Zionism carried, if only narrowly, 105 of 110 voting members approved the *Guiding Principles of Reform Judaism*. [57]

The *Guiding Principles* [58] are in three parts—beliefs, ethics, and practices —and the very title reminds us once again of the fact that these are not credal or doctrinal statements, but guides or recommendations. Just as an abundant number of Reform rabbis and congregations deviated considerably from the Pittsburgh Platform, so too no uniformity would be laid down for Reform Judaism in what came to be known as the Columbus Platform. Morris M. Feuerlicht (1879–1959), rabbi of the Indianapolis Hebrew Congregation for more than forty years, opposed political Zionism throughout the 1930s and 1940s, arguing that "Palestine is not the national homeland of the Jews." As late as the 1950s, Ferdinand M. Isserman (1898–1972), who served St. Louis's Temple Israel for more than four decades, opposed the Bar Mitzvah ceremony. Fifteen years after the Columbus decision, Rabbi Irving Reichert (1895–1968) could argue that "Judaism [was] a . . . religion, *and a religion only,*" and that "Zionism represented a retreat from the highway of Jewish destiny and achievement in America to the dead-end street of medieval ghettoism." And in 1943, by a vote of 632 to 168, Houston's Beth Israel congregation approved a resolution that not only reaffirmed the Pittsburgh Platform and repudiated the Columbus Platform but denied voting rights and elected office to all members who would not subscribe to the congregation's "Basic Principles." Both Reichert and Beth Israel, as did many other layment and rabbis, remained within the ranks of Reform Judaism because, despite Pittsburgh and Columbus, individual and congregational autonomy was always defended by the CCAR and the UAHC. The *Guiding Principles* were merely guides, no more. [59]

Part 1 of the *Guiding Principles*—beliefs—unlike the 1885 statement, stressed the particular, or unique, aspects of Judaism ("the genius of Judaism"). It had much to say about Torah (both the "written" and "oral," i.e.,

Hebrew Scriptures and Talmud), and its "unique insights"; noting that it was not only the product of a "continuing process" of revelation and "confined to no one group and to no one age," but that it remained the "dynamic source of the life" of the Jewish people. The *Guiding Principles* introduced, alongside Torah, another new concept, the Jewish People, which replaced the "religious community" of 1885.

True, Jews were bound together by a "heritage of faith," but by even more—a "common history," which expressed the Reform Jew's sense of peoplehood or common identity with Jews of other denominations. Finally, this sense of identity leads to an attachment to Palestine, and the Reform movement not only puts on the record its sense that Palestine is a land "hallowed by memories and hopes," but affirms its "obligation" to make it a "Jewish homeland." By this the rabbis meant that it should become both a "haven of refuge for the oppressed" as well as a "center of Jewish culture and spiritual life." This language, which some viewed as too mild (why not any mention of political goals?) and others as too strong ("Jewish homeland" represented the adoption of the Zionist movement's language), was the product of an extremely adroit tactical compromise. It clearly reversed the previous direction of Reform Judaism by embracing several elements of Zionism but managed to avoid a serious clash, which would have been disastrous, over the issue of nationalism.

Part 2—ethics—was an outgrowth of the strong commitment to social justice already demonstrated by the CCAR and the UAHC in the half-century since the Pittsburgh Platform's strong affirmation of Reform Jewish involvement in North American society. The demand for justice to "all, irrespective of race, sect, or class," introduced the section, and then at substantial length the document delineated a variety of pressing social issues in which Jewish assistance was needed, including the search for world peace through international disarmament.

Part 3—practice—together with the statements on Torah and the Jewish People in Part 1, revealed the extent to which Reform Judaism had begun to integrate aspects of the Jewish tradition, once discarded, into its ceremony and ritual. The emphasis was on Judaism as more than just a "religion" or a set of beliefs, for the rabbis gathered in Columbus in 1937 affirmed the centrality of Sabbath and festival observance in the synagogue and home, as well as the increased use of Hebrew in worship and study. While this emphasis did not, itself, radically change Reform Jewish ceremonies, it served as a catalyst and an indication of the direction in which Reform would be heading in the following decades. Even David Philipson, the only rabbi alive in 1937 who had been at Pittsburgh and who had faithfully defended the latter's platform until the final vote, understood that the *Guiding Principles* symbolized the end of an era of North American Reform. It was he, in fact, who moved their adoption at the end of the conference.

Institutions and Organizations

The Union of American Hebrew Congregations

In the half-century following the adoption of the Pittsburgh Platform, the Union of American Hebrew Congregations, still a lay organization of Reform Jewish congregants, steadily grew in congregations and departments. From 34 at its origin in 1873, it grew to more than 200 congregations in 1920 and nearly 300 by 1930 (see Table 1). Its Department of Synagog and School Extension, established early in the century, initially sought to create congregations and religious schools in smaller Jewish communities or in isolated sections of the land, and later expanded to serve various groups of Jews (prisoners, students, and those institutionalized as well as Jewish vacationers at popular summer resorts) who could not be organized into congregations, and to distribute informational releases (brief descriptions of a holiday, for example, to morning and evening newspapers) around the country.

The Committee on Circuit Preaching, established in 1895, arranged for rabbis to make visits—for worship and religious education—to small towns approximately every other month, while the Board of Delegates on Civil and Religious Rights sought to defend North American Jews against defamatory attacks and to aid overseas Jewry. The Committee of Social Justice, recreated in 1929 to aid "those who are struggling for more equitable and just conditions of life in fields of industry, commerce and social relations," continued the UAHC practice of taking vigorous (and sometimes bold) positions on issues affecting not only beleaguered Jews in Europe and elsewhere but on such domestic issues as child labor legislation, registration of aliens, release of political prisoners, and lynchings. The Commission on Jewish Education, which by the 1920s and 1930s, under the guidance of Dr. Emanuel Gamoran (1895–1962), was publishing books for nearly every grade level of Reform religious schools, together with the National Federation of Temple Sisterhoods (founded in 1913) and National Federation of Temple Brotherhoods (founded in 1923), both of which established religious, cultural, social, and philanthropic programs in nearly every congregation, became vigorous extensions of the UAHC.[60]

For the first half-century or more of its existence, the UAHC devoted most of its energies to religious education. By the time of its inception, the

United States public schools had become stable, free, and nonsectarian institutions, and the few Reform congregations that had organized day schools (combining Jewish and secular subjects) in the middle of the nineteenth century had converted these to weekend schools.

Philadelphia's Mikveh Israel and Charleston's Beth El organized the first Jewish Sunday school (1838), and by the end of the first decade of the UAHC's existence about 90 percent of the congregations had weekend religious schools. The UAHC, from its inception, tried to promote a "uniform course of instruction," to identify and train potential teachers, and, shortly after its formation, to survey schools and publish books and pamphlets as well as curricula, textbooks, and teachers' guides.

With the inception of the Department of Synagog and School Extension in 1903, the UAHC began to help organize religious schools, convene teachers' conventions, publish syllabi, manuals, and even a magazine for children. The Commission on Jewish Education expanded these efforts further, primarily by surveying religious education programs in Reform Jewish synagogues and responding to the needs identified. A 1924 survey of 125 such schools found the major subjects of study to be the same as in the 1880s (Jewish history, Bible, customs, Hebrew, religion, and ethics), and discovered the average class met for two hours (versus three hours in the 1880s). Textbooks and teachers' manuals published by the UAHC in the 1920s and 1930s reflected these subjects and the brevity of the school day.[61]

The Central Conference of American Rabbis

One of Isaac Mayer Wise's dreams was the unification of the North American rabbinate, and he undertook his first attempt at unity as early as 1855 at a conference in Cleveland. It failed, because the Conservative and liberal wings of the rabbinate found themselves too far apart ideologically for unification. Wise tried again at the conference convened by Samuel Adler and David Einhorn at Philadelphia in 1869 to create "the agreement of like-minded Rabbis" with many of the veterans of the German rabbinical conferences of the 1840s (the discussions were in German), but the "Radical" platform, including the resolution stating that "in prayer . . . Hebrew must yield to the vernacular," received little support from the traditionalists.[62]

The creation of the UAHC in 1873 proved to be the most important step in the direction of a rabbinical organization, if not of all North American rabbis, for it provided a common link on the congregational level. When Wise finally succeeded in bringing rabbis together in an organization, despite his claim that he sought to "maintain . . . a union of all American rabbis," it was almost exclusively rabbis of UAHC congregations who formed the Central Conference of American Rabbis (CCAR) in Detroit in 1889. This rabbinic arm of the Reform movement, with Wise as the first president, set modest goals, including publishing an annual yearbook and establishing a pension fund, but grew steadily from ninety "rabbis, ministers, preachers, or whatever titles the appointed teachers of the ninety congregations may claim" to nearly four hundred by the time of the 1937 convention in Columbus, Ohio.[63]

Although the CCAR responded tentatively at first to the social justice plank in the 1885 platform ("to solve, on the basis of justice and righteousness, the problems presented by the contrasts and evils of the present organization of society"), when it finally affirmed a vigorous commitment to a better life for all North Americans it did so with comprehensiveness if not boldness. "In no other area," one CCAR member has argued, "has the impact of the Conference been more substantial or profound than in that now commonly known as social action." The three dominant factors in the emergence of a strong program of social justice in the years between Pittsburgh and Columbus were the platforms or positions of the Protestant and Catholic religious organizations, the conditions of United States society, and the prophetic tradition of Judaism.[64]

While a few resolutions dealing with social problems were approved in the 1890s and early 1900s, including a declaration to work toward the elimination of child labor (1908), not until the progressive movement revealed the underside of United States society in unmistakable tones (growing industrialism, poverty-stricken immigrants, expanding slums, embittered unionism) and clergymen of other faiths began to play leading roles in issues of social significance (especially the Social Gospel movements in Protestant churches) did the CCAR create the Committee on Synagog and Industrial Relations (1913).

Together with the Commission on Social Justice, in 1918 it submitted a detailed program, the first official platform of principles of social justice, seeking to achieve "industrial democracy through social justice," and committing the Reform rabbinate to a liberal program (minimum wage, eight-hour working day, abolishment of child labor, sanitary working conditions, collective bargaining, unemployment and health insurance, and much more). Although strongly liberal in tone, most of the provisions had not only been affirmed by the Federal Council of the Churches of Christ in America (1908 and 1912), as well as the Catholic clergy, for several years, but many of them were already being enacted into legislation in a wide range of industrial states. Joseph Rauch (1881–1957), of Louisville's Adath Israel, noted that "most of the rights here stated are already on the state books," and thus the CCAR was "discussing matters which are already the law of the land." Nevertheless, if it didn't take the lead on the North American religious scene it did so among North American Jews and it surely kept pace with the courageous spokesmen of other faiths.[65]

By 1920 the CCAR took cognizance of the difficulties in black-white relationships, criticized the racial bias in the Immigration Act of the same year, expressed its abhorrence of the hysteria and threat to civil liberties inherent in the hunt for anarchists and Bolsheviks, and in 1928 and 1930 adopted a new statement scoring the "inequalities of wealth," pointing to the dangers of rising unemployment, and proposing several solutions for the amelioration of the latter dilemma. These later platforms were the first CCAR statements on social justice to touch on "international relations," and they affirmed the right of conscientious objection to war, denounced "economic imperialism," urged that "a popular referendum precede any declaration of war," and disapproved of compulsory military training in the educational system. On the domestic scene, well ahead of Protestant national religious organizations, the CCAR urged the use of "birth regulation" to aid in "coping with social problems." All these pronouncements laid the foundation for the lengthy and vigorous commitment to social action sealed in the Columbus Platform.[66]

These resolutions and platforms of the CCAR were accompanied by political action, especially with Catholic and Protestant religious bodies. On its own, however, the conference petitioned the courts to conduct a fuller investigation into the Sacco and Vanzetti case and lobbied in Congress for an antilynching bill. Especially during the 1920s and 1930s the CCAR joined the Federal Council of the Churches of Christ in America and the National Catholic Welfare Conference in vigorously protesting the twelve-hour day in the steel industry, in investigating grievances in the railroad industry, and in securing parole for IWW workers arrested with tremendous haste in the aftermath of a 1919 Armistice Day shoot-out in Washington State.[67]

The prophetic influence runs all through the CCAR statements as well as the pronouncements of individual rabbis bringing the message of the conference back to their congregations and communities. Abraham Geiger, the intellectual leader of nineteenth-century Reform Judaism, emphasized prophetic Judaism, and in the twentieth century it is scarcely an exaggeration to say that the majority of the Reform rabbinate saw the essence of Reform Judaism as ethical monotheism and that this was understood to be the central meaning of the prophetic faith. Samuel S. Cohon asserted that "the prophet holds the place of preeminence in the religious history of Israel," and the CCAR's 1928 platform, in its preamble, stated that it "deriv[ed] its inspiration for social justice from the great teachings of the prophets of Israel." Earlier discussions at CCAR conventions on the synagogue and social service also spoke of the "social ideals of prophetic Judaism" as well as of the "immortal prophetic cry for justice."[68]

Abba Hillel Silver, who strongly supported and often participated in programs for civic and social betterment in Cleveland, invoked the prophets, the "fearless spokesmen of God's moral law to men," for his affirmation of Reform Judaism's demand of "unremitting action" and "unwearied moral effort" to "build the good society." "At the heart of the message of Hebraic prophecy," he argued, "is a summons to men not to rest content with the evils of society . . . but to set to work to correct them." This explains, for Silver, why the prophets were such a potent symbol of social involvement and never divorced from society; "they were interested primarily in the moral tone of their nation and of society generally," especially in "social righteousness and human brotherhood."[69]

Samuel S. Mayerberg (1892–1964), who served Kansas City's B'nai Jehudah for years, gained extensive national exposure for his battle against the corrupt Pendergast political machine between 1932 and 1940. As he entered the political battle "with all the courage and strength" he could summon, Mayerberg invoked the "fearless, God-intoxicated prophets of Israel" as the "human ideals" that "impelled his conscience." As he began to translate the exposure of corruption into positive constructive action, the rabbi quoted Jeremiah's description of his own mission: "to root out and pull down and to destroy and overthrow; to build and to plant."[70]

Jacob J. Weinstein (1902–1974) left San Francisco's Shearith Israel in 1932 after "failing to win [the members] over to . . . the saving power of the prophetic teachings of Judaism." He was convinced that the prophets, "by some rare intuition, taught the need of social responsibility for the sins that were socially engendered," and considered it "the keenest failure in my ministry among you" that he was not "free in this synagogue to preach the prophetic ideals of Judaism." However, he used his nearly three decades (1939–1967) of leadership at Chicago's K.A.M. congregation to preach and practice (if not hurl himself into) prophetic Judaism, especially in the areas of fair housing and draft resistance, and to become, as he himself put it, an "Amos in the secular city."[71]

The "synthesis of religion and human service," Hyman G. Enelow pointed out in 1916, is what "Amos and Isaiah stood for." They, and their colleagues, he preached in 1924, taught that there is no separation between the individual and the community and that "if your religion is genuine" and is "to do any good," then "it must find expression in communal action [and] in social relations." And Stephen S. Wise, only one of numberless colleagues of Enelow and Silver who linked the prophets to the Reform Jewish involve-

ment in society, founded New York's Free Synagogue to preach and participate in prophetic Judaism. During the second decade of the twentieth
century, Wise's vigorous speeches on women's suffrage, clean city government, Jewish communal democracy, social welfare programs, and especially the United States labor struggles, were filled with prophetic utter-
ances. He attacked not only evil but also, as he saw it, evildoers, and based
these personal attacks ("Judge Gary has Cossackized the steel industry")
on the biblical prophet Nathan who "did not hold a meeting when he
wished to speak to David but went quietly into his chamber and said, 'Thou
art the man.' "[72]

Hebrew Union College

The prophetic thrust of Reform Judaism was institutionalized in the
Hebrew Union College, primarily through the college's deep commitment
to the study of the prophetic literature. By the time of the Pittsburgh
Platform, as we have noted earlier, the HUC had already graduated its first
class of four rabbis and seemed to be capable of permanency. The relationship between the UAHC and the HUC had been intimate ever since the
former founded the college in 1875 in Cincinnati. Even at the end of Wise's
presidency (1900), when the UAHC's activities had already become diverse,
virtually all its budget (raised largely by imposing a "tax"—a percentage
of the congregation's budget—on each member institution) was used to
support the college; it owned the college's property, and its leadership
elected the college's board of governors. Obviously, the growth of the
UAHC was vital to the college—UAHC growth meant the possibility of
both an increased budget as well as new congregations for HUC graduates
to serve—but the number of congregations in the UAHC was less in 1900
than in 1879.

Growth and expansion came, therefore, only with the new century. The
steady rise in individual membership (if not always in congregations) from
1900 through the late 1920s—especially between 1900 and 1910, when congregations and members nearly doubled, and between 1920 and 1930, when
membership doubled (see Table 1)—surely pleased college officials. Even
when the growth was not great, during the second decade of the century,
the college did well. Its own endowments enabled it to attain some financial
security; the Wise Centenary Fund—a successor to the Wise Memorial
Fund, which brought in $400,000 by 1911—collected over $300,000 in 1919,
and by the end of Kaufmann Kohler's presidency (1921) the college had a
yearly budget of $141,000 and an endowment fund in excess of half a million
dollars.

The Depression years were a time of great financial difficulty for the

Reform movement, although the college itself fared satisfactorily. Even before the stock market fell in 1929, the UAHC's growth was stagnant: there was only one more congregation in the UAHC in 1928 than in 1924, and there were fewer Reform memberships in 1928 than in 1927. In the early years of the Depression the situation worsened, as membership in Reform congregations declined each year between 1930 and 1935, and then virtually stood still, failing to return to the 1930 level even by 1940. This situation not only put the UAHC in debt but also made it almost impossible, in the late 1920s and early 1930s, to find jobs for newly ordained rabbis.

The college, unlike the UAHC, rode through these years in relative security: a generous endowment fund—conservatively invested (largely in railroad bonds rather than in common stocks)—helped it through the worst years. But the size of the entering classes was drastically cut (in 1931 only fifteen of forty-five and in 1932 only eight of twenty-six applicants were admitted), numerous pledges to the endowment were not paid, the library budget was reduced in half, faculty salaries were cut by 25 percent, and with the budgetary prognosis unfavorable, the student body was steadily reduced by weeding out the less qualified and by admitting fewer students. From 120 in 1928–1929, the college student body sank to less than half that number in 1934–1935.

The college faculty, while never large in this period (nine in 1903, two of whom were full-time Cincinnati rabbis; fifteen in 1932–1932, the highpoint during the presidency of Julian Morgenstern), was surely distinguished. Kaufmann Kohler had an outstanding reputation as a theologian and scholar, Morgenstern as a critical biblical scholar; Samuel Cohon wrote widely on Reform Jewish theology, and Jacob Mann gained international stature for his studies of medieval Egyptian and Palestinian Jewry. Jacob Lauterbach and Solomon Freehof achieved distinction in rabbinics; Moses Buttenweiser, Sheldom Blank, and Nelson Glueck became well-known Bible scholars; Jacob Marcus brought distinction to the college in history; and the *HUC Annual,* which attracted the leading Jewish scholars in the United States and overseas, emerged in the 1920s as one of the most distinguished journals of Judaica. Together with the library, whose generous endowment (even in 1930–1931 its allocation of $50,000 was 15 percent of the total college budget) and vigorous pursuit of private collections made it the major North American repository of Jewish scholarship, the faculty gave the college, during Morgenstern's administration, a reputation as an important center of Jewish scholarship.

The size and quality of the student body, as in other professional schools, varied considerably from year to year. The thirty-six students enrolled in 1903 was only half that of five years earlier, and by 1906–1907 it was down to twenty-eight—each of them examined by faculty members (and sometimes the president) in order to gain admission. Indeed, only seventy-five rabbis had been ordained in the college's first twenty-five years. But the student body grew steadily—at least until the Depression and its informal quota of seventy-five students reduced the student body to fifty-eight in 1934–1935— ascending to a peak of ninety-three in 1915–1916 during Kohler's administration and 120 in 1928–1929 during Morgenstern's presidency. Most rabbinical students, in the first six decades of the college's existence, came from poor families—poor German parents during Wise's presidency and poor East European parents subsequently—most had little Hebrew background, and in addition to pursuing and obtaining a bachelor of arts degree at the University of Cincinnati the rabbinic program required four or five years of Hebrew and Jewish studies, although for some time these could be taken concurrently with the bachelor of arts program. By the 1920s more and more students began to enter the college with a bachelor's degree in hand, and they could complete their rabbinic studies in as few as three years As the number of graduate years required of students steadily increased from none in Wise's years to one in Kohler's and, finally, after 1930, to four, the depth and breadth of the rabbinic program grew. By the time the Columbus Platform was issued, the college was turning out rabbis who were rigorously trained in Bible, literature, language, liturgy, and history.

The Jewish Institute of Religion

For a decade and a half before the Columbus Platform, Stephen S. Wise's Jewish Institute of Religion (JIR) in New York had also been training men destined (almost exclusively) for Reform pulpits, although the JIR was ostensibly nondenominational in its Jewish outlook. The first group of rabbis (ten) completed their studies in 1926, after a rigorous, four-year, graduate program that included a faculty and administration overwhelmingly sympathetic to Zionism. Wise felt that New York City, where perhaps half of United States Jewry lived, could sustain his rabbinical school and that North American Jewry was large enough to support two "liberal" seminaries. Wise, the most well-known rabbi in America, was dissatisfied with the anti-Zionist tone of the HUC and was determined to guide rabbinic students toward an appreciation of the social activist rabbinate. He gave direction to the school (together with, sometimes in spite of, and frequently while in the midst of rabbinical duties) until the end of its independent existence and merger with the HUC in 1949. Wise died in that same year, aware that he had guided a school that had trained nearly 200 rabbis and gathered a faculty of distinction.[73]

3. History, Ideology, and Institutions: 1937–1983

The Columbus Platform did not, in itself, cause a major shift in Reform Jewish practice but rather served as one sign of the gradual changes that had been occurring in the Reform movement for a generation. Zionism had become a stronger element in congregational programming; Hebrew prayers, classes, and songs had already begun to appear in synagogue worship and education; and ceremonies and observances once ignored or rejected had slowly begun to reappear in Reform Jewish life as the children of immigrants flowed steadily into the movement.

Nevertheless, despite the gradual adoption of some elements of tradition, Reform Judaism of the decades following 1937 remained firmly distinguishable from traditional forms of Judaism. This pattern was clearly evident in some of the central areas of Judaism as new forms of expression surfaced in the postwar decades in the areas of beliefs, ceremonies, and organization.

Beliefs

God

Of the classic trilogy of Judaism—God, Torah, Israel—the non-Reform Jewish denominations have laid primary emphasis on Torah (revelation) and Israel (people, civilization, culture), while Reform Judaism has been chiefly concerned with God and his ethical demands. This focus helps to explain the countless essays by Reform rabbis on what they understand by God and his moral will, as rabbi after rabbi, almost all with slightly different perspectives, offers his individual explication of this fundamental theological issue.

Few, however, write anything resembling systematic theology, or even, as was so popular in the nineteenth century, a theology that collected and arranged, under various headings, scriptural and rabbinic passages and added an interpretation or two to contemporize the "theology." The result is that no one theological system dominates Reform Judaism; instead, a multiplicity of Jewish theologies constitutes Reform Jewish thought and affirms, as Professor Alvin Reines (1926–   ) of the Hebrew Union College has explained, that "all opinions" are "equally valid."[1]

The Pittsburgh and Columbus platforms did little to resolve the ambiguities of competing views about God, his will, and his revelation. Both, as Professor Jakob Petuchowski (1925–   ) of the Hebrew Union College has argued, the concept of revelation in the 1885 statement and the 1937 revision as well as the view of God are purposefully ambiguous, satisfactory to those who believed in direct divine revelation and to those who could not conceive of God as actually revealing himself. And why not? For those documents, as Petuchowski himself took note, represented "a compromise between divergent views."[2]

Since even the 1937 platform provided nothing close to a definitive statement, Reform Jewish thinkers have continued to articulate highly individual theologies. As already noted, this diversity is perhaps the essence of North American Reform Judaism. As one rabbi stated in 1967, "No member of the CCAR or UAHC need ever feel that he has been cramped or forced to comply with a very narrow kind of theological view which is uncongenial to himself."[3]

We can say with some sense of confidence that the abstract and rational views of the nineteenth- and early twentieth-century reformers have yielded in recent years to an increasing number of Reform thinkers who have moved toward a personal concept of God, or the insistence that prayer must be directed or addressed to someone other than the worshippers themselves. Samuel S. Cohon, the principal architect of the Columbus Platform, suggested this when he noted in the 1930s that "Personality is characteristic of the Jewish idea of God. He was conceived as personal before He was recognized as cosmic." In his book, *What We Jews Believe,* Cohon argued that God is a reality, and that he hears prayer, gives strength to humanity, and blesses us with peace.[4]

Bernard Martin (1928–1982), a Reform rabbi who taught at Case Western Reserve and wrote widely on theology, argued that "He is *personal* . . . in the sense that He lives, acts, is conscious, and enters into personal relationship with man, addressing him and demanding his personal response." Arnold Jacob Wolf (1924–   ), a widely read Chicago Reform rabbi, has also consistently articulated such a view of God. He is, to Wolf, "more like what we call a person than like anything else we know," and while acknowledging the diversity of Jewish notions of God, Wolf argues that "the one thread that runs through all of them is that He is like a Person . . . who cares about us."

Although Arthur Lelyveld (1913–   ), rabbi of Fairmount Temple in Cleveland for many years, acknowledges that "when I say 'God is my Father' . . . I am making use of terms accessible to me to express an experience of relationship" and that "when I address God as person I am using a metaphor," he too affirms a personal God. He is troubled by those who insist "that God is 'cosmic process' and not 'cosmic person,' " "feels in prayer a sense of direct relationship . . . I describe . . . as personal," and argues that what one experiences in prayer is presence, and "we may, without apology, call that Presence 'Father' and 'King.' "[5]

Emil Fackenheim (1916–   ), a rabbi and professor of theology at the University of Toronto who has greatly influenced Reform rabbis and lay-people, has also tried to clarify the notion of God as a person. For him too, "God surely resembles a human person far more closely than He does an impersonal force"; "the most exalted picture we can make of God is as a person"; and "personality comes closer than any other human concept to the true nature of God." Robert I. Kahn, rabbi of Houston's Emanu-El, described "moments in my life when I felt God spoke to me," for God is not only Creator and Father but a "Friend [who] calls to us constantly." And Eugene Borowitz (1924–   ), a professor of religious thought at the Hebrew Union College, whose theological writings dominate Reform Jew-ish thinking, also emphasizes a personal God whom we meet and confront. "He hears us"; He "is always ready for prayer" (although men and women are not); and he urges us to "care about Him and to base our lives on the intimacy we share with Him." Jakob Petuchowski also rejects the intellec-tual "God concepts" of the earlier reformers ("some*thing* is not very likely to address me") for "some*one,* " and claims that "the tradition speaks of God as a Person." He further argues, "Tradition does speak of God's will, and of God's love, and of God's concern. And to have a will, love, and concern means that one is so constituted as to have them; and, in our human language, that kind of constitution is called 'personality.' He has this in mind when he speaks of God as the One 'who led the ancestors out of Egypt . . . and who watched over His people throughout their many wander-ings.' "[6]

Others, however, have suggested both more views of God and have actively publicized their theology among their rabbinic colleagues and the laity, for, as Petuchowski has noted, "our tradition is broad enough to include all kinds of views about God." Roland Gittelsohn (1910–   ), a Reform rabbi in Nassau County's Central Synagogue and in Boston's Temple Israel for years, wrote much and lectured widely on his "naturalist" view. Gittelsohn notes that "increasing numbers of modern religious Jews no longer think of God as a Person" and rejects the idea "that God [can] be encompassed within the terms of personality." "I did not conceive God as a Person," he writes, but as "a Process or Power or Thrust within the universe," for God "inheres within nature." God "is the creative, spiritual Seed of the universe—the Energy, the Power, the Force, the Direction, the Trust . . . in which the universe and mind find their meaning." Prayer, for Gittelsohn and his fellow religious naturalists, is not directed to a God who hears, to a personal God, but inward to oneself. It is "a reminder of who I am, of what I can become, and of my proper relationship to the rest of the universe." Its goals are to "articulate my true, unique, quintessence as a human being," to "reinforce my knowledge of nature's laws," and to "show us a vision of our noblest selves." A prayer of thanksgiving, according to Gittelsohn, is never valid if it requests something specific for the petitioner, but is valid only if "it moves us to share generously with others the gifts for which we are in the process of giving thanks."[7]

Another view of God popular among many Reform rabbis recently rejects the omnipotent and omniscient descriptors widely used by nineteenth-century reformers and understands the Deity in a much more limited manner. Widely popularized in weekly radio sermons and writings by Levi Olan (1903–1984), of Dallas's Temple Emanuel, in the 1950s, and for nearly five decades by Henry Slonimsky (1884–1970), a professor of theology at the JIR, it denies God's perfection and unlimited power and sees God as "becoming, even as is the universe and man." God too, therefore, "struggles against evil," with human help, and hence there is much that he is unable to do (e.g., prevent the Holocaust). This approach explains the senseless cruelty and meaningless suffering that so fills our world: God simply does not have the power to do all he might wish to do.[8]

This brief survey of some Reform Jewish theologies demonstrates, as Alvin Reines has noted, the existence of mutually exclusive elements of belief. And since no individual—rabbi or congregant—or document provides absolute authority or even "normative" doctrine, Reform Jews, on principle, will subscribe to different understandings of God.[9]

Torah

The attitude toward the Torah, while no less individualistic than that about God, also found a consensus in the decades after the Columbus Platform. First, as the children and grandchildren of East European Jewish immigrants began to dominate synagogue life, the actual use of the Torah steadily increased in Reform congregations. Bar Mitzvah (boys of thirteen) and Bat Mitzvah (girls of thirteen) ceremonies became commonplace, especially at Sabbath morning services, and the young men and women would read from the Torah—the unvocalized scrolls of Hebrew kept in an ark and containing the Hebrew text of the Pentateuch. Secondly, while nearly every rabbi would publicly declare these sacred scrolls, or more precisely, the biblical text, to be the product of human intellectual and spiritual creativity, the argument of the philosopher Emil Fackenheim that "the concept of revelation lies dead and buried" is not completely apropos. Reform rabbis, nearly everywhere, have retained the traditional blessing over the Torah— "Blessed art Thou O Lord our God who has given us the Torah"—a blessing that has appeared in every edition of the *Union Prayer Book* and the new *Gates of Prayer.* [10]

Rabbi Gittelsohn, for example, when editing and writing a "naturalist" creative liturgy for a UAHC Biennial Convention, wherein prayer is replaced by "meditation" and "quiet reflection," nevertheless blesses the Torah with these words: "Praised be the Eternal our God, Ruling Spirit of the Universe, who has chosen us from among all peoples to give us the Torah." Although Gittelsohn's "Spirit" has many limitations, the act of revelation is not one of them. Other rabbis would speak (albeit vaguely) of "divine inspiration" or "divine insight" or "self-disclosure" or similar notions in an attempt, on the one hand, to distinguish scripture from Shakespeare and, on the other, to deny "divine revelation," or, in the language of Abraham J. Heschel, the philosopher, the notion that "God spoke to the prophet on a long distance telephone." Few rabbis or congregants were bothered by the inconsistency.

Third, whatever the variety of Reform understandings of revelation, they all not only reject the fundamental belief that the contents of revelation are written down, *literatim,* in a book or books, but affirm a notion of "progressive" revelation. This means, in effect, a rejection of the traditional position that revelation occurred at only one time and one place (Sinai), and an affirmation of the notion that men and women, everywhere and always, have the potential to understand God's will, and that their insights are becoming (although not in a linear fashion as the nineteenth-century reformers imagined) generally progressively more clear. As Rabbi Maurice Eisendrath (1902–1973), president of the Union of American Hebrew Congregations for thirty years (1943–1973), expressed it succinctly, "God is a *living* God—not a God who revealed Himself and His word once and for all time at Sinai and speaks no more." [12]

Shortly after the Columbus Platform appeared, Rabbi Solomon Freehof (1892–   ) of Pittsburgh's Rodef Sholem and for many years head of the CCAR Responsa Committee, urged his colleagues to "restudy our relationship to traditional Jewish law" and to "revive the concept of *mitzva,* of Torah, and thus attain orderliness and consistency and authority in our Reform Jewish life." Both these requests, although not completely accomplished in the subsequent decades, were taken seriously by the Reform movement.[13]

The renewed interest in the *halacha* (Jewish law) was dominated by Freehof himself. Beginning in 1944 with his *Reform Jewish Practice*—an attempt to delineate the relationship between traditional Jewish law, or "the vast treasury of Jewish practice in the past," and "present reform practice" —and then with a second volume and another half-dozen or so volumes of Reform *responsa* (answers to questions about individual and synagogue observance), Freehof has sought to uncover—although not to "lay down the norm of practice"—the *halachic* background to current Reform Jewish practices. While Freehof frequently diverged from the *halachic* precedents, his sympathetic presentations served to drastically turn Reform Judaism from a movement disdainful of Jewish law and *mitzvot* to one that, in the past few decades, has seriously sought guidance (if not authority) from the Jewish legal tradition. Freehof's rich collections of *halachic* precedents not only served to provide those rabbis and congregants who introduced traditional ceremonies and observances into their congregations with the tools to relate their practices to those of the tradition, but reawakened the discussions that called for a "guide" or Reform *halacha* of ritual practices.[14]

Although those opposing such a guide have loudly argued that such a volume would bind Reform Jews by inhibiting individual freedom or by establishing minimum norms that would codify a level of minimum practice in Reform Judaism, there have been many efforts to promote such a guide among Reform Jews. Although one such attempt was made by Leopold Stein (1810–1882) in Germany in 1877 with his *Torat Hayim* (*The Torah of Life*), and another by Rabbis Voorsanger (1903) and Krauskopf (1904) in their attempt to convince the CCAR that it needed a "collective authority" or "a strong and correct definition" of "religious practice" (the "authority" was opposed by those who feared excessive coerciveness), neither had any significant influence. The influential steps in the direction of manuals or guides to Reform Jewish observances began with the recognition, at Columbus, that Reform rabbis were willing to listen with respect to suggestions for more, rather than less, ceremonial.[15]

In 1938 the CCAR Commission on Synagogue and Community recommended the creation of a code of Reform Jewish observances and ceremonies; in 1948 Leon Feuer (1903–1984), rabbi of Toledo's Collingwood Avenue Temple, reaffirmed the need for a "clear and simple code of reform Jewish practice," and by the 1950s individual rabbis began to produce such guides.

None of those compendiums received anything like official sanction by the Reform movement, but each one indicated a growing trend among Reform Jews to have a guide to ceremonies and observances drawn from the treasury of *halacha*.[16]

Rabbis David Polish and Frederick A. Doppelt wrote a *Guide* (1957) that sought to guide (not legislate) conduct and observance, and argued that the authority or criterion for observances ought to be the Jew's historic memory. Thus those ceremonies and rituals *(mitzvot)* that remind the Jew of historic experiences in which the Jewish people encountered God's moral nature (covenant, Exodus, Sinai) are "mandatory observances" (such as the Sabbath), for they concretize spiritual moments in Jewish history. The authors provide abundant "elective" observances, suggested by rabbinic authorities, in order to flesh out the mandatory observances. For the *mitzva* of Sabbath, for example, the possibilities include blessings of the Sabbath dinner, family worship and/or Torah discussion, and private study. All have the goal of leading the Reform Jew to the "self-imposed discipline of observance."[17]

The steady accumulation of individual guides, and the vigorous demands by rabbis such as W. Gunther Plaut for a CCAR-sponsored guide, led the CCAR, in 1972, to issue not a comprehensive guide for Reform Jews but a guide for Sabbath observance, *Tadrikh le-Shabbat (A Shabbat Manual)*. Plaut, in a 1965 address to his rabbinic colleagues, had recommended "the creation of a Sabbath guide" as "a pilot project for the larger, more comprehensive guide," and the *Shabbat Manual* was intended to serve precisely that function. The widespread use of the *Manual* in Reform Jewish households in the decade after its publication suggested a greater receptivity by Reform Jews to a higher measure of observance in their personal and collective lives.[18]

The most significant feature, in addition to much background on Sabbath observance and a substantial amount of Hebrew, was the list of recommendations *(mitzvot,* or "do's" and "don'ts") for the individual Jew: it is proper to "prepare for *Shabbat* . . . to light *Shabbat* candles . . . to recite or chant the kiddush . . . to maintain and enjoy the special quality of *Shabbat* throughout the [Saturday] afternoon." It is best not to "engage in gainful work on *Shabbat* . . . perform housework on *Shabbat* . . . [shop] on *Shabbat* . . . participate in a social event during *Shabbat* worship hours . . . [or engage in] public activity which violates [the *Shabbat*]." This emerging Reform *halacha,* while obviously not obligatory on any Reform Jew, provided concrete evidence that the Reform movement was strongly interested in helping individual Reform Jews enrich and maximize their level of ceremony and ritual through exposure to the varieties of Sabbath observance and celebration followed by those Jews committed to Jewish law.[19]

Israel

Although the Columbus Platform did not represent an overwhelming change of direction in either the rabbinic or lay enthusiasm for a Jewish state in Zion, the decade following the *Guiding Principles,* with its painful lesson of what actually happens to Jews when they have no homeland to which they may turn, witnessed the steady increase of Reform Jewish support for a Jewish state. The eventual birth of Israel in 1948 was embraced enthusiastically by congregants and rabbis, although the impact of the new state on Reform Jewish life was not large for the first twenty years of Israel's life.[20]

These two decades were dominated by two changes in Reform Jewish life. First, Israel began to permeate the programs of Reform synagogues. The pronunciation of Hebrew, long standardized in an Ashkenazic or East European style, yielded to the Sephardic sounds of the new state in prayer, Torah readings, and synagogue music: an entire generation of North American Jews was to be raised on the pronunciations *shabbat* (not *shabbos*), *shalom* (not *sholem*), and *adonai* (not *adonoy*). The study of Israeli culture and civilization became a standard part of UAHC curricula in the 1950s, and a more and more prominent part of Reform Jewish education throughout the 1960s: Essrig and Segal's *Israel Today* (1964) was only one of several texts widely used in intermediate and junior high grades, while Hebrew singing and Israeli dancing became as much a staple of Sunday School as the assemblies and services. Synagogues in places as diverse as Boston, Miami, Los Angeles, Cleveland, and Philadelphia joined with a large number in the New York area to assign Israeli pen-pals in Sunday School, adopt entire Israeli villages for *keren ami* ("charity") collections, and encourage visiting Israelis of diverse kinds (counselors, teachers, musicians) to participate in Reform Jewish congregational and summer camp life. It came as little surprise to most, then, that in 1969 the CCAR declared 5 Iyar, Israel Independence Day, an official holiday.[21]

Secondly, Reform Jewish congregants became more and more conscious of the fate of Reform Judaism in Israel. They began to learn that there were only a few Reform rabbis in Israel, that the minority Orthodox religious parties imposed their (generally extreme) will on the rather indifferent majority, and went out of their way to defame and discourage all attempts to establish a non-Orthodox religious alternative. While this information did little more, for two decades, than spur money-raising efforts in North America (through the World Union for Progressive Judaism) on behalf of the struggling Reform congregations in Israel, it succeeded in raising the level of consciousness of North American Reform Jews sufficiently for major changes to occur in the decade after 1967. The distribution of this information was aided by a variety of work-study programs in Israel for Reform high school and college students and an emerging generation of Reform rabbis who, ever since 1970, have been required to spend their first year of rabbinical school at the Jerusalem campus of the Hebrew Union College. Their presence in Israel, together with that of the Hebrew Union College, not only gives support to the small but rapidly growing Reform movement in Israel, but enables them, eventually, to speak to their congregations as observers, not just conduits, of Reform Judaism's struggle for acceptance in Israel.[22]

The Synagogue

When the Columbus Platform described the synagogue as "the oldest and most democratic institution in Jewish life" and "the prime communal agency by which Judaism is fostered and preserved," it provided a description of the Reform synagogue that became increasingly accurate in the postwar decades but that by no means captured the varieties of synagogue expression.

The democratic nature of the Reform synagogue became more apparent, especially in the 1960s and 1970s. First, in many congregations the amount of time one contributed to the synagogue's maintenance, rather than the amount of money contributed, became a more important factor in determining one's election to the board of directors and to offices. Second, more and more members who were not affluent, adult middle-aged men moved into positions of leadership. Women served as presidents; youth group leaders joined boards of directors; and converts—an increasing phenomenon with the rise in intermarriages—became presidents of sisterhoods and brotherhoods. Third, the rabbinic selection process was increasingly democratized. Men, women, and students sat on search committees; interviews and/or gatherings with rabbinic candidates were frequently open to the general membership; and the entire membership almost always voted on the search committee's selection.[23]

During the post–World War II years, the Reform synagogue continued —although no longer unrivaled—as the "prime communal agency by which Judaism is fostered and preserved" and reversed a trend toward the "synagogue-center," which, as we have seen, characterized the 1920s, 1930s, and even 1940s. While the amount of "sacred space" did not grow generously, Judaica programs of all kinds surely did.

For the first half of the twentieth century, the synagogue had little or no competition in fostering Judaism, but beginning in the 1950s, and especially in the next two decades, other communal institutions made major efforts to do the same. Jewish centers added to their recreational, cultural, and social events programs that would increase Jewish identity; the Jewish Family Service began to express a concern over the Judaic commitment— not just the counseling expertise—of its professional staff; the Jewish Federations and/or Welfare Funds introduced programs for their lay and professional fundraisers on "Jewish" values and other areas of Judaica; while colleges and universities everywhere developed courses, and even programs, in Judaism or Jewish studies. The synagogue was no longer unrivaled.

Despite the "competition," the synagogue by no means ceased to be the "prime communal agency" where Reform Jews went to foster and preserve Judaism. Together with Reform Jewish summer camps staffed by rabbis, rabbinic students, and other staff committed to Jewish content, and even before Reform Jewish day schools—sponsored and housed in synagogues —emerged from coast to coast in the 1970s, elective high school programs, and especially adult study groups grappling with Jewish texts, steadily replaced the more general or "nondenominational" topics of an earlier generation of guest speakers ("lecture series") and introduced Reform Jews to the treasures of the Jewish past. The *havurot,* small, independent groups of congregants who worshipped, played, and studied together independent of the institutional arrangements, also emerged in the 1970s in dozens of Reform congregations, and provided members with frequent opportunities to enrich their Jewish identity in less structured and more intimate ways.[24]

At the same time, synagogue worship radically changed in many congregations. Cantors, or *hazzanim* (singular, *hazzan*) as well as guitar playing music leaders, replaced or supplemented choirs; contemporary Israeli (Hebrew) melodies and songs replaced or supplemented English anthems; rabbis descended from pulpits and lecterns to speak less formally and even lead discussions in place of "sermons"; Bat and Bar Mitzvah celebrants individualized their "speeches," which traditionally followed their reading from the Torah, with discussions, commentaries, and even musical "explorations" of the scriptural story; and (especially in the 1960s) mimeographed creative liturgies and (in the 1970s) a new Reform prayer book substantially changed the worship content as well as format. A few congregations, of course, retained a formality more characteristic of the 1920s and 1950s than the 1960s and 1970s, especially on the high holidays. Worshippers here demonstrated their affluence by their finery and/or their seats in front pews; musical instruments and a large choir entertained the worshippers prior to and during worship; the order and decorum resembled that described by Israel Jacobson in 1810; elaborate electronic systems dimmed lights, modulated voices through sound systems, opened and closed ark doors, and, not infrequently, the spectators rose as the rabbi(s) ascended and descended the pulpit. Not surprisingly, such congregations were not usually those moving toward *havurot,* creative liturgies, and women rabbis.

In the second half of the nineteenth century, at least half dozen rabbis produced their own prayer books, and some, such as Wise's *Minhag America* (1857), Gustave Gottheil's *Morning Prayers* (1889), Kohler's *Sabbath Eve Service* (1891), and Einhorn's *Olat Tamid* (1858) were adopted outside the author's congregation. To solve the "disunion and dissension" that Rabbi Wise noted (1890) resulted from the multiplicity of new books of worship, the CCAR established a committee to begin the process of compiling a "Union Prayer-book," and in 1892 published the *Union Prayer Book* and gave Reform Judaism an official liturgy.[25]

The *Union Prayer Book,* modeled after Einhorn's prayer book (this is true of both Volume 1, *Sabbaths,* and Volume 2, *High Holydays*), is a drastically attenuated version of the traditional Jewish prayer book, the *siddur.* The latter is a rich compilation of devotions, supplications, prayers, and study passages that developed within the synagogue over centuries. The Reform prayer book, even in its three revised versions (Volume 1 was revised in 1894, 1924, and 1940; Volume 2, issued in 1895, was revised in 1922 and 1945), is a response to the mood of a specific age—the incredibly optimistic mood of the late nineteenth-century America. What the reformers did was to take the sense of security that late nineteenth-century Jewry felt in the United States ("the happier circumstances under which we are living in this blessed free country") and translate it into a messianic future, a permanent sense of progress and safety. This could only be done, on the one hand, by excising from the *siddur* all references to exile and suffering, and on the other, by adding English readings or "original productions" rather than "mere translations." This shift resulted in the Hebrew parts of the service either being rendered in English or having an English substitute.[26]

As already indicated in the Pittsburgh Platform, the reformers were not averse to expunging from their construction of Judaism those beliefs that they were convinced "we reject." Hence their prayer book, published less than a decade after the Pittsburgh Platform, rejects the sacrificial cult, a personal messiah, miracles, political (and even religious) Zionism, and the doctrine of resurrection of the body by eliminating such fundamental prayers of the *siddur* and by writing new ones. The *Union Prayer Book* begins a reading on Zion thus:

> Not backward do we turn our eyes; but forward to the promised and certain future . . . and though we cherish and revere the place where stood the cradle

of our people, the land where Israel grew up like a tender plant, and the knowledge of Thee rose like the morning dawn, our longings and aspirations reach out toward a higher goal.[27]

The *Union Prayer Book* also rejects individual, petitionary prayer, substituting in place of God as a cosmic complaint clerk a variety of moral improvements or benefits for the "inner being." It greatly reduces the amount of Hebrew in the service, and even includes some services with virtually none. The Hebrew text of the *Kol Nidre* (release from vows) for Yom Kippur and the *kiddush* for Sabbaths (sanctification of wine), for example, are omitted, and for many traditional prayers only an English translation rather than the original appear. Rabbinic materials, as opposed to biblical, are virtually absent; responsive readings are frequently composed of a series of biblical quotes.[28]

But reason and science did not consistently subordinate what the nineteenth century viewed as superstition. Besides repeated references to God giving the Torah through Moses, God's annual notarial judgment of men and women ("Book of Life") is retained ("On the first day of the [new] year it is inscribed and on the day of Atonement it is sealed: How many shall pass away and how many shall be born"), his "throne of judgement" is invoked, and the rewards of the afterlife (though not resurrection) for "those who suffer innocently" are repeatedly intoned, for the reformers are committed to the notion that "death is not the end, but a beginning."[29]

In addition to its sustained optimism, the *Union Prayer Book*—original and revised—emphasizes reason, beauty, and artistic expression rather than spirit or human emotion. Mystery, fire, and excitement, as well as awe, are carefully subordinated by prayers that seek to be almost *vérités de raison* and by a liturgy so rigorously constructed. The liturgy is structured in a manner that enables rabbi and choir to conduct an esthetically beautiful and coherent service *for* the congregation—with the dignity and decorum of High Church Christianity—but one without opportunities for spontaneity, creativity, more than a minimum of congregational participation, or the likelihood that one worshipper will recite the words of a prayer one or two syllables faster or slower than the rest of the audience. (Indeed, the authors-editors even indicate precisely when the "sermon" is to be delivered in the course of the service.)

The construction and arrangement of both the Sabbath and high holiday services demand that the rabbi pray for the congregation, indicate that the worship is but a prelude to the essence of the service, the sermon, and maximize the opportunities for worshipper passivity in prayer and song. Worshippers were usually prayed for, preached to, and sung at, and when criticisms of the *Union Prayer Book* became frequent in the 1950s, and especially in the 1960s, they focused frequently on this feature of the liturgy. Critics pointed to the *Union Prayer Book's* format, arguing that it left little room for informality, spontaneity, creativity, and emotion, took little cognizance of either tradition or of theological views inconsistent with an omniscient and omnibenevolent deity, and went out of its way to appeal to Christian visitors rather than Jewish needs. When one Reform rabbi, speaking to his colleagues in 1948, applauded the "newly revised" *Union Prayer Book* for "the delight which liberal Christian ministers have expressed in possessing the book and in utilizing its prayers," several of his colleagues voiced their objections to such a concern. Still other critics expressed dissatisfaction with the archaic English, and some with the omniscient, omnipotent, omnibenevolent God appearing on page after page.[30]

The result was the emergence, in scores of congregations, of mimeographed services written and/or compiled by the rabbi, as well as printed, softcover prayer books assembled by rabbis and also ritual committees. These experimental services eventually began to flood the executive offices of the CCAR with the hope, in most cases, that the conference would produce a new prayer book. Many of these liturgies initially developed around the weekly headlines (civil rights, brotherhood, opposition to war, social justice); others consciously sought to deal with the theological problems of worshipers who disliked the idea of God contained in the *Union Prayer Book,* congregants who sought a greater amount of Hebrew as well as spontaneity, participation, and spirit, and the desire, by rabbis and those praying, for the use of a vernacular language that would speak to the "Me" or "Now" Generation. This plethora of "creative" liturgy formed the foundation of what became in the 1970s the first new Reform prayer book in nearly a century: *Sha'are Tefilla* (*Gates of Prayer,* or *The New Union Prayer Book*).[31]

The new book boasted a Hebrew title, absence of sexist language, special services for Israel Independence Day, and complete reinstatement of Zion. It ran to hundreds of additional pages compared to the "old" *Union Prayer Book,* lacked formal instructions to the leader or the worshippers (congregational readings are merely italicized), and presented ten different Sabbath services reflecting radically different systems of thought and belief (including the very traditional and the very humanistic). It offered words to popular (Israeli) Hebrew melodies, explicit reflections on the Holocaust, and an abundance of traditional materials from the *siddur.* Thus *Gates of Prayer* concretized the varieties of religious expression (naturalist, organicist, existentialist, traditionalist, classicist, nontheist, polydox) to be discovered in Reform Jewish worship in the 1960s and 1970s, and had become, by the early

1980s, the standard prayer book of Reform Judaism. But it still remained the prayer book of a people who hardly ever prayed.

The Rabbi

During the period between the Pittsburgh and Columbus platforms, the role of the rabbi remained that of administrator, counselor, teacher, and preacher. From time to time a few congregational rabbis gained prominence for their Judaic scholarship (Hyman G. Enelow, for example), or for their position as Jewish communal spokesmen (Stephen S. Wise and Abba Hillel Silver)—but by the 1960s and 1970s Judaica scholars in universities and Jewish professional lay leaders had usurped these positions. The rabbinic role continued to be defined essentially in terms of those functions already listed. And in the decades after 1937 little had changed in the rabbinic role, except its demands:

> He must be a philosopher who can answer the ultimate questions about life and the universe; a theologian who can respond to the "show me God" demands of a confirmand, who can justify the mystery and anguish of death to grief-crushed parents who have just lost a child; a teacher who can reveal and illumine the drama of Jewish history and the glory of Jewish literature and relate them to contemporary Jewish living; a preacher and minister at the altar who can interweave faith and worship with reverence and moral fervor; a pastor who knows his people and is their listening ear and friend, who participates in every significant personal and family occasion from infancy to death; an organizer and administrator who can conduct a religious school, direct young people's activities, and correlate and harmonize laymen's committees and auxiliary groups; a community representative and ambassador who will interpret Judaism with dignity to the non-Jew (and with self-satisfaction and pride to his fellow Jews), and who will be a ready worker for all worth-while civic causes. To discharge [these tasks] he must possess not only highmindedness, dedication and superlative gifts of mind and heart, but also the physical energies that would tax a perfectly conditioned athlete and the psychic equilibrium of a saint.[32]

What had changed, however, were the areas of employment of Reform rabbis. By the late 1970s, with close to 1,000 members of the almost 1,400-member CCAR in the active rabbinate, more than 20 percent were employed outside of the pulpit. These included men and women in academic positions, staffing local and national Jewish institutions, directing Hillel foundations on college campuses, serving in the chaplaincy, and employed as temple educators. The image of the Reform rabbi as one who exclusively conducted worship services and delivered sermons dissolved in the 1960s and 1970s.[33]

Also changing was the exclusive male-dominated nature of the rabbinate. Although women had been welcome at both the HUC and JIR, at least in theory, for a century, and the CCAR had recommended the ordination of women as early as 1922, the first woman rabbi ordained was Sally Prei- sand, in 1972. By the early 1980s more than seventy-five women had been ordained, and they were no longer asked "You're a rabbi? Where's your beard?" for nearly every Reform congregant had become familiar (and quite comfortable) with women rabbis.[34]

The backgrounds of the post-Columbus generation of Reform rabbis had also changed dramatically. Twice as many rabbis came from Reform Jewish backgrounds in the early 1970s as did thirty years earlier, and this, many felt, enriched the congregation's active involvement in Reform Jewish institutional life, especially the UAHC, National Federation of Temple Sisterhoods, the National Federation of Temple Brotherhoods, and the National Federation of Temple Youth (founded in 1939). Rabbis from Reform backgrounds seemed especially committed to UAHC youth pro- grams (summer camps, programs of work-study in Israel, youth groups) and to deepening congregational programs about Reform Judaism.[35]

Judging from workshops and practica at CCAR conferences in the 1950s, 1960s, and 1970s, rabbis tended to spend their daytime working hours in two major areas: preparation for teaching and speaking; and meeting with individual members of the congregation. In addition to preparing Sabbath eve (and sometimes Sabbath morning) sermons weekly (unless blessed with an assistant with whom to alternate), rabbis taught youth and adults and spoke frequently outside the congregation. Much of their day was also spent in conversations with congregants who wished to discuss personal prob- lems, Jewish values, committee or synagogue business, forthcoming life cycle events, or just about anything. Without doubt, the rabbi's most effec- tive work was done outside the public arena of the pulpit—as a religious teacher of individual Jews. It was no longer true, as David Philipson had argued at the turn of the century, that "the rabbi stands and falls with his pulpit work."[36]

The rabbis emerging from the HUC-JIR in the 1960s and 1970s not only came from Reform backgrounds more frequently than before, but had other characteristics that made them much different, demographically and theo- logically, than the pre-1937 ordinees. The majority of HUC-JIR students were now married (virtually all were single in the 1920s and 1930s), and hence there was much more serious discussion, in class and out, of the spouse's role in the rabbinate. And a very large number of students were agnostic, causing them to experience acute dilemmas as they began to fulfill their roles as leaders of Jewish worship. For many of them, the alternatives to the congregational rabbinate were particularly appealing, not only because they provided the opportunity to use different professional skills but also because of theological reservations connected with public and private prayer.[37]

Many of these post–World War II trends and developments in Reform Judaism were crystalized in the San Francisco Platform of 1976, the third and most recent of Reform proclamations of the central directions of the movement. This "Centenary Perspective," to a great extent the work of Eugene Borowitz, begins with a statement noting, accurately, how much, once unique to Reform Judaism, has become a common denominator of most Jews, notes the impact of both the Holocaust and the state of Israel on Jewish identity and thought (and, implicitly, on this "Perspective"), and adumbrates the essence of Reform—the "autonomy of the individual." Such autonomy, as I have noted often, promotes and encourages diversity, and the body of the platform searches for the uniformity amidst the diversity.

The San Francisco statement about God is much more personal, even existential, than the previous statements of 1885 and 1937, for it speaks of not only conceiving but experiencing God, and of "ground[ing] our lives, personally and communally, on God's reality." The paragraph acknowledges the impact of modernity on belief and understanding, affirms the need for new conceptions of the divine, and asserts, if rather vaguely, that humans "share in God's eternality" after death.

More so than before, the San Francisco Platform emphasizes that peoplehood is an integral part of Judaism, and hence Israel, Hebrew, and Jewish history and culture are "inseparable from . . . religion." Torah is part of this "union of faith and peoplehood," and the existential dimension of revelation is stressed ("Torah results from meetings between God and the Jewish people") as is the continuous nature of this revelation ("Torah continues to be created even in our own time").

As in 1937, there is an increased interest in religious practice, but now a detailed list of "duties and obligations," despite the need to "exercise . . . individual autonomy," is provided for the individual Reform Jew, including "keeping the Sabbath and the holy days." Unlike 1937, however, there is nothing equivocal about the commitment to Israel: "we have both a stake and a responsibility in building the State of Israel, assuring its security, and defining its Jewish character." And yet the emphasis remains on North American Jewry and its responsibility in "building the State of Israel, assuring its security, and defining its Jewish character."[38]

The 1,000-word document concludes with an affirmation of a pluralism, such as that of the United States, where a group can develop its particular values while, concomitantly, struggling for "a universal concern for humanity." That is, this statement as well as earlier declarations attempts to simultaneously satisfy particular and universal obligations. The obligations to humanity are hardly new; this statement's innovation lies in the stress on "devotion to our particular people," in its particularity.

Institutions and Organizations

The Union of American Hebrew Congregations

The "religious revival" or "return to religion" of the 1950s affected Reform Jews no less than it did the Protestants and Catholics of America. Perhaps the anxiety and insecurity of the Cold War and the possibility of imminent attacks by the Russian atheists affected Jews thus? Or perhaps they felt the postwar drive for respectability among millions of middle-class Americans—that is, suburban social pressures—that fueled the revival? Or perhaps they felt a genuine interest in, and concern with, religion, which stimulated everything from university religious organizations and departments of religion to synagogues "springing up in firehouses, banks, and even Protestant churches."

Whatever the reason, and whatever the real quality of the movement, the quantity cannot be denied. From a base of $26 million in 1945, the amount spent on new churches and synagogues rose steadily: 1946, $76 million; 1948, $251 million; 1950, $409 million; 1954, $593 million; 1956, $775 million; 1958, $863 million; 1959, $935 million; 1960, $1,016 million. Obviously, millions of people were convinced that in addition to adding a new phrase ("under God") to the pledge of allegiance, one pledged allegiance to the Deity with generous capital improvements.[39]

The Union of American Hebrew Congregations grew spectacularly in the two decades or so after World War II. In 1947–1948 there were 364 congregations with 100,000 member "units" or families with 3 to 5 members; less than ten years later (1955), there were 520 congregations with 255,000 memberships; and by January 1963 the UAHC comprised 646 congregations (see Table 1). In one 12-month period alone (1954–1955) fifty congregations joined the UAHC, while the UAHC budget skyrocketed from $150,000 in 1943 to $1,370,000 in 1953, and to $2,780,000 in 1964–1965. By and large, this growth was the result of spontaneous combustion: groups of young Jews getting together in newly emerging neighborhoods created by the postwar housing boom; deciding to form a congregation; exploring the denominational alternatives; and, frequently, contacting the UAHC for assistance in establishing a Reform congregation.

The UAHC would provide an ark, prayer books, and a Torah on loan to the new "congregations," arrange for a student rabbi from a HUC campus to conduct services, and work vigorously to encourage the group to become a Reform synagogue. The result was an explosion in Reform congregations as Judaism hit the suburbs: Nassau County, with less than 150,000 Jewish residents, had twenty-two Reform synagogues in 1954, while between 1946 and 1958, according to the UAHC Department of New Synagogues, sixteen new Reform temples emerged in northern New Jersey, four in Rockland County, six in Westchester, and thirty-one on Long Island.[40]

This growth in United States religious institutions was paralleled by a sizable increase in affiliation with, and attendance at, these same institutions. In 1954 George Gallup reported that 79 percent of adults polled belonged to a church or synagogue; and, according to a Gallup poll a year later, the United States population set an all-time attendance record at worship services: Whereas in 1940 only a third of the United States adult population polled had "attended a church or synagogue in the past seven days," in 1955 one-half had done so. These same polls indicated that while Jews gathered for prayer much less frequently than either Protestants or Catholics, they too did so in record numbers. It became especially fashionable to enroll children in programs of religious education (the number of children in Jewish schools doubled between 1946 and 1955), and rabbis who served the larger congregations in the bigger cities often found themselves with so many Bar Mitzvah candidates and so few Sabbaths that they celebrated "double" ceremonies week after week.[41]

The administrative center of the UAHC, housed in the eleven-story House of Living Judaism on Manhattan's Upper East Side ever since it moved from Cincinnati in 1951, was a large and generously staffed institution serving congregations in nearly every state of the land.

Rabbis and lay professionals in the New York center administered the various UAHC divisions: Department of Youth Programming, Department of Worship, Department of Synagogue Administration, Department of Adult Education, Department of Jewish Education (which, among other things, was the largest publisher of Jewish teaching aids in the country), Department of New Synagogues, Commission on Social Justice, and so on. Rabbis supervised the congregations in the seventeen (as of 1962) UAHC regions; there were seven (as of 1965) Reform Jewish summer camps, run by the UAHC, in Massachusetts, Wisconsin, Indiana, California, Pennsylvania, Georgia, and New York. The UAHC operated three Schools of Jewish Studies. And, by the early 1960s, replacing the Social Action Committee established at the 39th Council of the UAHC in 1946, there was a UAHC Social Action Center in Washington, D.C.

This large network of people and institutions was supported financially by the members of UAHC congregations. For two decades after World War II the Combined Campaign raised large sums of money and, as at all other times, divided the proceeds equally between the HUC and the UAHC. Between 1948–1949 ($732,638) and 1962 ($2,500,000) the Combined Campaign raised more money each year, and its totals were collected from congregational dues (50 percent), individual supplementary gifts (40 percent), and various communal grants (10 percent). For some years members of UAHC congregations paid a flat amount for UAHC dues ($6 per member unit in the 1950s), but there was increasing pressure to "tax" congregations more equitably. The UAHC Toronto Biennial of 1957 adopted a proportional dues plan (the ["Louis] Broido Dues Plan"), which mandated that beginning 1 July 1958 each congregation would send 10 percent of the dues collected to the UAHC. This plan worked successfully, and it was still in effect (though raised to 12 percent) in the early 1980s, although in 1965 the Combined Campaign had changed its name to the Reform Jewish Appeal.[42]

To understand the place of UAHC dues in a congregation's budget, we might note how one midwestern congregation of 1,000-member units (2,200 people), allocates it budget. For fiscal year 1983 the synagogue spent $500,000; of this amount, 54 percent went for salaries (two rabbis and a rabbi emeritus; a religious school principal and teachers; a preschool director and staff; choir direction and singers; administrator and office as well as maintenance staff). In addition, 16 percent was needed for maintenance expenses, 10 percent for office materials, 10 percent for "operations" (youth activities, special events, and transportation of elderly residents to worship services), 5 percent for religious and Hebrew school subsidies, and, finally, only 5 percent to meet the congregation's obligations to the UAHC.

Under Maurice Eisendrath's leadership (1943–1973), the most distinctive and prominent mark of the UAHC was to be found in its commitment to social action. Eisendrath busied himself encouraging social action committees and programs in nearly every congregation, and called on Reform Jews "to apply the precepts and practices of prophetic Jewish faith in combating all forms of injustice and bigotry." When asked, on being chosen clergyman of the year by Religious Heritage of America in 1959, why he placed such emphasis on injustice and bigotry, he replied, "That's religion! The heart of religion concerns itself with man's relation to man." The effect of Eisendrath's commitment to social justice on the congregational level meant that the Reform movement, rather than individual rabbis, now gave a high priority to social action programs.[43]

Eisendrath devoted special attention, during the 1950s and 1960s, to efforts to integrate blacks into the mainstream of American society. The

1955 biennial conference hailed the previous year's Supreme Court decision (*Brown* v. *Board of Education*), and the national executive board "enthusiastically" reaffirmed this resolution on desegregation. The Toronto biennial conference strongly denounced both segregated schools and segregated housing, while Eisendrath (as well as other UAHC leaders) made a strong plea for racial integration in a press conference. The 1959 biennial in Miami Beach approved a Social Action Center in Washington, and in 1961 the Emily and Kivie Kaplan Center for Religious Action opened in the Capital despite the opposition of two (of the more than 600) UAHC congregations.[44]

As might have been expected, the strongest opposition to the UAHC efforts to end segregation came from southern congregations. Northern rabbis and laypeople rode Freedom Buses through the South, together with Christian leaders, and their congregations sent moral and financial support. Young men and women from northern and western Reform congregations came south to try to desegregate public facilities. And when a southern rabbi, such as Charles Mantinband (1895–1974) of Hattiesburg's B'nai Israel, worked to improve race relations by "applying [Judaism's] principles to day-by-day living," some of his congregants offered verbal opposition. The president of B'nai Israel felt that Mantinband's "identification with liberal causes [he had in mind the Mississippi Council on Human Relations] does the Jewish people no good," while one congregant, at a congregational meeting attended by every member, asked, "Why must the rabbi mix with the niggers?" Such local complaints, despite their stridency, did little to slow the steady commitment to civil rights in the national Reform movement of the 1950s and 1960s.[44]

The nine UAHC summer camps in 1983 were dedicated to intensive Jewish programming as well as to summer fun. One of the most noticeable features of camp life in the early 1980s was the return to tradition or, perhaps more precise, the movements toward traditions, observable in the worship services at several of the camps. At the UAHC camp in Zionsville, Indiana, campers learned how to genuflect during the *aleynu* or adoration prayer in the twice-daily worship services; at Warwick's camp, traditional chants pervaded some services; while at Camp Swig in California the youngsters were told to face east during parts of the service and vigorous discussions took place over whether or not to install completely kosher dining facilities. If it is true, as some rabbis claim, that the trends of Reform Judaism are first revealed at the UAHC camps, then Reform and Conservative worship services will probably become less distinct in the years ahead, and the "perceptive move in the direction of more traditional observances" that one UAHC survey revealed will continue.[46]

With its numerous regions well-staffed, its camps filled, its educational programs immensely diverse, and its involvement in North American society broad and deep, the UAHC entered the 1980s, if not with any hopes for dynamic growth, very much content with its strength and contributions. And with its attention turned from civil rights to the attempts to strip the federal judiciary of jurisdiction in several areas, budget cuts and human needs, the nuclear arms race, abortion, the situation of Soviet Jewry, and right-wing extremism, there was abundant evidence of renewed social action in congregations all over the land.[47]

The Hebrew Union College and the Jewish Institute of Religion

Julian Morgenstern, despite the Hebrew Union College's financial problems during the 1930s, responded to the increasingly dangerous situation facing German Jewry by bringing five rabbinic students, with all expenses underwritten, from the Hochschule für Wissenschaft des Judentums (the German liberal seminary) to the college, and, in addition, providing jobs for eight Jewish scholars (including Abraham Joshua Heschel) and three refugee professors. This generous act of salvation, which came at great expense to the college, was remembered by some as Morgenstern's most important single effort.[48]

Morgenstern retired in 1947, and Nelson Glueck (1900–1971), a Cincinnati native ordained at the HUC in 1923, was inaugurated that same year. Glueck had received his doctorate in Germany in 1927, served as the director of the American School of Oriental Research in Jerusalem for much of the 1930s and 1940s, and was an internationally known archaeologist when chosen as Morgenstern's successor.

Glueck presided over the combined HUC-JIR during two decades (the 1950s and 1960s) of tremendous expansion for Reform Judaism and, as a direct result, of the college. The UAHC doubled its member congregations in the decade and a half after World War II, and its dues-paying members also doubled. Glueck worked out a 50–50 split of revenues raised by the UAHC-HUC Combined Campaign for Reform Judaism as well as member congregation dues early in the 1950s, and this enabled him to expand the HUC administration, student body, faculties, and physical plants in these years.

The faculties consisted of twelve full-time people in 1947, but reached forty in 1970. The student body, only 120 in 1950 (New York and Cincinnati), doubled by 1970, as the explosion of new congregations and the growth of old ones created an enormous demand for solo as well as assistant rabbis.

The California school of HUC was established in 1954, and after developing from a prerabbinic to a rabbinic program covering the first two of the five required years, it dedicated its new campus in 1971 adjacent to the University of Southern California. The New York campus established a School of Education (offering degrees in Jewish music and training cantors), directed, initially, by Abraham Franzblau (1901–1982) and Eric Werner (1901–   ), and the HUC Biblical and Archaeological School, despite vigorous Orthodox opposition, was founded in Jerusalem in 1963, and by 1970 it served as the site for a required "Year in Israel" for all entering HUC rabbinic students.

In Cincinnati, the American Jewish Archives was established and greatly expanded in a short time under the direction of Jacob Rader Marcus (1896–   ) and soon became the major depository of Judaica Americana; a new library, capable of housing hundreds of thousands of volumes, was built in 1959–1960; while a graduate department took shape, with generous fellowship support, and by 1971 had issued fifty doctoral degrees, more than half to Christian interfaith fellows.

When Glueck died, and Alfred Gottschalk (1930–   ), a German-born but U.S.-educated HUC graduate replaced him in 1972, the HUC and JIR, independently and together, had ordained over 1,300 rabbis, were receiving nearly all their incoming students from the Reform movement itself, and were successfully running four major campuses, including a new five-story building in New York City dedicated in 1979. As the 1980s unfolded, the HUC-JIR was in marvelous health.

The Central Conference of American Rabbis

The Central Conference of American Rabbis, which had been organized by Isaac Mayer Wise in 1889 as he and about thirty other rabbis were attending a Union of American Hebrew Congregations biennial assembly, grew steadily in numbers and strength. By the 1980s its membership exceeded 1,400. Its publications—especially prayer books—yielded more than a million dollars in sales in 1980 and hence funds for conference expenditures; its members had active roles in the Jewish as well as general community; and it sponsored a quarterly, the *Journal of Reform Judaism* (formerly the *CCAR Journal*), which combined practical rabbinics and scholarship. In addition, it played a vigorous role in the Synagogue Council of America, the umbrella organization for all Jewish rabbinic and congregational organizations; it published a comprehensive "Code of Ethics for Rabbis"; and its members seemed never to tire of studies and reflections on the "state of the rabbinate."[49]

While an executive board is responsible for the conduct of business between annual conventions, at these CCAR conferences the membership expresses its position—always nonbinding on its members—on the issues of the day and approves the executive board actions. At the 1983 convention in Los Angeles, the resolutions included pleas for increased Soviet Jewish emigration, "food banks" for the hungry, assistance to the unemployed and disabled, support for the single rabbi, and a declaration that the child of a marriage involving one Jewish parent of either sex—when that child affirms his or her identification with the Jewish faith and people—is "under the presumption of Jewish descent." But much of the CCAR work is performed by committees, with thirty-four standing committees on such matters as conversion, education, family life, interreligious activities, liturgy, Reform Jewish practice, and retirement. In addition, there are several commissions, task forces, and ad hoc committees.[50]

After years and years of complaints about pulpit hiring, a placement commission, jointly run by the CCAR and UAHC, was approved by the CCAR in 1950. Despite vigorous lobbying by the rabbis within their congregations, the UAHC rejected its most important parts, approving instead a much diluted version consisting of a Provisional Rabbinic Placement Commission with one representative from the CCAR, the HUC, and the UAHC. Only in 1961 was a plan made mandatory for rabbis and a placement director on the CCAR staff approved, and the UAHC and HUC both approved the Rabbinic Placement Commission, which has functioned smoothly for two decades.[51]

The biggest crisis the CCAR faced in recent years was the 1973 convention debate on the issue of rabbinic participation in mixed (i.e., interfaith) marriages. Although a 1909 resolution had discouraged such participation, some Reform rabbis—unlike their Orthodox and Conservative counterparts —officiated at such ceremonies, and by the early 1970s a very large minority of Reform rabbis did so. After periodic discussion of the proper stance of the Reform rabbinate in the wake of rising intermarriage rates—a threat to the survival of a minority faith—a 1973 resolution declared the CCAR's "opposition to participation by its members in any ceremony which solemnizes a mixed marriage."[52]

A vigorous and lengthy debate on the convention floor—widely predicted and even feared by Reform leaders—took place. Rabbi Harvey Fields (1935–   ), for example, felt that this debate and vote would "split asunder the reform rabbinate." But his fears and those of others were exaggerated. Although the resolution was approved by more than 3 to 2 (321–196), it neither deterred a significant number of rabbis from continuing to officiate at interfaith marriages nor caused the CCAR to split apart. A few rabbis did form the Association for a Progressive Reform Judaism, a caucus within the CCAR, but the primary impact of the resolution was to give those who refused to officiate at mixed marriages the authority of a conference majority resolution to use in explaining their position.[52]

The CCAR itself, headquartered in New York City for the past thirty years, has had only two executive vice-presidents, as Rabbi Isaac Marcuson, administrative secretary for a few decades, ran the conference from his synagogue study. The conference appointed Rabbi Sidney Regner (1903–   ) the first executive vice-president, and he served from 1954 to 1971. Rabbi Joseph Glaser (1925–   ) has directed conference affairs since that time.[52]

One of the most striking developments in recent years has been the movement of CCAR members into leadership positions of the UAHC. The president of the UAHC remains, as always, a layman, but rabbis dominate nearly every executive-level position in this once lay-dominated organization. The implications of this change, while rarely discussed at CCAR conventions, are increasingly the topic of informal conversations among congregational presidents and national leaders, and if the decline in influence among the laity continues, one imagines that this decline will become a more volatile issue.

PART II

CONSERVATIVE JUDAISM

---

4. History and Ideology: 1886–1983

Unlike Reform Judaism in North America, which began to train rabbis for its own congregations two decades after many of those congregations had identified themselves as Reform and two years after a sizable number of those congregations had formed a union, Conservative Judaism began in North America with a seminary (1902)—albeit a "reorganized" one—and a decade later (1913) a union of congregations, nursed by this seminary, was formed.

At the founding of this congregational union, the United Synagogue of America, the president of the Jewish Theological Seminary (JTS) sought to extend the roots of this twentieth-century movement deep into the previous century. He paid tribute, in 1913, to "such men as Isaac Leeser, Sabato Morais, Marcus Jastrow, Benjamin Szold, Alexander Kohut and many others," identified them as the creators of the Conservative movement in North American Judaism, and had the good fortune to have this claim repeated by virtually every supporter of Conservative Judaism ever since.

His claim is, however, erroneous. It is based on (1) a misunderstanding of the Judaic expression of the so-called founders, an attempt to apply the threefold divisions of American Judaism (Reform, Conservative, Orthodox) in the twentieth century to that not-so-neatly-divided in the nineteenth, (2) a confusion between the generic *conservative* and the specific *Conservative,* and (3) an exaggerated conception of the role played by the original Jewish Theological Seminary.[1]

German-born Isaac Leeser (1806–1868), although not a rabbi, performed many rabbinical functions in his position as *hazzan* (in this case a bit more than "cantor"—perhaps cantor-minister) of Philadelphia's Sephardic congregation Mikveh Israel (1829–1850). He conducted religious services, preached sermons, supervised religious education, officiated at weddings and funerals, published feverishly, and performed pastoral duties. He has been widely hailed as the "unofficial founder" of Conservative Judaism, "the prototype of today's conservative spiritual leader," and the man who "set an example for the conservative rabbi of the twentieth century."[2]

None of these claims is true. Leeser did battle, especially in the last decade or so of his life but as early as the 1830s, against Poznanski in Charleston and the reformers—especially Isaac Mayer Wise—and could be claimed as a founder just as easily by Orthodox Judaism. In fact, one early biographer has called him "the foremost pioneer leader of Orthodox Judaism in America," and his most recent biographer called him a man who "articulated a consistent bibliocentric, doctrinal orthodoxy."

Since neither Conservative Judaism nor Orthodox Judaism, as such, existed in North America during Leeser's lifetime, and since Leeser clearly could not be labeled a Reform Jew, he could be called either a Conservative or Orthodox *hazzan*. But the term *conservative* bears little in common with what became, more than three decades after Leeser's death, Conservative Judaism.

If either term must be used, in its nineteenth-century context, describing Leeser as Orthodox would be most accurate. "In the well nigh two score years of his pulpit and public activities," one biographer noted, Leeser "evidenced not the slightest change in his rigidly orthodox standpoint," while another argued that Leeser's theology was "typical of any supernaturalistic Orthodox Jew." He was uncompromising on the matter of observance, condemning those who abolished the second day of certain holidays or used the vernacular for prayer. He defended a literal belief in every miracle just as the Bible recorded it, he tried to rally his supporters around the sanctity of the oral Law ("the Talmud contains the divine tradition given to Moses"), and he sought to create a rabbinical union in which the members pledged to reject the "abandonment of a single ritual principle, or a single act of religion." Another of Leeser's biographers has argued that he was "a strict traditionalist, adhering to the dictates, decisions, and documents of the past," while his bitterest enemy, Isaac Mayer Wise, eulogized Lesser with the claim that "we know of no man in America who will replace Isaac Leeser in the orthodox camp."[4]

Benjamin Szold (1829–1902) came from Hungary to Baltimore's Oheb Shalom in 1859 and, a few months after his arrival, wrote to Isaac Mayer Wise that "I, too, like you, am against the fresh reform . . . I am . . . neither of the two [Orthodox or Reform] or both at the same time." Szold was surely not both at the same time, and perhaps what he instituted at Oheb Shalom was not "fresh reform"; but Reform it surely was—not much different from that of several other Reform congregations. And this Reform position was not a sudden shift for Szold. Before his election at Oheb Shalom, he had applied (1859) for a rabbinical position in Stockholm, with a letter of recommendation from Zacharias Frankel of the Jewish Theological Seminary in Breslau, and when asked by the board of directors there to state his views on Reform he replied that "wherever the necessity for reforms generally would become known within a community" [organ, vernacular prayers, choir, abridged prayer book], he "as a rabbi never would oppose such a desire and its realization."[5]

Szold used a denationalized prayer book (*Abodath Israel*) with English translations (and another with German), an organ, a mixed choir (Jews and non-Jews), and family pews (men and women together). He eliminated the second day of some festivals (1867) as well as the use of head covering during worship (1869), and even the reading of certain scriptural verses (1869). He argued, in the case of the biblical chapters on sacrifices, that they were without "significance to us today," and in his "catechism" for youth he explicitly denied the divine revelation of scriptures and argued that the Pentateuch was "written by different authors." Outside the congregation Szold was also viewed as a reformer: he led Oheb Shalom into the Union of American Hebrew Congregations by 1885, and was invited by Wise to be the main speaker at the first graduation of the Hebrew Union College (1883). In fact, the commitment of Oheb Shalom to Reform Judaism was so firm that when Szold died, William Rosenau (1865–1943), a HUC graduate, was selected as rabbi and served the congregation for nearly half a century.[6]

Marcus Jastrow (1829–1903) was ordained in Germany, received a doctorate from the University of Halle (Saxony) in 1855, came to Philadelphia's Rodef Shalom in 1865, and served as its rabbi until 1892 when Henry Berkowitz, a HUC graduate, succeeded him. The hiring of a Reform rabbi seemed rather inevitable, for Jastrow himself had introduced many reforms, including an organ, late Friday evening services, family pews, a mixed choir, Szold's revised prayer book, and had even led the congregation into the Union of American Hebrew Congregations in 1878. Little had changed by the time of Jastrow's forced "retirement"; indeed, in his last year the congregation even voted to eliminate nearly all Hebrew from the Sabbath service. Jastrow, in describing the congregation during his rabbinate, noted that it "championed the cause of reform," albeit with a "wholesome conservatism."[7]

Alexander Kohut (1841–1894), who received his ordination in Breslau at the Jewish Theological Seminary (1867) and his doctorate at the University of Leipzig (1864), spent only the last decade of his life in the United States, where he served as rabbi of New York's Ahavath Chesed and as professor of Midrash and Talmud at the Jewish Theological Seminary of America. Kohut is not easy to classify, although there is nothing in his writing or rabbinic career to suggest that he had much in common with Reform

Judaism, something he described as "a deformity—a skeleton without flesh and sinew, without spirit and heart." His claim to being a founder of Conservative Judaism rests on his use of that term—one of the earliest recorded—at the opening exercises of the JTS of America (2 January 1887). But the rest of his writing, especially his 1885 debates with Kaufmann Kohler, suggests that it is difficult to say more than that Kohut was in what he called the "Mosaic-rabbinical" tradition. Some of his views subsequently became identified with North American Orthodoxy (Jewish law is "un-changeable") and others with Conservative Judaism (the "exigencies of the times" may serve as the guide for "what may be discarded"), and Kohut has been claimed by both groups.[8]

The final "founder" of Conservative Judaism identified by Solomon Schechter was Sabato Morais (1823–1897), an Italian-born and trained *hazzan* who arrived in the United States in 1851, succeeded Isaac Leeser at Philadelphia's Mikveh Israel (a congregation he tried to bring into the UAHC), remained there until his death nearly five decades later, delivered the commencement address at HUC in 1878, and also served as the founding president of the Jewish Theological Seminary (1886–1897). Although in his case too we have precious little, despite his abundant writing, to link him directly with Conservative Judaism, in his thinking and especially in the institution he presided over there were intimations of the movement that exploded on the scene of twentieth-century North America.

Morais spoke of the need to "preserve historical Judaism," a phrase that suggested his discomfort with both Reform and traditional Judaism. Reformers in the last few decades of the nineteenth century spoke more of discarding than preserving, while the small but growing traditional community resisted the notion of change or development and hence felt uncomfortable with "historical," or evolving, Judaism. Morais's "love of the observance[s] of Judaism," especially those which "recall[ed] the events at Sinai," set him apart from the reformers, while his desire to make changes "without trenching upon the essentials of our religion" posed the fundamental thrust, and dilemma, that later faced Conservative Judaism.[9]

The Jewish Theological Seminary, which the aging Sabato Morais founded in 1886 and which began course instruction in January of 1887, emerged simply as a counterseminary to the Hebrew Union College, and not specifically as a Conservative Jewish institution. In fact, if anything is appropriate as a label, it would be *Orthodox* and not *Conservative.* Not only did Morais suggest calling it the "Orthodox Seminary," and one of its earliest instructors, Bernard Drachman, noted that it was organized with "uncompromising adherence to the tenet of Orthodox Judaism," but Solomon Schechter, president of the seminary from 1902–1915, called Sabato

Morais "the greatest leader of Orthodox Judaism in this country" and called the earlier seminary "orthodox." Furthermore, in the preamble to the constitution of the Jewish Theological Seminary Association, the stress is on remaining "faithful to Mosaic Law and ancestral traditions," to "faithfully expound[ing] rabbinical literature," and to the "establishment of a seminary which demonstrates," as Morais argued the HUC did not, "a spirit of fidelity and devotion to the Jewish Law."[10]

The Jewish Theological Seminary, then, was first and foremost a rabbinic seminary dominated by Orthodox Jews committed to rejecting Reform Judaism—as taught in the classrooms of the HUC and expressed in the Pittsburgh Platform—and not a specifically denominational school. The founders of the seminary also hoped that the school would contribute to Jewish learning: Cyrus Adler (1863–1940), a future president, spoke of the seminary as early as 1892 as the center of a "renaissance of Hebrew scholarship in America," and Alexander Kohut voiced similar expectations. Yet it cannot be a coincidence that the founders of this anti-Reform institution chose a name already in use in Europe, that Kohut spoke of "Conservative Judaism" in this address at the opening exercises, and that the object of the Jewish Theological Seminary Association (JTSA), its founders announced, was "the preservation in America of the knowledge and practice of historical Judaism." These factors were to provide the twentieth-century creators of Conservative Judaism as a movement the grounds for linking the JTS of the nineteenth century to the later denomination.[11]

"Jewish Theological Seminary" is a precise translation of the German name of the important school in Breslau that had produced, in the last half of the nineteenth century, most of the great rabbinic leaders and scholars of European Jewry. The first president of the Breslau Seminary was Zacharias Frankel (1801–1875), who assumed the position in 1854 and retained it until his death, and both Frankel and the institution were committed to what the Jewish Theological Seminary Association would call "historical Judaism."

Frankel, who was born and raised in Prague, received his doctorate in classical philology at the University of Pesth and his rabbinical ordination in the same year (1831). He then held rabbinical positions in Teplitz, Bohemia (1831–1836), and Dresden, Saxony (1836–1854), before accepting the position at the Jüdisch-Theologischen Seminar in Breslau. Frankel rose to prominence in the 1840s via his writing and preaching, and while modifying tradition (he called it "moderate reform") both within his congregations (choir, organ, vernacular sermon, elimination of the secondary celebration of some holidays, omission of some parts of the liturgy) and in his writings ("we must omit certain unimportant actions"), he demonstrated a much stronger attachment to it than did the reformers in either Germany or North America.[12]

Committed to an historically evolving dynamic Judaism (in contrast to the Orthodox), Frankel viewed the essentials of Judaism, especially law, through the prism of history (like the reformers) and feeling (unlike the reformers). While the reformers applied primarily intellectual and historical criteria in deciding what to retain and what to abolish, Frankel asked not only what part a particular ritual, custom, belief, or law played in the people's past (for Frankel the past was a source of values, inspiration, and commitment) but also what the feeling and sentiment of the Jewish people of his own day was toward that item. He was not bothered at all by the possibility that certain rituals or observances might be discarded or even cease to exist, for if that was the "will of the entire community," then so be it. The "people . . . will not hurt itself and will not destroy its practices; its own sense of religiosity warns against it." Thus "positive historical Judaism," as Frankel would call it, sought to discover not only the origins of his people's *Volksgeist* (national spirit) but their *Gesamtwille* (collective will) as well, so both the past (historical) and present (sociological) had a say in any attempt to determine what to change, what to retain, and what to discard. The past (tradition) and the present (the total will, or at least the majority will, of the Jewish people) had a vote, as it were, in contemplated change, and the "ultimate" arbiter, or source of authority behind Jewish law, was, apparently, the religious consciousness of the people.[13]

Frankel made a memorable public exit from the 1845 rabbinical conference in Frankfort, because a majority of the participants had voted that there was no "objective necessity" to use Hebrew in the Jewish worship service. Abraham Geiger had argued that since Hebrew was merely a "national" element in the service and since Reform Judaism replaced the nationalistic elements with universal symbols, Hebrew was unnecessary. Frankel knew, of course, that Hebrew was not a religious factor and that even the strictest of Jewish legalists could have no fundamental objection to prayer in the vernacular. He responded with the argument that Hebrew was one of the most vital positive historical elements in Judaism, the sacred tongue in which Jews over the centuries expressed their beliefs and ideas, and that it was an emotional or mystical element—even when not understood—as well. When the rabbis voted 15–13 in support of Geiger (although not actually carrying out their decision), Frankel stormed out and, in a subsequent letter to a Frankfort newspaper, affirmed his commitment to "positive historical Judaism," that is, the special role of the Jewish people as the source and carrier of Judaism. Thus he became, in the words of a JTS professor a century later, "the father of the 'positive historical school.' "[14]

Frankel did not fit easily into the compartmentalization of German Judaism of the mid-nineteenth century. Although he shared much with Geiger and the other reformers, he strongly disagreed with them over the legitimate criteria for religious change in his insistence on limiting the role that scientific scholarship, relevance, reason, and precedents for change might have in determining such change and in his deep commitment to traditional piety and observance. He also fought bitterly with the Orthodox over his view that the Oral Law (Talmud) was completely rabbinic in origin rather than Sinaitic, that this law *(halacha)* was dynamically evolved, and that the source of observance (e.g., the Sabbath) was not in the divine origin of the *halacha* but in the role the various rituals and observances had for the Jewish people over the centuries. This position, what Kaufmann Kohler called "Conservative reform," a kind of mediation between Reform and Orthodox (at least in their extreme forms) that, in one scholar's words, "would reserve to itself absolute freedom of thought but otherwise keep up the traditional form of religious worship," was to provide, eventually, the ideological basis of Conservative Judaism.[15]

Little more than the name, as far as we know, linked the rabbinical school of the Jewish Theological Seminary Association to that of Frankel in Breslau, although the founders, as we have seen, were conscious of the associations the name similarity would offer. Alexander Kohut, who taught rabbinic literature in the waning years of his life, had studied at the Breslau seminary, but one could as easily identify the JTS—during its first fifteen years of existence—as Orthodox as one could call it Conservative. Kohut, in fact, urged the founders not to permit the seminary to be labeled either Conservative or Orthodox, but merely an alternative to the HUC.

Morais, the first president, insisted that it not "deny Moses the authorship of the Pentateuch," while Cyrus Adler, the second president of the "reorganized" (1902) Jewish Theological Seminary, noted that "when the Seminary was founded . . . it was the institution of the Orthodox, or Historical, or Conservative School." What Adler meant was that the seminary was a protest against the radicalism of Reform Judaism and that little about its early years besides its name and its proclamation linking it to "historical Judaism" enables us to say more about it than that it was a non-Reform, or vaguely "traditional," institution, as were the synagogues to which nearly all the faculty, students, and eleven or twelve of the fifteen original trustees belonged. To call the founders, or their synagogues, or the seminary they founded *Conservative* is to adopt a term rich in meaning only in the twentieth century but without specific demarcation in the nineteenth. In any event, the impact of the seminary on the North American religious scene was minimal. Unlike the HUC, it had little congregational or financial support; by 1900, the cash deficit was so severe that the president, Joseph Blumenthal (died 1901), was forced to advance funds. And through the commencement of June 1902 only seventeen rabbis had graduated (six of them in 1902), and one of the only two graduates to pursue a successful rabbinic career, Joseph H. Hertz (1872–1946), quickly left North America and served, eventually, as chief rabbi of the British Empire![16]

The seminary stood on the brink of bankruptcy in 1901–1902. Default was averted when a group of extremely affluent (and mostly Reform) Jews, under the prodding and direction of one of Morais's disciples, Cyrus Adler, and the initial largess of Louis Marshall (1856–1929) and Jacob Schiff (1847–1920), two members of New York's leading Reform congregation, Emanu-El, assembled an endowment fund of over $500,000. The impetus for their involvement was the awareness that there was no institution providing traditional, Americanized (English-speaking) rabbis to serve the nearly one million East European Orthodox Jews who had arrived in North America in the previous two decades. The seminary, an editorial in the *American Hebrew* explained, "afford[s] the surest and safest means of handling the downtown problems of Americanizing the foreign element by sending among them trained and well-equipped rabbinical teachers." The integration of these newcomers into North American society, Schiff and others realized, could be hastened by supplying them with religious leaders trained in North America rather than Europe, and yet, unlike the HUC graduates, sensitive to and comfortable within a world of traditional customs and observances.[17]

The generous endowment enabled the directors of the reorganized seminary (Reform financiers and the Americanized but observant Adler) to woo and to finally entice Solomon Schecter (1847–1915) to leave his position at Cambridge University and assume the presidency of the seminary in 1902. Schecter was an ideal person to lead the revitalized institution, for his Rumanian background, traditional Jewish education, and strict observance made him acceptable to traditional Jews: "the observance of the Sabbath, the keeping of the Dietary laws, the laying of *Tefillin,* the devotion to Hebrew Literature and the hope for Zion in Jerusalem," he noted, "are all things as absolutely necessary for maintaining Judaism in America as elsewhere."[18]

At the same time, his Western training, international scholarly reputation (he discovered the Cairo *Genizah* manuscripts), and commitment to the scientific study of Judaism enabled him to build "a school of Jewish learning, which should embrace all the departments of Jewish thought . . . scientific thoroughness and finish which alone deserves the name of research." It was, in fact, only a short time before "Schecter's Seminary" rivaled the Hebrew Union College as a serious institution of Wissenschaft des Judentums, for Schechter took seriously his commitment to modern scholarship: "I am just as anxious for the truth, whatever it may be, provided it is based on real scholarship."[19]

Schecter began his presidency with the hope that the reorganized seminary would avoid denominationalism and, instead, "give direction to both orthodox and reform." He frequently emphasized the term *America* in the institution's full name—Jewish Theological Seminary of America—and felt that the founders used this designation to demonstrate "their intention of avoiding sectarianism; for it is an especial American feature that no preference is given to any denomination or sect." Schechter never came close, however, to winning the support of the reformers and the traditionalists for his adjectiveless Judaism and making the seminary a "theological centre which should be all things to all men, reconciling all parties, and appealing to all sections of the community." In response to Schechter's acceptance of modern biblical criticism, the Union of Orthodox Rabbis (UOR) issued a writ of excommunication against the seminary in June 1904, despite Schechter's assurance that Jews, in North America, "need not sacrifice a single iota of our Torah." That same year the Slutzker Rav, Rabbi Jacob David Willowski (1845–1913), came to the United States and reportedly announced that English preaching had no place in a synagogue. And the Reform movement quite quickly and decisively demonstrated its lack of support. Cut off from the left and right of North American Judaism, Schechter, truly "THE founding father of the movement in this country," began to delineate the contours of what he and others, self-consciously, would call Conservative Judaism.[20]

The phrase "Conservative Judaism," with a capital "C," was first used regularly by Schechter, and he borrowed it from English-speaking Orthodoxy in Great Britain. He nicely summed up the specific task of a seminary dedicated to such an interpretation in a 1907 letter: "Conservative Judaism can only be saved in this country by giving to the world trained men on scientific lines, and proving to the world that Wissenschaft and history are on our side." A few years later, in another letter to the same former student, Schechter emphasized that although Conservative Judaism was a distinct trend in Judaism, it combined important elements of traditional and nontraditional Judaism: "Conservative Judaism unit[es] what is desirable in modern life with the precious heritage of our faith . . . that has come down to us from ancient times."[21]

This blend of the modern and the ancient in Schechter rejected both Reform ("Lord, forgive them, for they know nothing") and Orthodoxy ("a return to Mosaism would be illegal, pernicious and indeed impossible"), and he affirmed, as the central thrust of Conservative Judaism, an emphasis on the "Tradition." This emphasis meant, for Schechter, a far greater appreciation of, and commitment to, the rituals, customs, observances, laws, and beliefs in the Jewish past, as understood by the Jewish people ("people's will," he called it), while at the same time using science and history to probe, challenge, and uncover that past.[22]

Unlike his Orthodox opponents, Schechter respected much of modern, scientific biblical criticism, including the conclusions that Solomon did not write Ecclesiastes, that David did not author the entire Psalter, and that Isaiah 1–40 is not the same as Second Isaiah—all of which, incidentally, had already been suggested or hinted at by the ancient rabbis. He even raised the question of whether Moses actually existed and if he had any connection with the Pentateuch! But most of all, he rejected (or at least minimized) the notion of a divine revelation and emphasized instead the need for constant reinterpretation of the tradition by "catholic Israel"—the totality (or at least the vast majority) of the Jewish people. He wrote, "The Torah is not in heaven; its interpretation is left to the conscience of catholic Israel." Hence Schechter spoke of "development, progress, and retrogression," and of the "subjective notions of successive generations regarding religion," in order to emphasize not only the evolutionary character of Judaism by the responsibility of each generation of Jews—rabbis and laypeople—to change (albeit slowly and deliberately) the revered tradition in "accordance with its own spiritual needs."[23]

To advance his conception of Judaism, Schechter, together with members of the Alumni Association of the seminary, began work in 1909 to establish a union of congregations that could be sympathetic to, as well as "promote, Conservatism," and felt this would be "the greatest bequest which I shall leave to American Israel." This effort—to institutionalize catholic Israel in something distinct from Reform or Orthodoxy—resulted in the organization of the United Synagogue of America (USA), in February 1913, a union of twenty-two congregations seeking institutional sanction for emerging deviations from Orthodoxy yet committed to "maintaining Jewish tradition in its historical continuity." It represented, with its continual emphasis on tradition without Orthodoxy, perhaps the clearest beginnings of Conservative Judaism in North America.[24]

It took three or four years to hammer out, but in the preamble to its constitution the United Synagogue explicitly separated itself from the Reform movement (Schechter had specifically eliminated from the United Synagogue congregations that used the *Union Prayer Book* and worshiped with bare heads), while spreading the broadest possible net with which to lure any and all congregations ("essentially loyal to traditional Judaism") not affiliated with the UAHC. The commitment to a heterogeneous, traditional Judaism was clear, if not yet always explicitly called Conservative Judaism, for the United Synagogue hoped to further the observance of Sabbath and dietary laws, the use of Hebrew in worship, "traditional observances" in the home, and the study of Hebrew language and literature.[25]

But what gave Conservative Judaism its special flavor was Schechter's rejection of a European form of tradition and his insistence that Conservative Jews must be "thoroughly American in habits of life and mode of thinking . . . and imbued with the best culture of the day." This helps us understand why Schechter insisted that this "Conservative Union" ought to have as its goals: demonstrating to the East European immigrants that a secular education and rigorous observance are compatible; supporting rabbis, trained at the JTS in "scientific research," who insist on preaching English (rather than Yiddish) sermons and creating "proper order and decorum" in worship; and publishing modern textbooks and building an organizational structure as sophisticated and strong as that of the UAHC.[26]

Schechter was convinced that the survival of traditional Judaism in North America depended on its Americanization via Conservative Judaism, for without the United Synagogue, he predicted, "traditional Judaism will not survive another generation in this country." The JTS had served as "a bulwark of Conservative Judaism within the last ten years," and now (1913) there existed a sufficient number of JTS rabbinical graduates and sympathetic congregations to "establish Conservative Judaism on a firm foundation for posterity." The purpose, therefore, of the United Synagogue was to "conserve all those positive elements" that these rabbis and congregations "have in common."[27]

The congregations that joined to form the United Synagogue of America represented a blending of the "thoroughly American" and "Tradition," of Orthodox congregations seeking North American-trained, English-speaking rabbis, or as Max Drob (1887–1959), rabbi of Philadelphia's Bnai Jeshurun put it, the "thesis that there is no discrepancy between modern culture and the ancient faith." Cleveland's B'ne Jeshurun, already by the 1880s consisting of "prosperous immigrants" who "no longer adhered to Orthodoxy in its European form," has been described as "quasi-Orthodox" or "modified Orthodox." A JTS graduate served as its rabbi from about 1906–1908, and was followed by a graduate of the HUC who neatly delineated the type of congregation that founded the United Synagogue: "orthodox with a touch of liberalism." This meant that, on the one hand, the regular Orthodox Sabbath morning service was chanted, as was the entire weekly Torah portion, but there were mixed seating (family pews), late Friday evening services, and an English sermon. Conservative Judaism, it has been said of B'ne Jeshurun, was that "for which they might be said to have been groping."[28]

Among many of the other congregations of the fledgling United Synagogue similar patterns emerged, including Syracuse's Adath Yeshurun (the "Neustadter Shul"), served by the first JTS graduate, Joseph Hertz, from 1894–1896, immediately following his ordination, and by subsequent JTS graduates; Birmingham's K'nesseth Israel, by 1900 consisting of "gentlemen whose devotion to Judaism has never permitted them to diverge from its most orthodox aspects"; Chicago's Anshe Emeth, where there was a "mode of worship that would reflect somewhat the modern tendencies and still retain the essential features of the old orthodoxy"; St. Paul's Temple of Aaron, where "conservatism was absolutely necessary to promote Modern American Judaism [and where] the old traditional form of the Jewish Ritual should be followed, omitting such portions of it that would not interest the younger folks and the coming generation"; Sioux City's Shaare Zion synagogue, which sought "a modern form of Jewish worship that would appeal to the growing generation of American Jews and at the same time safeguard the best Jewish traditions"; and Norfolk's congregation Beth El, a charter member of the United Synagogue, which "combined the sanctity of traditional Jewish worship with innovations" such as mixed seating. Perhaps none of these synagogues expressed the dilemma and challenge as succinctly as did Far Rockaway's Shaaray Tefila:

> Divine worship is conducted according to the orthodox ritual, retaining the authority of Israel's past, yet expressing that authority in the accents of America's present; designed especially to attract the young and yet hold the old, the result is a decorous and beautiful service.[29]

In the Newton, Massachusetts, Temple Mishkan Tefila, a founding member of the United Synagogue, Conservative Judaism represented a "new synthesis of tradition and the modern spirit." The newly developing movement offered some Newton Jews a "more esthetic and dignified setting" for the "traditional synagogue service"; the opportunity to cloth the "inherent beauty and majesty of our traditional synagogue" with "dignity, decorum, and glorious musical settings"; and "a new type of religious service in which the hallowed, traditional ritual of the synagogue was invested with a beauty and dignity." At Tifereth Israel, in Columbus, Ohio, an "old, rigid Orthodox" congregation until the 1920s, the majority of the congregation could "not join in sympathy with Orthodox Judaism" and found Reform unappealing. Its rabbi, Jacob Klein (1870–1948), in explaining why the synagogue affiliated with the United Synagogue, said, "It was the middle ground which they chose." At the Troy, New York, Temple Beth

El, the congregation's founders wanted a synagogue where whole families might worship together and English prayers would be read—in brief, a temple where "the demands of the tradition would be met but where new interpretations would be considered." Everywhere, then, United Synagogue synagogues attempted to concomitantly retain "tradition" and make changes in response to the new environment. As the Propaganda Committee of the United Synagogue explained at the 1919 convention, these synagogues were "battling for traditional Judaism" with "decorum, congregational singing, and the English sermon"; or, as New York's Inwood Hebrew Congregation put it, "Tradition is observed throughout, but by translations of portions of the prayers."[30]

While the cultural and social activities of Conservative congregations expanded tremendously in the 1920s and 1930s, a certain uniformity—despite much variety—began to be noticeable in the Sabbath worship services. Worship commonly occurred on late Friday evening and early Saturday morning, with the latter being about double the length of the former because of the practice of reading or chanting the Torah portion (several chapters of the Pentateuch) at this service. All congregations required men to wear head covering, had rabbis who actually conducted the worship service and preached English sermons, emphasized dignity and decorum (i.e., the elimination of constant conversations, random moving about of worshippers, unsynchronized recitation of congregational prayers, and public auctioning of Torah "honors"), used a prayer book other than the *Union Prayer Book* of the Reform movement, and were filled by men, on Sabbath mornings, who usually wore prayer shawls *(tallitim)* and many of whom often remained for an afternoon of study with the rabbi.[31]

Some aspects of the service, however, though everywhere traditional in content yet dignified in form, varied from congregation to congregation, for, as the organ of the Conservative movement put it, "no one is asked to yield aught of his belief and of his observance," and hence, it noted, the only thing Conservative congregations have "in common [is] that they have agreed to cooperate." Many had organs, mixed choirs, family pews, only one-day festival observance, *minyons* (a group of ten men) that met twice daily for worship, abundant English translations of prayers; and the reading of the prophetic selection *(Haftarah)* in English; some had none of these. Others had a junior congregation, where younger members—usually the second generation not yet removed, physically and spiritually, from the neighborhood and Orthodoxy of its parents—elected their own officers and board of trustees, conducted their own high holiday and Sabbath services, and generally resembled in their organizational structure the popular sisterhood and brotherhood. Other congregations rejected such a division and included younger people with their elders. Thus the pattern, from place to place, would vary significantly and be, sometimes, with modest reforms, quite similar to some Reform worship services and, at other times, not unlike those of Orthodox congregations. Israel Goldstein (1896–   ), for example, speaking to his colleagues in 1927, noted that "Reform Judaism [is] becoming more conservative," while orthodoxy now represents itself as the "exponent of the true American Judaism." Thus he wondered "wherein we conservatives, so called, differ from this revamped orthodoxy which permits decorum in the service and English in the sermon." This remained an issue regularly addressed by Conservative rabbis and other sympathetic observers.[32]

Sometimes "orthodox" congregants of "conservative" synagogues had their own definition of Conservative Judaism, in part because the leaders of the new movement refused to define precisely which innovations constituted Conservative Judaism. Thirteen members of Cleveland's Jewish Center, an affiliate of the United Synagogue, went to Cuyahoga County Court of Common Pleas in 1925 to force their rabbi, Solomon Goldman (1893–1953), to restore Orthodox Judaism to the congregation. Their uncertainty as to where to draw the line between Orthodoxy and Conservatism was a genuine dilemma, for no one could say for sure whether this or that specific reform (late Friday evening services, mixed seating, English preaching) was a prerequisite for Conservative Judaism. The court petitioners argued that Rabbi Goldman deviated from Orthodoxy and affirmed Conservatism by publicly stating the the Torah was neither authored by God or Moses, carrying books on the Sabbath, omitting part of the worship service, and eating at public restaurants that were not kosher.[33]

The direction and development of Conservative Judaism lay not only in the rapidly expanding number of congregations affiliating with the United Synagogue of America, but in the ideological expression, provided by the men ordained at the JTS, such as Solomon Goldman, and the faculty of that seminary (together called "Seminary men"). The congregations that joined the United Synagogue looked to the JTS not only for rabbis to serve them but to its faculty for ideology. This was especially true as Conservative Judaism sought to determine how it differed from Reform and, to a greater extent, Orthodoxy.

As early as 1919, a group of six rabbis and professors, including Mordecai Kaplan (around whom efforts to clarify Conservative Judaism always seemed to center), urged colleagues to make their "beliefs and practices . . . clear to the rest of the world." But Louis Ginzberg, the acting president of the JTS while Cyrus Adler was in Paris, refused even to let the men meet at the seminary. Rabbi Goldman noted, in 1931, that "Conservative Judaism has nowhere been defined, its program has never been clearly stated." Rabbi Robert Gordis (1908–   ), in the middle of the 1940s, bemoaned the fact that "many of our most distinguished scholars and thinkers have declined to formulate a specific program" or to "enunciate the philosophy of Conservative Judaism," and Ira Eisenstein (1906–   ), rabbi of Chicago's Anshe Emet, pointed out in the late 1940s that the Rabbinical Assembly of America (RAA) "seems to be a group of rabbis in search of a philosophy." Morris Adler (1906–1966), of Detroit's Shaarey Zedek, bemoaned the fact, during the 1960s, that "our members sense that they are not orthodox, they are not moved by reform, but they have yet to learn that they are conservative." They have no "unified purpose," according to Adler, "specific enough to confer upon [them] a corporate identity," and hence they are simply "between" Orthodox and Reform Judaism.[34]

Hillel E. Silverman (1924–   ), then of Sinai Temple in Los Angeles, opened the decade of the 1970s by scoring the lack of any ideology in Conservative Judaism, describing the movement as "a 'catch-all' for the dissatisfied, a conglomeration of many needs, pluralistic in approach to the extreme, boasting a left, a center and a right, a tepid orthodoxy and at the same time a timid reform." Conservative Judaism, he concluded, "is *nisht a hin und nisht a her,* a synthesis that avoids extremes and yet stands for little that is novel and authentic." In the middle of the decade, Benjamin Z. Kreitman (1920–   ), of Brooklyn's Shaare Torah, scored the "organizational diffusion and confusion" of Conservative Judaism and called for the fixing of definitions by the institutions of the movement. And David Lieber (1925–   ), president of the University of Judaism in Los Angeles, the West Coast division of the JTS, urged the Conservative movement, at the end of the 1970s, to "articulat[e] a definition of Conservative Judaism which is intelligible and unambiguous; . . . a clear and persuasive definition."[35]

Conservative Judaism has never produced an official declaration of principles, unlike Reform, and therefore there has always been a certain vagueness, what Mordecai Kaplan called frequently "inchoate and amorphous," which veiled the fundamental aims and ideas of Conservative Judaism. In fact, throughout the 1920s and 1930s, Cyrus Adler, the JTS president, vigorously rejected all attempts to set down "any set of resolutions or platforms," to a great extent because of the steady growth of the movement in the decade after World War I. Critics within the Conservative movement, such as Kaplan, described this amorphousness with the imagery of the dietary laws *"nicht milchig"* and *"nicht fleischig"*—"not dairy" and "not meat"—and underscored its liability for the movement, while its defenders noted that "our lack of a definite and definitive ideology . . . was one felicitious manner in which diverse and divergent numbers were attracted to our movement." Despite this lack of a platform, it is possible to determine some of the parameters of the movement as they unfolded in the twentieth century.[36]

Most of the JTS graduates and faculty who wrote or spoke about Judaism agreed that the Judaic expression of the East European Jewish immigrants must become adjusted to entirely new social, economic, and intellectual conditions. But in this process of adaptation, and even change, all sought to "conserve" the abundance of customs, beliefs, traditions, rituals, and various other elements, including the Hebrew language, that had constituted Judaism as they knew it, despite the apparent hostility of the environment. As Max Arzt (1897–1975), of Scranton's Temple Israel and later vice-chancellor of the seminary, put it, "We are anxious to conserve those tangible visible and time-honored elements of Jewish life which make for continuity with our past and which have intrinsic value and content." Congregations and individuals, as in the Reform movement, often operated entirely on their own in certain matters—thus the wide differences in ritual and worship of those calling themselves "conservative," but all sought ways to conserve rather than to eliminate.[37]

Conservative Jews, and Conservative Jewish congregations, therefore, appeared to many observers identical to Orthodox Jews and Orthodox Judaism. Solomon Goldman, then of Chicago's Anshe Emet, asked, "Suppose the angel Gabriel were overnight to teach all the members of the *Agudat Harrabbanim* [an Orthodox rabbinical group] to speak English, and suppose that the orthodox synagogues were to introduce decorum, what then would be the function and purpose of the conservative group?" But behind the desire to observe and perpetuate traditional ceremonies and laws, in the personal lives of congregants and in their institutional life as well, was much that separated the Conservatives from the Orthodox, and these differences were to become more and more clear as Conservative Judaism struggled to define itself.[38]

First, there was a commitment to the conception of Judaism as a developing religion, articulated most clearly by Frankel and later by Schechter, Louis Ginzberg, Louis Finkelstein, and others. Judaism was a changing and growing organism that sustained its vitality by adjusting to environmental conditions and adapting to cultural differences. It was, according to Schechter, "constantly liable to variation . . . through the subjective notions of successive generations," and this notion was adumbrated by most of the men Schechter brought to the seminary. The result of this conviction was that Conservative Jewish thinkers spoke of observances that had become obsolete and others that were actually in the way of the continued growth of Judaism. Such "obsolete practices" were not abrogated (unlike the reformers) nor were they observed anyway despite their irrelevance for many (unlike the Orthodox), but simply ignored.[34]

Second, unlike the Orthodox, there was rarely pressure to conform to any theological doctrine, such as the divine revelation of the Torah at Mt. Sinai. There was, in contrast, often encouragement or at least respect for various attempts to harmonize Jewish belief and modern thought. Thus a wide variety of theological positions, many at odds with each other despite sharing some commonalities, characterized the JTS faculty, the Conservative rabbinate, and even the laity. And the laity said it wanted to hold on to traditional forms and memories, to be significantly involved with traditional Judaism, but it wanted to do so on its terms and thus to choose which aspects of the tradition it wished to keep and in which manner.

Third, there were persistent efforts to establish the proper legislative machinery, or authoritative body, to adapt Judaism to what one JTS professor, Louis Ginzberg (1873–1953), called the "modern progress of thought" or what a lay leader described as the tension between "mental integrity and our Jewish observance." The chief obstacle, early on, was the near impossibility of enforcing any decisions such a body would make, for the United Synagogue permitted, in Ginzberg's words, "a good deal of autonomy to its members, the individual congregations." Nevertheless, there seemed to be considerable interest, as early as 1918, in establishing a "body of men learned in the law who will be able to advise us concerning the great questions that arise in our present day religious life." There was considerable difference over whether such a body should establish a distinctive "conservative" interpretation, thereby cutting itself off from the traditionalists as the reformers had done, or whether it should try to rally all traditional Jews around its banner. But both schools of interpretation acknowledged that the *Halacha* was not divine and that it was subject to careful change or adaptation.[40]

Fourth, there was a strong commitment to some of the adaptations the reformers had made in order to prevent congregants from "despis[ing] and hat[ing] the House of Worship, and with it Judaism." These adaptations included the English sermon, order and decorum in the synagogue, families sitting together during worship, modern religious schools, rabbinical leadership by men "scientifically" trained, and even more. A 1947 ritual survey of 170 Conservative synagogues, presented to the 1948 convention of Conservative rabbis, noted that "there has definitely emerged a distinctive pattern of religious behavior in almost all our congregations" and that "it is the general practice in *nearly all our* congregations to conduct late Friday evening services, to permit mixed pews, to use a non-orthodox prayer book and to employ a mixed choir."[41]

All these steps were carefully justified; as Simon Greenberg (1901–   ), rabbi of Philadelphia's Har Zion for two decades (1925–1946), executive director of the United Synagogue, and later, professor of homiletics and education as well as vice-chancellor of the seminary, put it, "We accept and practice only that which is historically tested and authenticated and that to which an overwhelming consensus has given approval in theory and practice." What Greenberg does not mention explicitly, but which becomes more and more true, is that the "historically tested" refers to adaptations first instituted by the Reform movement and used, with some success, for a century. These small changes in the service more and more clearly separated the Conservative faction from the traditionalists who had not yet yielded to the new environment, while several elements of the liturgy— prayers almost exclusively in Hebrew, old chants, the wearing of prayer shawls and head covering by all men—told even the casual observer that this was not a Reform service.[42]

Additionally, a number of JTS graduates and faculty began to articulate a rather consistent ideology of Conservative Judaism. While it never took the form of a platform or even a series of creedal statements agreed on by any group, however small, and while aspects of the ideology were disclaimed by Conservative loyalists, sometimes immediately after their pronouncement, a sufficient number of men linked to the Conservative movement agreed with each other for us to speak of such an ideology.[43]

God

Although few Conservative thinkers offered the rich theological and philosophical speculation that characterized Reform conceptions of God, there was, with an exception or two, a rather unanimous affirmation of a creating, choosing, revealing, active, omnipotent, omniscient, omnibenevolent, personal God in the essays, lectures, and sermons of Conservative thinkers (i.e., someone produced by, or connected with, the Jewish Theological Seminary). Seymour Siegel (1927–   ), professor of theology at the seminary, affirms a "transcendent person" when he discusses the "living God" of Judaism, a god who "gave Israel its Torah" and who "is addressed and . . . addresses us, . . . reveals Himself, . . . and tells man what He wishes and what He expects of mankind."[44]

To be sure, already during the 1920s a naturalistic theology had emerged (God is the "power that makes for salvation"), constructed by Mordecai Kaplan (1881–1983), a maverick JTS professor of homiletics and *midrash* from 1913 to his retirement in 1963, founder of Reconstructionism (see p. 179), and the most original and consequential Jewish theologian produced by the seminary, but this naturalism had, initially, little impact on the Conservative movement. Supernatural conceptions of God-dominated Conservative Jewry throughout its history, and while there are surely theological liberals within the Conservative movement who reject the very metaphor of a transcendent and personal God who issues commands and holds humanity accountable, they are far less visible than among the Reform rabbinate. Far more common are men such as Wilfred Shuchat (1920–   ), of Westmount Quebec's Shaar Hashomayim, who affirms the "two way communication between man and God" and the "reality of God to whom, above all other powers . . . man can relate in communication."[45]

Torah

Conservative Jewish thinkers largely affirmed revelation, setting the movement clearly apart from Reform Judaism, but they were vague enough on what constituted revelation to leave Conservative Judaism without the literalism of the traditionalists who believed that God dictated every word of the Torah to Moses (verbal revelation). The typical view of revelation found expression in Louis Finkelstein (1895–   ), a professor of Talmud and theology, and later provost, president, and then chancellor of the seminary, who stated that the "codes of law in Exodus, Leviticus, and Deuteronomy, though expressed in prosaic form . . . can only be recognized as prophetic and divine, in the same sense that the fiery words of Isaiah and Jeremiah are prophetic and divine." No Reform thinker ever made such a claim for the legal material in the Pentateuch, but in contrast to the Orthodox, there is little certainty as to what Finkelstein meant by "divine." Later, in the same 1927 address to his rabbinic colleagues, he referred to the laws of the Torah as "prophetically inspired," and despite the vagueness of the term *inspiration*, it was used frequently by Conservative thinkers who discussed the Torah. In contrast to the Orthodox, who spoke of verbal revelation, and the reformers, who spoke of the Torah as a human (albeit exceptional) product (progressive revelation), the Conservative position bridges the two extremes by suggesting a divinely "inspired" human composition, or "continuous" revelation, for, as one rabbi noted, "the vast majority of the members of the Rabbinical Assembly do not believe in supernatural revelation."[46]

As to what precisely constituted the divine impingement on the human mind, or what is human and what is divine in revelation, the answers varied, from Conservative thinkers who argued (1) that human beings loosely recorded the divine will revealed at Sinai, to those who claimed (2) that the human beings who wrote the scriptures were divinely inspired, to those who (3) viewed the scriptures as the human record of the encounter between God and humankind. They all agreed, however, in acknowledging greater divine "involvement" in the Pentateuch (Torah) than in the other books of the Hebrew scriptures—whatever that involvement might be—and in rejecting the Orthodox notion that the human agents of God's revelations presented to Israel a literal copy, God's *ipsissima verba*, of what he had communicated.

God's Word

The view that asserts that God revealed himself at Sinai, but that human beings (imperfectly) recorded the revelation, has been most popularly articulated by Abraham Joshua Heschel (1907–1972), a professor of Jewish ethics and mysticism at the JTS from 1945 to 1972. Heschel, for whom God was a shattering reality, an "overwhelming presence," explained that "the speech of God is not less but more than literally real"; that "if God is alive, then the Bible is His voice"; and that God took Hebrew words and breathed into them of his power. Revelation, for Heschel, was not "inspiration" but speech, although the human or humans who heard this revelation recorded more what they understood than what they heard. Heschel claimed that revelation was the transmission of thought and will from heaven to earth, but since heaven remains heaven and the earthly remains earthly, revelation must be translated into human language. Heschel's view was affirmed by (1) Gilbert S. Rosenthal (1934–   ), rabbi of Cedarhurst New York's Temple Beth El, who has argued that the "biblical kernel of Jewish law . . . is Divine —the revealed will of God"; (2) David Novak (1941–   ), of Far Rockaway's Congregation Darchay Noam, for whom God is "a person *who* reveals and *who* elects"; (3) Ernst Simon (1899–   ), a visiting professor at the seminary, who described the Bible as "a human echo of the Divine voice," a "human translation of God's word," and who sought, in his teaching, to find "traces of the original word of God"; and (4) Simon Greenberg, who felt that the Israelites, "*as a group,* experienced with unprecedented clarity and intensity, an ineffable awareness [and] . . . communicable content . . . of the Divine Presence."[47]

Inspired Documents

The view that revelation is fundamentally inspiration has been most often associated, in the Conservative movement, with Ben Zion Bokser (1907–   ), rabbi of the Forest Hills Jewish Center in Long Island, New York. For Bokser, divine revelation is that power beyond oneself that brought "new visions of truth and beauty to the world," or, in the production of scriptures, the "breathing in" by humans of the message they felt compelled to record. (Words such as *compelled,* of course, leave unidentified the source of the compulsion: humans? God?) This breathing in, or inspiration, is synonymous with revelation, and is the way in which God disclosed his will to his people. Bokser, like so many of his colleagues, cannot accept without embarrassment the notion of God speaking to human beings and dictating his pronouncements, and yet he also cannot accept the view that Moses, Jeremiah, Amos, and others simply prefaced their words, for greater effectiveness, with "Thus says the Lord." Hence a special vocabulary suggesting that, on the one hand, human creativity and initiative is involved, but, on the other, that this statement issues from God.[48]

Human Documents

The position that the Hebrew scriptures are a completely human document, devoid of divine inspiration, that recorded the people's sense of an encounter between the sacred and profane—what Abraham J. Karp (1921–), then rabbi of Rochester's Beth El, called "God's lure to holiness" —and their response to this "meeting," is a popular view among some Conservative thinkers. They have given up all claims for divine origin or inspiration, and accept the scriptures as an expression of human creativity and genius. For them, the scriptures are the human recordings of the experience of revelation, or the encounter of the human with the divine, and it is this existential dimension, or the record of humanity's feeling of having met God, that they emphasize.[49]

Halacha

Conservative Jewish writers, from Schechter on, have emphasized both the necessity of "conserving" or observing the laws of classical Judaism— dietary, Sabbath, holiday or festival, liturgical, and ethical—and the necessity of modifying, changing, and even discarding some of these traditional laws. Hence, while acknowledging Jewish law and observance to be required for a full Jewish life, Conservative Judaism admits that change and renewal, as people meet life, gain new ethical sensitivities, or no longer share a particular observance's social assumptions, are necessary. Its thinkers have, generally, emphasized less *halacha's* rootedness in divine revelation than its importance historically, its insights and wisdom, its growth and development through time, its ability to maximize human potential—and its changeability. As Bokser explained,

> Conservatism admits the propriety of change. It admits the divine origin of the Torah; but it asserts that, as we encounter it, every divine element is encumbered with a human admixture, that the divine element . . . rests in specific forms which are historically conditioned. These historically conditioned forms are . . . subject to adjustment.

There is, as we have noted, no comparable sense of conserving the tradition in Reform Judaism (none of the specifics of the law are binding), nor, as I shall note later, has Orthodox Judaism agreed to many of the modifications and changes instituted by the Conservative movement.[50]

The awareness that such changes must be made deliberately led the Conservative movement to make decisions in a communal manner, with the "conscience of catholic Israel," to use Schechter's phrase. Communal change was a direction urged on the movement in the early years of the United Synagogue, especially by Louis Ginzberg, and drew on Schechter's suggestion, vague as it was (is "catholic Israel" the majority of Jews? the observant Jews? the Conservative Jews? the accepted practice of the Jewish people?). The result was that "catholic Israel" came to mean Conservative Jews—both the "98 percent of the membership of our congregations who have learned disrespect for the law" and the "[2] percent which has, more or less, rigidly adhered to the letter . . . of the law"—and they came to be represented by Conservative rabbis. Ten of them (four "liberal" and four "Conservative," chosen by the RAA's executive council, and two chosen by the other eight), formed the Committee on Jewish Law (1928–1948) and, subsequently, following extensive dissatisfaction with its inflexibility and a bitter debate at the 1947 convention, twenty-five of them constituted the Committee on Jewish Law and Standards (CJLS) and ruled on issues of Jewish law.[51]

The committee prided itself on considering the vertical, as well as horizontal dimension, of catholic Israel—the practices of those generations no longer present. That is, it made, in the words of Kohut, "the teaching of the ancients its starting point," while not losing "sight of what is needed in every generation." Unlike among the Orthodox, the past alone cannot exercise a veto; but, unlike among Reform Jews, it must not be deprived of a vote. Nevertheless, until the committee's reorganization in November 1948, Louis Ginzberg and Boaz Cohen's Conservative (some argued, reactionary) domination so successfully bridled the committee that the slow and almost immobile *halachic* stance of the committee guaranteed that the past almost always carried the day, and change, in response to altered conditions, was minimal (some say nonexistent). As the chairman of the committee, Louis Epstein (1887–1949), admitted at the 1938 convention, after acknowledging complaints that "the committee is too conservative, too slow, too timid and too circumscribed in its scope," yet the committee "is not ready to lay down principles which would be in conflict with orthodox practice." This attitude changed quickly, however, with the expanded CJLS, as the new chairman, Morris Adler, vowed (and fulfilled the promise) no longer to halt between "fear of the orthodox and danger to reform" but to articulate "positive and unambiguous affirmations" and to "introduce into our thinking this revolutionary fact—the impact of an entirely changed world both outer and inner.[52]

Unless the committee made a unanimous recommendation (such as "no Conservative rabbi may officiate, and no synagogue may offer its facilities, for marriage of a Jew to a non-Jew"), each congregational rabbi was free to use his own authority to decide whether to follow the majority or minority recommendations (three votes were sufficient for a minority position to be established). This led, quite obviously, to charges of inconsistency in some quarters, but it is the way in which Conservative Judaism made only modest changes (by institutionalizing change) and the way the movement responded to differences among rabbis, congregations, and communities.

An example of the impact of the modern world on tradition, and the need to modify and conserve that tradition, concomitantly, within the Conservative movement, was the problem of travel on the Sabbath. As the automobile led to the development of the suburb, and Jews lived greater distances from the synagogue, it became increasingly difficult to have a suburban home, participate in communal worship, and observe the prohibition on Sabbath travel. The Committee on Jewish Law and Standards, in a majority report, resolved this dilemma (or affirmed the widespread reality, many cynics noted) in 1950 by exempting riding to the synagogue, for worship only, from the usual prohibition of travel on the Sabbath—thus conserving the prohibition on travel (for most of the Sabbath) and the obligation to pray with the community.

In so doing, the Committee on Jewish Law and Standards rejected the Orthodox view that every jot and tittle of the law must be observed, that the authority of any individual rabbi is minimal (each Conservative rabbi was expected to be the authority for his community, the final religious authority for his congregation), and that a rabbinically forbidden act (travel on the Sabbath) that comes in conflict with the obligation of public prayer ought to be sustained. At the same time, in wrestling with the *halachic* norm, and in filing a restrictive minority report, the committee rejected the Reform notion that Jewish law is outdated and no longer provides a meaningful precedent.[53]

Another example is what the Conservative movement did with the *ketubah,* the marriage contract. In Talmudic times the power to divorce rested with the husband only (according to the rabbinic interpretation of Deuteronomy 24:1 and the following verses) leaving the wife with many disabilities. Keenly aware of the inequity involved, the *halacha* took steps to reduce the power of the husband and to extend the rights of the woman by providing her a lien on the property of the husband and hence an automatic financial settlement on the dissolution of the marriage. This approach was adequate when the state supported the rabbinical system of authority, but in a country such as America, where rabbinic courts have little coercive power, if the man refuses a divorce initiated by his wife little can be done beyond strong persuasion. He must still authorize the divorce. In a relatively minor *halachic* modification, the Conservative movement, rejecting the Reform solution (eliminating the need altogether for a Jewish legal divorce), merely added a paragraph to the *ketubah* providing that at the request of either party both must appear before a rabbinic court and abide by its decision. Both parties affix their signature to this provision, so that if one refuses the other can sue, in a civil court, for breach of contract, and the equality of access, for both husband and wife, to a *get,* or bill of divorce, was established. In other words, the court is able to grant a divorce without the consent and in the absence of the husband by having had the husband make out an instrument at the time of the marriage authorizing the court to grant his wife a divorce. Thus did Conservative Judaism adapt Jewish law to new values and circumstances, and the new *ketubah* was used in thousands of marriages.[54]

Change—controlled, to be sure—here emanated from catholic Israel, from Jews who respected the authority of Jewish law. The committee had affirmed what one of its members, Robert Gordis, of Rockaway Park's Temple Beth-El and the of the JTS faculty, had proclaimed as the "fundamental philosophy of Conservative Judaism: *growth is the law of life, and Law is the life of Judaism.* "[55]

If change, at whatever pace, emanated from catholic Israel, it did not emanate from the divine nature of revelation. Without the authority of *torah misinai,* God's dictation of the law to Moses, with which the Orthodox felt secure, the Conservative movement found the authority of the law in the human, not the divine—in what Harold Kushner (1935–   ) called *torah mitoldot ameinu.* By that he meant that "generations of our people have found holiness in performing them [laws] and continue to do so today." Thus both the vertical and horizontal dimensions of Jewish law give the law authority for Conservative Judaism.[56]

Halacha also offers another way to demarcate Conservatism from the other denominations. There is universal agreement among Conservative leaders, lay and rabbinic, that *kashrut* (dietary rules) is one of the key elements of Judaism, essential to any proper pattern of the Jewish way of life. In this the Conservative movement differs from Reform, for the latter rarely, if ever, devotes any attention to matters of *kashrut*. There is, however, far from universal agreement as to the exact manner, form, and degree of *kashrut* that is necessary and proper for the faithful Conservative Jew. So while Orthodox Jews debate how to be more "strictly" (*glatt*—literally, "smooth," i.e., meat that is kosher without any suspicion whatsoever) kosher than just kosher, Conservative Jews discuss adjusting the legal interpretation of *kashrut* to permit, for example, strict obedience at home and leniency in public. Generally speaking, therefore, Orthodox Jews consider the whole traditional pattern binding, in all its details, while Conservative Jews, especially in the past three decades, have considered the main outlines of the pattern as binding but have permitted individuals to fill in the amount of detail they wish to select.

The Jewish People

Without doubt, neither Orthodox or Reform Judaism has placed as much emphasis on peoplehood *(k'lal yisrael* or just "Israel") as has Conservative Judaism from its inception. Frankel, and especially Schechter, contributed to this emphasis, and their disciples amplified it—thus the embracing, very early in the Conservative movement, of Palestinian and East European Jewry.

There has not been, however, such unanimity over the notion of the chosen people. Although the official Sabbath and high holiday prayer books of the movement retained the traditional formula—"You have chosen us from all the nations"—there are widely differing, and generally quite diluted, interpretations among JTS faculty and congregational rabbis. For Robert Gordis, "no other people has produced a group of men comparable in spiritual insight and moral character to the Hebrew prophets," and therefore chosenness means service: "Israel is 'the chosen people,' chosen . . . for the service of humanity." For Simon Greenberg, chosenness is not "innate biological superiority," nor is it "privileges denied any other human being," but "a greater obligation to study and obey the Torah." For Ben Zion Bokser, anxious to avoid "tribalism," chosenness is not unique for the Jewish people. "All groups," he wrote in 1941, "are equally God's chosen, the unique vehicles of His revelation and the instruments of His purposes in history." To Louis Finkelstein, who even in 1927 was keenly aware of the dangers of attributing "singular excellence" to any one people and mimicking the "preposterous claims of Teutonic and Nordic superiority," any claims of chosenness were to be avoided. The Jewish people, Finkelstein pointed out, had "done great things," but it also had its share of "weaknesses of which we are aware." The formal language, therefore, of the prayer book may suggest election, but Conservative writers have radically altered this concept, for they are not willing to defend contrasts between Jews and others, they do not see the Jews as more conspicuously dedicated to God's purposes than other groups, and they emphasize rather that the Jews "chose" God in the sense of consecrating themselves to his service.[57]

Zionism

From, practically speaking, its inception, the Conservative movement—seminary faculty, rabbis, congregations—enthusiastically supported the Zionist movement, arguing that religion and nationality were intimately related, or, in Louis Ginzberg's felicitous phrasing: "Jewish nationalism without religion would be a tree without fruit, Jewish religion without Jewish nationalism would be a tree without roots." Several of the men connected with the Jewish Theological Seminary Association and the seminary in the nineteenth century affirmed this symbiotic relationship: Marcus Jastrow, professor of Talmud at the JTS, became a vice-president of the Federation of American Zionists (FAZ); Joseph Hertz wrote a lengthy pro-Zionist essay affirming Palestine as both a haven of refuge and a source of pride for world Jewry; seminary students formed the first collegiate Zionist society (Young American Zionists), which became, in 1899, an exclusive Zionist fraternity (ZBT, whose initials stand for three Hebrew words) at JTS, Columbia, New York University, and City College; and Schechter too affirmed and probably indelibly impressed this attitude on the movement. One year after his death, the class rosters of the seniors and juniors reveal that nearly every student at the seminary belonged to a Zionist organization (Hebrew League, Menorah, Zion League, Young Judea, Sons of Israel, Herzl Zion Club, and so forth).[58]

Schecter was convinced that "you cannot sever Jewish nationality from Jewish religion" (nor, for that matter, would he support an irreligious Jewish nationalism), and in a 1905 address explaining why he joined the FAZ he provided a public declaration of his pro-Zionist position. His subsequent devotion to the group and its ideology was so strong, despite the lack of support that he received from JTS lay leaders such as Jacob Schiff and Felix Warburg, that Louis Lipsky, years later, noted that "Dr. Schechter . . . made the JTS an institution for the graduation not only of rabbis, but also of Zionists. Without exception, its rabbis . . . have carried the message of Zionism to all parts of America."[59]

At the JTS, Louis Ginzberg, a delegate to the Sixth Zionist Congress, Israel Friedlander (1876–1920)—professor of biblical literature, history, and philosophy, the first president of Young Judea, a founder of Young Israel, and a member of the FAZ executive—and Mordecai Kaplan, as well as Louis Finkelstein, who argued that Palestine ought to be "established as a Jewish community [and] if possible as an autonomous one," were all dedicated Zionists, and students left the seminary with a very positive attitude toward Zionism. As early as 1927, Israel Goldstein, rabbi of New York's B'nai Jeshurun and a national Zionist leader, reported that the Zionist Organization of America (ZOA) looked on the Conservative rabbinate "as the rabbinical bulwark of American Zionism"; in 1944 Solomon Freehof, a Reform rabbi, noted that almost the whole Conservative rabbinate and the membership of Conservative congregations were pro-Zionist; and in 1983 more than a hundred rabbis ordained at the JTS had left America and were living in Israel. While the Reform movement may have entered the 1980s more vigorously Zionist, this commitment of the JTS, United Synagogue, and Conservative rabbinate to Zionism, and later, to the state of Israel, has never wavered, despite the difficulty Conservative Judaism has experienced in establishing its legitimacy as a movement in Israel.[60]

Judaism as a Civilization

As early as 1916 and then steadily in the following two decades, Rabbi Mordecai M. Kaplan, a Jewish Theological Seminary professor, forcefully articulated the notion of Judaism as a religious *and* secular civilization. Kaplan was not the first Jewish thinker in North America to suggest such an idea. Several years earlier Israel Friedlander, in a 1907 lecture, developed the concept of Judaism as a civilization. But Kaplan greatly expanded Friedlander's suggestion: "Judaism is," he wrote as early as World War I, "the *tout ensemble* of all the elements of what is usually termed the cultural life of a people, such as language, folkways, patterns of social organization, social habits and standards, creative arts, religion, etc." By this he meant to convey the idea that the totality of activities of a Jewish group—especially art, dance, drama, literature, music, play, philanthropy, study—not just the more obvious "religious" functions, are to be considered part of Judaism, even of the synagogue. While the reformers placed their overwhelming emphasis on the Jewish religion, generally neglecting Hebrew language and literature, Palestinian (Hebrew) music, and the like, and the Orthodox largely stressed God, Torah, and the commandments, the Conservative movement—particularly after 1920, when Kaplan's writing (especially in the *Menorah Journal*) began to have a profound impact on seminary graduates—witnessed the emergence of more and more synagogue-centers: religious institutions combining some of the secular activities of the Jewish community center under one roof.[61]

By 1916 Kaplan had established the first synagogue-center in New York City, and in 1920 Israel Levinthal (1888–1982) established the Brooklyn Jewish Center, the most well-known prototype of the synagogue-center. Levinthal argued that "in our community all the Zionist work, all the work for Hebrew culture, for philanthropy, for every phase of Jewish life, is being done through the center." Similar synagogue-centers were established, during the 1920s, in Cleveland, Philadelphia, Newark, Chicago, Manhattan, Jacksonville, and several Long Island Jewish communities, with great hopes. The synagogue-center (or "shul with a pool") showed movies, housed orchestras, fielded athletic teams, and made space available for Scout troops, dramatic clubs, and adult classes. Some had rabbis directing their social and educational activities; others had full-time recreational leaders guiding the swimming, basketball, and gymnastics. All these activities brought hundreds and even thousands of Jews into the facility.[62]

Samuel M. Cohen (1886–1945), the executive director of the United Synagogue for twenty-seven years (1917–1944), had "no doubt that the Center movement will gain in strength and ultimately become the sole form through which Jewish life will express itself." "Built on the theory," Israel Goldstein pointed out in 1928, "that there should be no cleavage between the religious and secular activities of man [and] to give full expression to all interests, physical, social, intellectual, within the province of the synagogue," these institutions were not without critics, most of whom argued that (1) few were asking what is "Jewish" about basketball; (2) Jews, "as a result of playing basketball in its very premises lose their reverence for the synagogue"; or (3) those who came to swim would not stay to pray. Nevertheless, as some Conservative Jewish congregations encompassed not only prayer and study and celebration but also Jewish music, Jewish literature, and Jewish basketball teams, the movement surely enriched itself and definitely attracted new affiliates.[63]

The 1920s were the most productive years for the emergence of synagogue-centers. By the 1930s and the 1940s few such institutions, if any, were being created, as the National Jewish Welfare Board successfully established hundreds of Jewish centers throughout the country in these years. After World War II, however, a number of conservative leaders, invoking Kaplan, called on the Rabbinical Assembly, the Jewish Theological Seminary, and United Synagogue to "remake the synagogue into the synagogue-center." Part of the impetus was the challenge of the centers, successfully attracting large numbers of Jews for secular activities, and part was the anxiety to provide a full range of "sacred and profane" facilities, within the synagogue, for the returning veterans so that their "re-discovery of the synagogue" will be "pleasant" and "the relationship of these veterans to organized religion . . . a happy one." Although the Conservative synagogues did experience an enormous postwar membership boom, and funds were not available for capital expansion, the centers had entrenched themselves so firmly that the Conservative movement almost unanimously decided to spend its available dollars on other items than replicating center gymnasiums and, in its stead, worked hard to make the centers more programmatically Jewish. In this aim they steadily, but very slowly, succeeded.[64]

Women

In a memorable 1947 address at a United Synagogue meeting, Mordecai Kaplan first spoke of three "schools of thought" or "distinctive groups" within the Conservative movement. The rightists, who accepted the "traditional belief with regard to the supernatural origin and character of the Torah," were most reluctant to make changes in ritual law and "put little faith in any existing rabbinical group as qualified to effect such change." The centrists, who no longer believed in the revelation at Sinai as a historical *event* but viewed it as a historical *process* continuing into the twentieth century, sanctioned change in ritual and law when appropriate precedents existed in that law. The leftists, such as Kaplan, did not hesitate to venture beyond Jewish law, when necessary, and render decisions based on the implications, consequences, or "spirit" of Jewish values. Hence, as Kaplan noted in this address, the status of women in traditional Jewish law is one of inequality vis-à-vis men, and the "only feasible remedy," for the leftists, "is to legislate that the woman be given equal status with the man."[65]

The Rabbinical Assembly Law Committee, reconstituted at the 1948 convention, attempted to represent all three tendencies within the movement—to walk a very delicate tightrope between those chanting "tradition" and those urging "change"—and one can note the impact of each group in the conservative movement's decisions about women. The leftists, responding, as it were, to Kaplan's early calls for changes in the legal status of women, together with the centrists, issued a series of rulings, especially in the 1950s and 1970s, which moved the Conservative movement closer and closer to Reform Judaism's position that all distinctions based on sex were to be eliminated in the synagogue.

The Committee on Jewish Law and Standards voted overwhelmingly in 1955 in favor of women being called to the reading of the Torah (ten said "sometimes," and five said "anytime"); it added to the *ketubah,* as noted earlier, a clause that virtually equalized women and men in Jewish marriage and Jewish divorce laws; and the committee ruled, by a 9–4 vote in 1973, that women counted equally with men in the quorum necessary for communal prayer. In addition, the United Synagogue had recommended to all its members in 1959 that married women have a voice and a vote equal to their husbands, that single women be entitled to membership, and that all women be eligible for any congregational office. The need for the latter became glaringly evident in that same year when a National Women's League of the United Synagogue survey revealed that only 35 percent of Conservative congregations permitted women to run for elected offices.[66]

The left and center were not, however, even by the 1980s, able to achieve their single most important desideratum—the ordination of women as rabbis at the seminary. Despite a growing and often tumultuous series of appeals, protests, manifestos and consciousness-raising events—spearheaded by the position paper of Ezrat Nashim, a New York-based Jewish feminist group, in 1972 ("Jewish Women Call for Change")—demanding the equalization of religious rights for women in Conservative Judaism, the Committee on Jewish Law and Standards voted more than 2 to 1 in 1974 against ordaining women as rabbis. Three years later, however, the Rabbinical Assembly did vote to have a commission of lay and professional Conservative Jews study the matter of whether the Rabbinical School of the Jewish Theological Seminary should ordain women, and convinced the chancellor of the seminary, Gerson D. Cohen, himself a "passionate advocate" of the ordination of women, to agree to advocate the recommendation of the commission to the seminary faculty.

The fourteen-member commission, in addition to its own meetings, held open hearings in seven U.S. and Canadian cities during 1978. It wrestled, first and foremost, with the demands of *hclacha* and concluded, by a vote of 11–3, that "there is no direct *halachic* objection to the acts of training and ordaining a woman to be a rabbi, preacher, and teacher." The seminary faculty, however, rejected the proposal, more responsive to the pleas from the rightists that this would mean an irrevocable break with Orthodoxy and with the most traditional among Conservative Jewry than to the leftist and centrist argument that 50 percent of potential spiritual leaders were being discriminated against. The JTS faculty senate voted 25–19, late in 1979, to postpone indefinitely any decision on the ordination of women. Despite a vote of 156–115 in favor of such ordination by the Rabbinical Assembly the following spring, the seminary faculty maintained its position. Mounting pressure, however, by responsible women and men, led the faculty, in October 1983, to approve (34 to 8) the admission and ordination of women.[67]

The position of women in Conservative synagogues in the early 1980s echoed the divisions Kaplan identified nearly forty years earlier. There were more than two congregations with women presidents (the 1959 figure), but the number was very small (less than 10 percent) and it was not until 1980 that a "major" Conservative synagogue (Sinai Temple in Los Angeles) elected a woman president. Many congregations called women to the Torah just as they did men, but in many others they were called only at "special" times or not at all, and, in their stead, girls, at "junior" services, received *aliyot.* Girls had a Bat Mitzvah that paralleled precisely the Bar Mitzvah at many congregations of the Conservative movement, but at many others the young women participated in a ceremony that, because of certain pre-scribed differences (such as being restricted to Friday evenings rather than Saturday mornings), did not equal that of the boys. And in a large majority of Conservative synagogues, congregational "honors" that occurred during worship were reserved for husbands, not wives. In short, much of Ezrat Nashim's manifesto remained to be accomplished, despite the changes in the wake of the 1972 protest (including Conservative Jewish women wearing multicolored patchwork, needlepoint, embroidered, or even designer prayer shawls), if women were to have full participation in the total religious life of Conservative Judaism.

5. Institutions and Organizations: 1886–1983

The Jewish Theological Seminary

I have already briefly discussed the forerunner of the JTS, the rabbinical school of the Jewish Theological Seminary Association and that school's reorganization in 1902 under Solomon Schechter. I noted that from January 1887 to June 1902 only seventeen rabbis had been ordained and that more than one-third of those men were ordained in the last class of the "old" seminary (1902). The most celebrated of the 1902 graduates was Rabbi Mordecai M. Kaplan, for many years a professor at the JTS and the founder of the newest Jewish "denomination"—Reconstructionism.[1]

Bernard Drachman (1861–1945), who taught fifteen hours of classes a week during the 1893–1894 winter term, provides us with a general idea of the rabbinic curriculum in the "old" or early seminary. On Sundays he offered Talmud (Senior B) and Jewish history (Preparatory A); on Mondays, Hosea (Juniors) and psychology (Preparatory A); on Tuesdays, Jewish philosophy (Senior B) and Hebrew grammar (Juniors and Preparatory A); on Wednesdays, Jewish philosophy (Senior B) and Hebrew grammar (Preparatory B); on Thursdays, philosophy texts (Senior A), philosophy works (Senior B), and Aramaic (Juniors); and on Saturday evenings (!) he taught Talmud to the Juniors. What strikes one, in addition to Drachman's breadth of learning, is the breadth of subject matter taught at the seminary. While students studied Talmud for more hours than any other subject, they were exposed to a significant number of nonrabbinic Judaica courses as well.[2]

With the advent of Schechter's leadership, the admission requirements as well as the depth and scope of coursework paralleled, except for this or that emphasis, those of the Hebrew Union College. During the 1890s, the small undergraduate student body, all of whom lived in the building (on Lexington Avenue between 58th and 59th streets) which housed the school, attended the City College in the morning, studied at the JTS in the afternoon, and were publicly examined, annually—at least once by Kaufmann Kohler, the future president of the HUC. Schechter introduced rigorous exams for entrance, presided over by himself, including the ability to translate, on sight, any passage of the Pentateuch and to prepare thirteen pages of Talmud, and, in addition to this Hebraica, an applicant was to possess a bachelor of arts degree. This latter requirement sought to guarantee that the emerging Conservative rabbinate had a thorough secular education and a fluency in English; in fact, of the eighty-four rabbis ordained between 1904 and 1917, almost all during Schechter's presidency, more than 50 percent received their bachelor's degrees from Harvard, Columbia, or the University of Pennsylvania, all three of which established special programs for students intending to enter the JTS.[3]

The tuition at the JTS was free, and nearly all the students (themselves immigrants or the children of recent immigrants—Schechter once wrote that the seminary would "sav[e] the souls of many thousands of Jewish immigrants") entered both college and rabbinical school with generous financial assistance. The students were not only poor but they were also rigorous in their observance of Jewish ritual. "Every student," under Schechter's presidency and ever after, was "expected to observe the Jewish Sabbath and to conform to the Jewish dietary laws." In the late 1950s a JTS catalogue stated that an applicant must "conduct and fashion his life according to Jewish law and tradition, including . . . the observance of the Sabbath and festivals, daily prayers, and dietary laws," and to participate in daily and Sabbath morning and evening worship services with the faculty. Unlike the HUC student body, where all observances were a matter of personal choice, the seminary and the rabbinical organization of seminary graduates strictly adhered to this code.[4]

The JTS launched its first $1 million fundraising campaign in October 1923 with Rabbi Max Drob as national chairman, and the campaign relied almost exclusively on congregational rabbis to solicit their members. They did this with much success; by the end of the year New York City congregations had supplied $450,000 of their $500,000 quota (led by B'nai Jeshurun's $50,000 and Anshe Chesed's $30,000), and congregations in Philadelphia had pledged $100,000. By the summer of 1924 $940,000 had been pledged nationwide and nearly $600,000 collected.[5]

The rabbinic program took a minimum of four years following the bachelor's degree, more if the student had Hebrew deficiencies and was placed in the three-year preparatory program. Its emphasis was in rabbinics (HUC's emphasis was in scripture), and the Hebrew skills necessary to complete it were great; only in the late 1920s and 1930s was the largely classical Hebraica curriculum supplemented by required courses in education, modern Hebrew literature, and practical rabbinics. For many years, the faculty was quite small: in 1902 it consisted of only Schechter; Louis Ginzberg; Drachman, who taught Hebrew and rabbinics; and Joshua Joffe, who taught Talmud and Codes, the post-Talmudic lawbooks. In 1912 the faculty was Schechter; Israel Friedlander; Ginzberg; Alexander Marx (1878–1953), librarian, bibliographer, and historian; Kaplan; Israel Davidson (1870–1939), who taught medieval Hebrew literature, philosophy, and liturgy; and Joffe. And in 1922 the faculty consisted of Ginzberg, Marx, Kaplan, Davidson, Finkelstein, and Moses Hyamson (1863–1949), who taught Codes. These men were, for the most part, very observant Jews and scholars of distinction who published extensively, and while most graduates spoke more effusively about the faculty's piety and learning than its pedagogical skills or concern with the world outside, they were clearly men who cared very much about the rabbis they were educating, if not always about the North American rabbinate.[6]

Cyrus Adler, a major figure in the 1902 revival of the JTS and the first recipient of a doctorate in semitics from a North American university, succeeded Schechter as acting president in 1916 after the death of the latter in November 1915, and remained in the presidency until his own death in 1940. He had served since 1908 as president of the Dropsie College for Hebrew and Cognate Learning, a nonsectarian graduate school of Hebraica, and continued to govern both Dropsie and the seminary for several years after 1916 while pursuing his own research and publication; then, in 1924, he became president of the JTS. Most importantly, Adler moved the institution into its present buildings on Broadway between 122nd and 123rd; built a library with an extraordinary collection of Judaica; established the Museum of Jewish Ceremonial Objects, which later moved into the former Warburg mansion on Fifth Avenue and became the Jewish Museum; vigorously maintained the "traditional" posture of the institution, especially for students who, he insisted "must be persons who live in accordance with the Jewish law"; and carefully nurtured the seminary's faculty and students. He drew most of the faculty of the rabbinical department from the ranks of its alumni, while the school continued to attract and ordain a large number of well-qualified young men, almost all of whom were reared, then and even later, in Orthodox or Conservative homes. In the years 1925–1929 alone, the seminary ordained fifty-five men.[7]

Of the men ordained during Schechter's presidency, several had rabbinical careers of note within the Conservative movement. Rudolph Coffee (1878–1955) was ordained in 1904 after studying at Columbia, later receiving his doctorate at the University of Pittsburgh (1908), and served Pittsburgh's

Tree of Life and Oakland's Temple Sinai for many years. Israel Levinthal —Russian-born, Columbia-educated, and ordained in 1910—developed, as noted earlier, the most oft-copied synagogue-center at the Brooklyn Jewish Center, where he served for fifty years. And Max Drob, Russian-born, Columbia-educated, was ordained in 1911 and served as president of the Rabbinical Assembly (1925–1927) and as rabbi of the Bronx Concourse Center of Israel for many years. In addition, the rabbis Jacob S. Minkin, ordained in 1910, Meyer Waxman, ordained in 1913, and Israel Efros, ordained in 1915, all students during the Schechter years, made significant scholarly contributions to Jewish intellectual life in America.

A comparable list for Adler's presidency ought to be many times longer, and is. It includes congregational rabbis who achieved national reputations, such as Solomon Goldman (ordained in 1918), Israel Goldstein (1918), Max Arzt (1921), Herman Hailperin (1922), Morris Silverman (1922), Louis Levitsky (1923), Simon Greenberg (1925), Milton Steinberg (1928), Albert I. Gordon (1929), Ben Zion Bokser (1931), Ira Eisensten (1931), Theodore Friedman (1931), Max Gelb (1932), Max J. Routtenberg (1932), Armond E. Cohen (1934), Morris Adler (1935), A. Judah Nadich (1936), and Aaron H. Wise (1938). And it includes scholars such as Louis Finkelstein (1919), Solomon Grayzel (1921), Moses Hadas (1926), Robert Gordis (1932), and Judah I. Goldin (1938).

Louis Finkelstein, who succeeded Adler in 1940, was born in Cincinnati, ordained at the JTS in 1919, received his doctorate from Columbia in 1918, and began teaching Talmud (later theology) at the seminary in 1919 while serving as the rabbi of the Orthodox congregation Kehilath Israel in the Bronx. In 1931 he became professor of theology—he was already well known for his highly acclaimed *Jewish Self-Government in the Middle Ages* (1924) —and, in a short time, thanks to Adler's decisions, moved from assistant to the president (1934), to provost (1937), and then to president (1940) and to chancellor (1951–1972). Finkelstein built a faculty that brought the seminary worldwide recognition, and he reorganized, expanded, and invigorated not only the seminary (with a ten-year $60-million campaign launched in 1955) but the Conservative movement; in the words of a colleague, Max J. Routtenberg (1909–   ), he "harnessed the latent forces of this large, prosperous, middle-class conservative community and created a dynamo."[8]

One of the most significant acts of Finkelstein's administration was the support he gave to a suggestion made by Mordecai Kaplan in 1945. Early that year, at the thirty-fifth anniversary celebration of the Teacher's Institute, Kaplan proposed that the JTS become a "University of Judaism," somewhat parallel to the Hebrew University in Jerusalem, and serve not only rabbis, cantors, Jewish educators, social workers, and graduate students but "become the main instrument of higher education" for North American Jewry.[9]

Finkelstein proposed that such an institution, under the auspices of the JTS, be established in the fastest-growing American Jewish community, Los Angeles. He and Kaplan, together with others, made several trips west to interest lay leaders in such a school and, in 1947, to set up the organizational structure and establish the University of Judaism, with Rabbi David Lieber as president. Housed, initially, in Sinai Temple (1947–1948) and then in buildings of its own on South Ardmore (1948–1957) and Sunset Boulevard (1957–1977), it now rests on top of the hills separating the San Fernando Valley from Los Angeles on Mulholland Drive. By the 1980s the University of Judaism not only fed into the seminary rabbinical program but, by offering a bachelor's degree, even competed with Los Angeles area college and university programs.

Finkelstein served as chancellor until 1972, when Rabbi Gerson Cohen (1924–   ), formerly a professor of history at Columbia University (1963–1970) and the Jacob H. Schiff Professor of History at the JTS (1970–1972), succeeded him and, two years later, launched a $6.5 million national campaign. During Finkelstein's tenure as head of the seminary, a sizable number of men were ordained who achieved national reputations as congregational rabbis, leaders of Conservative Jewish institutions, or as men of letters. These included pulpit rabbis such as Mordecai Waxman (ordained in 1941), Sidney Greenberg (1942), Herschel J. Matt (1947), Harold Schulweis (1950), Samuel Dresner (1951), Herbert Rosenblum (1954), Shamai Kanter (1955), Jules E. Harlow (1959), Harold Kushner (1963), and Dov P. Elkin (1964). The list also included administrators and executives such as Benjamin Kreitman (1942), Max Vorspan (1942), Bernard Mandelbaum (1946), Gerson Cohen (1948), David Lieber (1948), Wolfe Kelman (1950), Marc Tannenbaum, of the American Jewish Committee (1950), David M. Gordis (1964), and Elliot Dorff (1970). And the list also included Judaica scholars such as Moshe Davis (1942), Arthur Hertzberg (1943), Abraham J. Karp (1945), Stuart E. Rosenberg (1945), Jacob Milgrom (1946), Seymour Siegel (1951), Richard L. Rubenstein (1952), David W. Silverman (1952), Chaim Potok (1954), Moshe Greenberg (1954), Jonathan Goldstein (1955), Arthur Hyman (1955), Baruch A. Levine (1955), David S. Winston (1955), Seymour Fox (1956), Joseph Yerushalmi (1957), Edward Gershfield (1958), Yochanan Muffs (1958), Jacob Neusner (1960), Walter P. Zenner (1960), Robert L. Chazan (1962), Ismar Schorsch (1962), Shalom M. Paul (1962), Benjamin C. I. Ravid (1964), David Blumenthal (1964), Lee I. A. Levine (1965), George L. Berlin (1966), Arthur E. Green (1967), Jeffrey H. Tigay (1968), Marc Cohen (1970), Ivan Marcus (1970), and Joel Rembam (1970).

The seminary, as even this partial list reveals, stood second to none among graduate institutions in the number and quality of men who have enriched Jewish scholarship in the past few decades.

The United Synagogue of America

The United Synagogue of America, as noted briefly earlier, was organized by alumni of the JTS, by Solomon Schechter, and by delegates of twenty-two congregations in 1913. For the first five years, seminary faculty members directed the organization (Schechter, 1913–1915; Adler, 1915–1917; Ginzberg, 1917–1918); seminary alumni then took over (Rabbi Elias J. Solomon, 1918–1926; Rabbi Herman Abramovitz, 1926–1927); and in 1927 the first lay member of a Conservative synagogue, S. Herbert Golden (1927–1929), began a term as president. Rabbi Bernard Segal served as executive director and executive vice-president for twenty-three years (1952–1975), and he was succeeded by Rabbi Morton Siegel as executive director (1971) and Rabbi Benjamin Z. Kreitman as executive vice-president (1976).

Schechter and some other founders hoped that the United Synagogue would unite all non-Reform congregations into a single religious movement; even in 1921 the *Recorder* editorialized that the United Synagogue stands for "Catholic Israel as embodied in the universal Synagogue; it, therefore, appeals to no one section of the Jewish people." It became quickly apparent, however, that Conservative and Orthodox Judaism had sufficient ideological and administrative differences to prevent any unity, and that the United Synagogue would become, continually, more and more of a specifically Conservative organization. The United Synagogue, already in its initial years of existence, began a rigidly denominational program that made few compromises with Orthodoxy and fewer with Reform.[10]

The Committee on Education sought to develop curricular and programmatic texts, materials, and guidelines for United Synagogue afternoon Hebrew and Sunday religious schools; the Committee on Sabbath Observance issued calendars that noted precisely when the Jewish Sabbath began and ended each week and promoted increased observance in several ways. The Committee on Propaganda sent publicity to congregations that were potential United Synagogue members and tried to get area Conservative rabbis to visit such groups and recruit new members for the union. And the Committee on the Interpretation of Jewish Law sought to make both *tradition* and *change* meaningful words in the vocabulary of Conservative Judaism. Various other components of the United Synagogue were responsible for a *Kosher Directory* listing hundreds of eating places in more than a hundred cities, the regional divisions that made the United Synagogue into a more workable organization, and a vigorous affirmation of concern for world Jewry, including those Jews seeking to rebuild Zion.[11]

Within four years of its founding, the United Synagogue had an executive director, Rabbi Samuel M. Cohen, and together with the Committee on Propaganda Cohen could doggedly pursue groups of Jews who might potentially establish a Conservative congregation. Many of the nearly two hundred congregations that joined the United Synagogue in the 1920s were newly formed by rapidly Americanized immigrants and their adult children, and Cohen's procedure in Providence, Rhode Island, was rather typical.

The city of Providence contained three Orthodox congregations in the early 1920s, two with Yiddish-speaking rabbis and one with no rabbi, and these synagogues were far more closely identified with Old Europe than with the America that some Providence Jews, and especially their children, were embracing. On the other extreme was one Reform congregation, a bastion of classical Reform, wherein the use of Hebrew was almost nonexistent, visible ritual and tradition were absent, and the sense of warmth and intimacy some Jews prized was not easily felt with the rigid separation—physical and spiritual—of pulpit and pew.

Under such circumstances, Rabbi Cohen wrote a letter to one Providence Jew, with whom the Committee on Propaganda had initiated contact, noting (with some hyperbole) that "thousands of young people" were being "slowly estranged from the faith of their fathers." He urged this man, Philip Joslin, who happened to be the Speaker of the House of Representatives of Rhode Island, to bring together the "proper leadership"—that is, "a number of your friends"—and Cohen or an associate would join them and try to create the "right institution." The goal? "To save [Providence] for traditional Judaism."[12]

Joslin responded, less than two weeks later, enthusiastically. He pointed out what Cohen knew, that "numberless" and "estranged" young people, whose immigrant parents belonged to one of the Orthodox synagogues, revealed "indifference and apathy" and were on the verge of being "forever lost to the faith of their ancestry." Joslin noted the need for "an appeal in a tongue and under conditions which are most tasteful to our modern American life" (non-Orthodox), and yet "not forgetting the fundamentals [and] the traditions" (non-Reform). Six weeks later fifteen people met at Joslin's home, and Temple Emanu-El, a Conservative congregation, was born. It grew quickly; by the late 1940s, it was one of the largest Conservative congregations in the United States.[13]

The United Synagogue grew rapidly during the 1920s, claiming 229 congregations (as well as 262 sisterhoods and 119 young people's organizations) by 1927—more than 200 greater than when it was founded fourteen years earlier. It grew especially rapidly during the so-called religious revival of the 1950s, following on the massive migration of Jews from cities to suburbs and the combination of low-cost tract housing and G.I. mortgages: 130 new congregations joined the movement during 1956 and 1957 (requiring the United Synagogue to expand to fourteen regional offices to serve all local needs); eighty joined in 1958 and 1959; and by the end of 1965, when the boom had nearly ended, 800 synagogues, compared to 500 one decade earlier and 400 fifteen years earlier, belonged to the Conservative movement.

It was then, during the 1950s and early 1960s, that Conservative Judaism emerged as the branch with the most followers and the number of United Synagogue congregations exceeded—permanently—the UAHC affiliates. The late 1960s began a period of stability; for the next fifteen years the number of congregations did not fluctuate more than 4 percent. Nevertheless, the growth goals had been accomplished. From a movement with a negligible following at the beginning of the 1920s, it had clearly become the dominant branch of non-Orthodox North American Judaism; indeed, in nearly every large Jewish community of the early 1980s more Jews identified themselves as Conservative than as either Reform or Orthodox.[14]

Much of this growth in the Conservative movement, United Synagogue publications indicate, was the result of the fact that the majority of Jews in newly developing surburban communities who had anything to do with organizing the first synagogue in the community turned to Conservatism as a compromise movement that would best "satisfy everyone." What some saw, thus, as its weakness—"a loose umbrella-type ideology taking under its shelter a wide variety of apparently contradictory positions"—turned out to be, in at least one area, a strength.

The genuineness of this growth was debated, as in the Reform movement, by Conservative rabbinical and lay leaders in the pulpits and publications of the United Synagogue and Rabbinical Assembly. Stuart E. Rosenberg (1922–   ), rabbi of Rochester's Temple Beth El and then Toronto's Beth Tzedec, summed up one school of thought by labeling the rush to affiliate with Conservative synagogues "just another respectable social habit," while Bernard Segal (1907–   ), the executive director of the United Synagogue, noting that the new affiliates brought a "genuine hunger for Torah," argued that the sincerity of the revival was a fact, not fancy. Not all were convinced, of course, by Segal's portrait, and the United Synagogue congregations, in the midst of a revival that brought thousands of previously unaffiliated Jews into the synagogue as members, passed a nonbinding "Statement of Standards for Synagogue Practice" at the 1957 convention (it was approved in principle at the 1955 convention). Its goal was to boost the levels of observance among Conservative Jews and to establish, especially for those who were suddenly joining congregations for the first time, standards of religious behavior within the synagogue. The "Standards" prescribed the proper observance of the Sabbath, *kashrut,* various ceremonies and rites, as well as administrative procedures (public functions, fundraising, moral dignity), and they primarily confirmed or reaffirmed the existing procedures.[15]

The 1950s witnessed not only a burst in synagogue affiliations with the United Synagogue and a rigorous effort to make those affiliations more than just memberships, but a much greater involvement than ever before with the ills of North American society. In 1954 the Joint Commission on Social Action—acting on behalf of the Conservative synagogues, sisterhoods, and brotherhoods—was formed, and it played a vigorous role in the movement for civil rights throughout the 1950s and 1960s. Abraham Heschel, in his writings, speeches, and personal activism, prodded the Conservative movement to support various civil rights programs and attempted to supply the ideological basis for such involvement. Conservative rabbis, lay leaders, youth, JTS students, and even JTS faculty—no longer insulated as in the 1920s and 1930s—joined in marches through the South, urban Peace Corps (i.e., VISTA) projects, voter registration drives, anti-Vietnam War protests, and the nationwide March on Washington (1962) to muster support for the landmark civil rights bill pending in Congress. The march included a special prayer service at the seminary, in which the chancellor, Louis Finkelstein, identified the seminary with the purposes of the march, and a delegation of the top Conservative lay and rabbinic leaders marching behind a prominent United Synagogue of America banner. This type of involvement in civil rights continued throughout the decade, until, by the early 1970s, individual rabbis disengaged themselves from active programs of social concern as "the steam seemed to have gone out of the general civil rights movement."[16]

At the same time that the United Synagogue was developing its commitment to racial equality and civil rights, it was also encouraging the development of Conservative day schools and coordinating them through the Solomon Schechter Day School System of the United Synagogue's Commission on Jewish Education. One of the earliest, if not the first, Beth-El in Far Rockaway, New York, began with twenty-one kindergarteners in 1951 and before the end of the decade had 100 pupils enrolled in grades K–8 and sixteen fully certified teachers—all in a school supported by one congregation. By the late 1960s there were twenty-eight Solomon Schechter day schools with an enrollment of nearly 5,000 students; in 1968 the first Conservative Jewish high school opened at the Flatbush Jewish Center in

Brooklyn; and by the early 1980s this number had grown to sixty-five Solomon Schechter schools with 12,000 students. Despite the growth of these schools, the Conservative movement remained strongly opposed to federal aid for its schools, arguing that strict separation between "church" and state, in the long run, would best allow such schools to develop.[17]

Like the National Federation of Temple Sisterhoods in the Union of American Hebrew Congregations, the Women's League of the United Synagogue recruited thousands of women in congregations across the country to labor on behalf of not only local needs but also the JTS and overseas Jewry. Schechter himself, at the organizational meeting of the United Synagogue in 1913, noted that women's "influence is more far-reaching than that of their husbands," and five years later Mathilde Schechter (1859–1924), the widow of Solomon Schechter, formed the Women's League. It grew as rapidly as did the movement throughout the 1920s and continued, even in the 1970s and 1980s when larger numbers of women were working than ever before, to play a prominent role in the life of each Conservative congregation through its local constituency—the sisterhood. By 1982, 800 Conservative sisterhoods in North America had more than 200,000 members.[18]

The youth movement of the United Synagogue (Young People's League), although organized in 1921 with Rabbi Israel Goldstein as president, began to grow significantly after World War II, and in 1951 held the first United Synagogue Youth (USY) convention. By 1964 USY units throughout the Conservative movement had 24,000 teenage members, supplemented by 1,100 college students (in the organization called Atid), most of whom were USY graduates. Atid grew rapidly in the late 1960s, as thousands of Jewish college students sought organs of self-identity, and claimed 8,000 members in 1969. By the early 1980s 20,000 youth belonged to USY chapters, while Kadimah, the pre-USY age group, claimed 10,000. The latter served as a generous feeder for the Conservative movement's Ramah summer camps, while the former supplied the JTS with a large proportion of its students.[19]

The United Synagogue and the JTS were supported financially, as in the Reform movement, by dues paid by congregants and by a combined campaign. Unlike the UAHC and HUC, which split the funds raised, the seminary received the bulk of the campaign distribution (90 percent when the campaign began). The National Enrollment Plan, adopted at the 1957 United Synagogue convention, required every United Synagogue congregant to contribute $10 (or more) to the combined campaign of the seminary, Rabbinical Assembly, and United Synagogue. By the 1980s, however, the percentage that a given congregation sent to New York to support the national organizations was calculated from its membership and budget and distributed more equitably.[20]

The Rabbinical Assembly of America

The antecedent of the Rabbinical Assembly of America was the Alumni Association of the Jewish Theological Seminary, first organized in June 1901 with fifteen men—former students and graduates of the old seminary—who united in support of the institution and for fellowship. The lack of a specific ideology—a problem plaguing the Conservative movement ever since 1901 —was already evident, for an observer noted that "the question of religious policy seems to have been left out of consideration—the graduates of the Seminary as a body have considered the question of theology as non-germane to its *raison d'être.*"

In 1918 the Alumni Association decided to broaden its scope and include nonseminary graduates (Orthodox) who (primarily) served Conservative congregations, and it changed its name to Rabbinical Assembly of the Jewish Theological Seminary of America and, about fifteen years later, to just Rabbinical Assembly of America. Two hundred strong, it published annual *Proceedings* of its conventions beginning with the twenty-seventh annual convention in 1927; instituted an ethical placement system and policies on tenure, severance, salary, pension, and relief; established an active Social Justice Commission; and vigorously pursued a publications program, which included prayer books such as the *Festival Prayer Book* (1927), the *Sabbath and Festival Prayer Book* (1946), and the *Mahzor for Rosh Hashanah and Yom Kippur* (1972).[21]

The *Sabbath and Festival Prayer Book,* the first official Conservative prayer book—a joint effort of the Rabbinical Assembly and the United Synagogue—was based on the work of Morris Silverman (1894–1972), a Hartford rabbi who had compiled his own Conservative prayer manuals and published a widely used *High Holiday Prayerbook* (1939). The doctrinal principles of the book are delineated in the introduction, and they reveal the subtle influence of Mordecai Kaplan and some ideological compatibility with Reform Judaism on the following subjects: the task of the Jewish people in the world, an emphasis on spiritual immortality over bodily resurrection, a preference for people-centered rather than for theological readings, the rejection of a personal messiah, and the renunciation of hope for restoring the ancient Jewish temple in Jerusalem. In fact, however, the book is hardly different from the traditional prayer book, except for a hundred pages of supplementary readings and English translations filled with optimism. In only a few places (unlike Reform's, which changed far more) the Hebrew is emended; for example, wherever the original says that "in Zion, when God restores us, *we* shall offer again the ordained sacrifices," this prayer book changes the Hebrew to say "there *our fathers* offered the ordained sacrifices." The general pattern, however, is to assume that the worshipper will read new meanings into Hebrew words (such as "who gives life to the dead") whose ideas the editors reject and hence to retain these old formulas.[22]

The *Mahzor for Rosh Hashanah and Yom Kippur* (1972) moves considerably further from the traditional prayer book than does the Sabbath liturgy. First of all, two colors are used in this physically attractive volume, one highlighting the instructions and introductory medications. In addition, there is an explicit awareness of both the Holocaust and the state of Israel; sensitive and often gifted English translations; a poem, by Miriam Kubovy, grappling (affirmatively) with ambivalence and doubt; and an awareness of both ancient and contemporary martyrdoms. Subsequent books, the Rabbinical Assembly has indicated, will diverge even more from the traditional liturgy.

The Rabbinical Assembly grew rapidly in the decades after World War II, claiming 600 members in 1955, 900 in 1970, and 1,200 by 1983. Its executive council governed the assembly, under the administrative leadership of Rabbi Wolfe Kelman (1923–   ) ever since 1951, but numerous committees served the organization. It too, like its Reform counterpart, constantly struggled with the difficulties of the rabbinical profession, especially the demands of the pulpit and congregation; the lack of time for reading, studying, and thinking; increasing disenchantment and resignation; and the diminished role of the spiritual leader in contemporary America. Through the Rabbinical Assembly's journal, *Conservative Judaism,* and its annual convention, it continuously confronts the strengths and weaknesses of the Conservative rabbinate.

PART III

ORTHODOX JUDAISM

---

6. Origins and Early Development: 1654–1902

It has been the custom among historians of North American Judaism to describe all non-Reform Jewish life prior to the emergence of Conservative Judaism, as *orthodox,* although some have also used the word *traditional* to delineate those congregations that were a "little less orthodox" than the others. Such usage of the term *orthodox,* however, does not adequately convey the texture of Jewish life of those who joined congregations established before Reform Judaism emerged or congregations that remained outside the orbit of Reform Judaism during the middle decades of the nineteenth century. And it does not suggest the rich diversity of religious expression and institution constructed by the East European Jewish immigrants, and their children, in the twentieth century as alternatives, first to Reform, and then to Conservative Judaism. Thus, prior to the emergence of a Reform Jewish organization there existed a sizable number of synagogues, quite varied in their expression of Judaism, uncomfortable with the liberalizing steps undertaken by some of their kind, and committed to replicating, in some manner, much of Old European Judaism in its Dutch, English, German, or Polish form.

The earliest synagogues in America were Sephardic in their ritual, and all were established along the East Coast, where most of the Jews settled in the century or so after they first came to the United States in 1654. Aside from New York, which could boast of a congregation before the end of the seventeenth century, the several other seaborad cities that became the home of Jewish immigrants did not develop congregations and build synagogues until the 1700s. Charleston's Beth Elohim, Savannah's Mickve Israel, Newport's Yeshuath Israel (now Touro Synagogue), Richmond's Beth Shalome, and Philadelphia's Mikve Israel joined New York's Shearith Israel as the earliest United States synagogues, and all followed the Sephardic ritual and a relatively similar pattern of organization.[1]

Although acculturated Ashkenazic Jewish immigrants constituted a

larger and larger percentage—and sometimes the majority—of these congregations, the Sephardic leaders had come to North America, most recently by way of Holland, England, or their possessions, and usually looked
to London's Bevis Marks or Amsterdam's Spanish-Portuguese synagogue
as a model for the ritual, organization, and even architectural style of the
synagogue. Philadelphia's Mikve Israel sought approval from both London
and Amsterdam for the Sephardic design of its 1782 buildings—a design
quite similar to the synagogues in Newport and New York. It featured a
women's gallery as well as a reader's table, facing the ark, which would
enable the *hazzan* to lead services with the congregation, whose seats were
on the sides, on either side.[2]

Laymen tightly controlled these Sephardic congregations. Power—that
is, control of every aspect of congregational life—resided in the hands of
a *parnass* (president) and an *adjunta* (board of directors): together they
determined who received synagogue honors; kept rigorous records of births,
deaths, marriages, circumcisions, and deaths; approved marriages that took
place within the congregational family and burials in the congregation's
cemetery; maintained decorum and observance by fining and legislating
against backsliders; provided rules and regulations (as well as the time) for
the conduct and order of the service (according to the ancient Sephardic
custom) and Torah reading; supervised the baking of Passover *matzo* and
the free distribution of same for the needy; hired and supervised the *shochet*
(ritual slaughterer) and observance of *kashrut* (dietary laws); assigned and
sold seats in the synagogue; and strictly ruled the *hazzan* (cantor) or "minister." In 1782 Philadelphia's Mikve Israel *adjunta,* to give but one example
of its authority, informed its minister, Gershom Seixas (1745–1816) that
"You are not to marry Mr. Jacob Cohen to Mrs. Mordecai. Neither are you
to be present at the wedding, and you are hereby strictly forbid, to mention
said Cohen or his wife's name in any respect whatsoever in the synagogue."[3]

The *hazzan* (or cantor or minister—these terms are used interchangea-
bly) was hired by the directors to chant the liturgy, officiate at life cycle
events, and instruct the children, but rarely to preach (which was usually
done, if at all, by a knowledgeable member). Always instruments of the
board of directors, the most successful *hazzanim,* that is, those who remained at a congregation for a period of years, obeyed the *parnassim*
meticulously and acted only as instruments of the board of directors, not
as interpreters or administrators of religious law. It was undoubtedly too
tempting to interpret the law, given the lack of a single ordained rabbi in
the United States until 1840 and the generally low level of Jewish education
in eighteenth-century America, but most *hazzanim,* although sometimes
calling themselves *rabbi,* realized they were simply laymen who knew some

Hebrew and had pleasant voices for chanting, and they seem to have encouraged their *adjuntas* to write to European rabbinic leaders for legal interpretations.

Congregational boards of directors hired not only *hazzanim* but men who could supervise other Jewish ceremonial activities. Synagogue leaders sought to hire at least a *mohel* (circumcizer), *shochet* (whose job was, typically, "to kill sufficient Meat of all kinds fitting for the use of said Congregation"), *melamed* (teacher), and *mashgiach* (supervisor of dietary laws and Passover *matzzoth* preparation)—although usually the low level of compensation made it necessary for one man to combine several of these specialties.[4]

Morris A. Gutstein undoubtedly exaggerated when he claimed that "the Jews of Newport in the eighteenth century carried out the laws and customs of the Jewish people to the minutest detail," while Jacob R. Marcus was probably correct in pointing out that "most of the Jews whom we know by name in the eighteenth century were observant to some degree." But the degree was often slight. This negligence was certainly not for any lack of congregational effort, for boards of directors legislated, fined, threatened, and even considered excommunication to raise levels of worship attendance and observance (especially the Sabbath and *kashrut*) in the eighteenth century.[5] And Philadelphia's Mikve Israel directors brought charges against one member in 1782 for shaving on the Sabbath, while New York's Shearith Israel not only levied countless fines for such matters as disturbing "the devotion and quiet of our holy worship in any manner whatever," absenting oneself from the synagogue, and "indecent and abusive language," but threatened its members in the 1740s and 1750s with a more severe punishment, loss of salvation: "Whosoever . . . continues to act contrary to our Holy Law by breaking any of the principle commands will not be . . . buried according to the manner of our brethren."[6]

Throughout the eighteenth century, Jewish immigrants from Germany and even Poland trickled into North America, and by the time of the American Revolution, when perhaps 2,500 Jews lived in the United States, these immigrants were a clear majority. At first, however, the more acculturated of them found acceptance in the Sephardic congregations, and with the exception of Philadelphia at the very end of the century, no group of Ashkenazic Jews left a Sephardic congregation to start their own synagogue during the eighteenth century.

Philadelphia became the first United States city to have an Ashkenazic congregation when some recent immigrants left Mikve Israel, about 1795, to establish the German Hebrew Society or Rodeph Shalom. The influence of the Sephardic texture of North American synagogues was immediately present: Rodeph Shalom used the Spanish term *junto* to describe its board of directors. Not until 1825, when a group of acculturated Ashkenazim, members of New York's Shearith Israel, formed a new congregation (Bene Jeshurun), did another Orthodox Ashkenazic synagogue emerge. Cincinnati Jews established an Ashkenazic congregation (but not a synagogue) about the same time (Bene Israel), and in the following decade or two numerous such Orthodox German congregations or synagogues took root in eastern and trans-Allegheny communities.[7]

The New York secessionists expressed their dissatisfaction with the Sephardic ritual, the ceremonial laxity outside Shearith Israel (it was, as we have seen, anything but lax inside) and the oligarchy within, and Bene Jeshurun, like most of the Orthodox congregations to follow, created a much looser structure of power. First, there were usually far more directors and officers, thus distributing power; second, the German and German-Polish immigrants of the post–Napoleonic Wars brought with them a tradition of synagogue life in which the Sephardic oligarchical style was absent; and finally, in many communities, the new immigrants modeled their synagogue not after Shearith Israel in New York but after the democratic society they had entered. One could gain election to the board not only by generous financial contributions but by hard work as well.[8]

The lay leaders of these nineteenth-century Orthodox Ashkenazic congregations were just as eager as their Sephardic predecessors to achieve synagogue attendance and ritual observance, and they instituted no less long a list of fines and warnings. Philadelphia's Rodeph Shalom made it obligatory to attend Friday evening and Saturday morning services (or else pay a fine), while Buffalo's Beth El had fines for nonattendance and for undecorous behavior when one did attend. New York's B'nai Jeshurun fined members $25 for using "improper" language against the trustees, denied admission to services to a congregant who opened his or her store on the Sabbath, and prevented an intermarried member from serving on the board of trustees. The Baltimore Hebrew Congregation imposed fines for talking during services, singing louder than the *hazzan,* "shewing" tobacco (though spittoons were everywhere), leaving during the Torah reading, and (shades of Reform) "read[ing] or sing[ing] any prayer loud during the services."[9]

There is little evidence, however, to suggest the Jews of the first six or seven decades of the nineteenth century were any more observant than those of the previous century. They lacked religious leaders; often peddled long distances from home and from kosher food, synagogues, or the rest; and found few Jews to help reinforce their strict observance even if desired. When Abraham Rice, the first ordained rabbi to come to live in the United

States, arrived in Baltimore in 1840 to serve the Baltimore Hebrew Congregation, he discovered that his Orthodox congregants generously ignored the commandments. When he resigned in 1849, he wrote home to his former teacher, Wolf Hamburger: "The character of religious life in this land is on the lowest level; most of the people are eating non-Kosher food, are violating the *Shabbos* in public . . . and there are thousands who have been assimilated among the non-Jewish population."[10]

The Ashkenazic congregations, as did the Sephardic ones earlier, hired functionaries who specialized in, or were ritually qualified, to aid congregants to fulfill various commandments. These included a *shochet,* butcher; *mohel, hazzan, shamash* (beadle or superintendent); *mashgiach,* supervisor of the *mikveh*[11] (ritual bath); and, increasingly by the 1840s, a rabbi; and while some of these required no special training, many of the functions did. Best, of course, for these economically struggling congregants was to find one man, usually through an ad in the Anglo-Jewish press, who could handle multiple tasks; for example, "Rabbi" Mordecai Tuska, who was not an ordained rabbi at all, came to Rochester's Berith Kodesh in 1849 and served as rabbi, *hazzan, shochet, mohel,* and teacher.[12]

Isaac Mayer Wise, in his autobiography, described *hazzanim* such as Tuska in this exaggerated but not wholly untrue reminiscence:

> There was no room in the synagogue for preachers and rabbis. The *hazzan* was the Reverend. He was all that was wanted. The congregations desired nothing further. The *hazzan* was reader, cantor, and blessed everybody for *chai pasch,* which amounted to 4-1/2 cents. He was teacher, butcher, circumciser, blower, grave digger, secretary. He wrote the amulets with names of all the angels and demons on them for women in confinement, read *shiur* for the departed sinners, and played cards or dominoes with the living; in short, he was a *Kol-bo,* an encyclopedia, accepted bread, turnips, cabbage, potatoes as a gift and peddled in case his salary was not sufficient. He was *sui generis,* half-priest, half beggar, half oracle, half fool as the occasion demanded. The congregations were satisfied, and there was no room for preacher or rabbi. Among all the *hazzanim* whom I learned to know, there was not one who had a common-school education or possessed any Hebrew learning.[13]

The earliest of these Ashkenazic congregations, of course, were composed of German Jews, but well before the mass immigration of Russian Jews began in the 1880s there were sufficient numbers of these East Europeans to establish their own Orthodox congregations in cities such as Buffalo (B'rith Sholem, 1865), New York (Beth Hamidrash, 1852), Chicago (Anshe Kenesseth Israel, 1875), Rochester (Sheves Achim, 1870; Bene Sholom, 1871; Beth Israel [the result of a merger between the preceding two], 1874), Baltimore (Bikur Cholim, 1865), Cincinnati (Adath Israel, 1874), and

Boston (Beth Israel, 1849; Shomre Shabbos, 1870s; Shomre Beth Abraham, 1875).

There was little organizational unity among these Russian, German, and Polish Orthodox congregations; in fact, there was a steady defiance of all ecclesiastical authority beyond the limited boundaries of most congregations. Yet even before the mass migration began there was an attempt at a formal organization of twenty-six Orthodox congregations. In 1879 representatives of these congregations met to establish the Board of Delegates of Orthodox Hebrew Congregations, the first formal attempt to unite the Orthodox congregations, and to extend an invitation overseas to Rabbi Meir Loeb Malbim, a noted Talmudic scholar and vigorous opponent of Reform Judaism, to serve as chief rabbi. Despite the task the board of delegates wanted to lay on Rabbi Malbim—to end "the disintegrating process in our religious system, the open and flagrant desecration of the Sabbath, [and] the neglect of dietary laws"—he expressed interest in the position. However, his acceptance of a European position and then his death that same year doomed this attempt at unity.[14]

Early in the 1880s the East European Jews inundated the approximately 280,000 Jews already in the United States. By the outbreak of World War I, more than 2 million had found their way to the United States. The general press labeled 9 September 1881, when the first group of eighteen pogrom refugees arrived in New York, as the precise date when the mass migration of East European Jews began. These Jews came from Russia, Poland, Lithuania, Rumania, Hungary, Galicia, and adjacent areas, and often felt a keen sense of pride about their unique origins. The city, country, or province where they had lived usually served as an organizing principle for not only their social and cultural but their religious life as well. Thus, among those New York City synagogues contributing to the second attempt to attract a chief rabbi (1887) were the Suwalk, Kalvarie, Polish, Ungarn, Merimpol, Neustadt, Russian, and Augustov synagogues—all named for the members' places of origins. And in North Lawndale, a Chicago community of nearly 100,000 Jews in the 1930s, Orthodox synagogue life was still organized by region of European origin—a Russian *shul,* a Hungarian *shul,* a Rumanian *shul,* and so on.[15]

Surely, a self-conscious Orthodoxy does not begin at least until these immigrants arrived, and perhaps not even until the twentieth century with the Union of Orthodox Rabbis of the United States and Canada (1902), or perhaps a bit earlier with the Union of Orthodox Jewish Congregations of America (1898). When the great migration began, Nathan Glazer has pointed out, of the approximately two hundred major congregations in existence in the United States, only about a dozen were still Orthodox, while a contemporary noted that by 1906 91 percent of the Russian Jewish immigrants ceased to be strictly Orthodox in their religious practices.[16]

Even if Glazer's estimate is too low, it is certain that there were hardly that many distinguished Orthodox rabbis in America. The leading East European Orthodox congregation in New York, Beth Hamidrash Hagadol, had only a part-time rabbi of meager scholarship, while one Orthodox observer in Cleveland reported, in 1882, that "Sabbath observance is at a low ebb, and as a result the synagogues are poorly attended."[17]

The first to come, and to take an extended leave from Jewish communal apparatus, were probably the least religious; this helps to explain why one Orthodox observer could only find one Talmud Torah (Hebrew school) of any merit on the entire East Side of New York in 1887, and why there were only two Jewish day schools in the whole country until 1915. The bulk of these early East European Jewish immigrants probably had strong ethnic, but weak religious, ties, to Judaism. When they observed Judaism, they certainly intended to do it the "Orthodox" way, but there is much to question about the frequency of their commitment to observe Jewish law, study Jewish texts, maintain Jewish dietary laws, and worship on the Sabbath and holidays.[18]

The multiplicity of Orthodox synagogues not only in New York but in numerous other cities of East European Jewish immigration (twenty-five synagogues on Chicago's West Side early in the twentieth century totaled 2,000 members), is not in itself a strong sign of religiosity. As Charles Liebman has correctly pointed out, since the ritual was virtually identical in all these synagogues, and since they served as social forums and benevolent societies, their abundance is best understood as fulfilling social and cultural, rather than religious, needs of nominally religious folk originating from the same European community.[19]

Whatever their primary function, a number of synagogues organized themselves, in 1887, into the Association of American Orthodox Hebrew Congregations, corresponded with the leading rabbis of Europe, and invited Rabbi Jacob Joseph of Vilna (1848–1902) to come to the United States as "chief rabbi" of New York. The major desideratum, from the start, was the supervision of *kashrut,* an area marked by squabbles between butchers and accusations among the *shochatim* (slaughterers). Although Rabbi Joseph, a fine scholar, good preacher, and active organizer, received an enthusiastic welcome from thousands of immigrant Jews when he arrived in July 1888, his was a hopeless task. His salary was to be financed by congregational dues paid to the association, and by fees paid by the consumers for supervision (1¢ for the metal tag attached to each chicken's leg to certify its *kashrut*).

Protests and demonstrations erupted over this progressive-spirit "house-cleaning." Other Orthodox rabbis, envious of Rabbi Joseph's large salary, saw themselves losing a source of income; socialists and anarchists joined cause with rabbis to protest price gouging; many butchers formed an association (Hebrew Poultry Butchers Association) to resist control more effectively; housewives resented the additional charge. Rabbi Joseph, despite a small and appreciative following, could not overcome the centrifugal forces in the community, and was quickly reduced to being merely the chief rabbi of the Association of American Orthodox Hebrew Congregations, or perhaps merely the employee of the butchers who accepted his authority.[20]

The failure of Rabbi Joseph to "correct abuses which have appeared" in the religious life of New York Orthodoxy—as the association's charge to him required—was less a reflection on his skills, which were considerable, than on the resentments and jealousies among the Orthodox immigrants and the unfortunate meeting between an Old Europe rabbi and a U.S. community. The New York correspondent of Isaac Mayer Wise's *American Israelite,* even before Jacob Joseph arrived, described him as a man "whose vernacular is an unintelligible jargon," while Dr. Henry Pereira Mendes, of Shearith Israel, told the association itself (before Rabbi Joseph arrived) that he doubted that a chief rabbi, by virtue of the authority he possessed in the old country, "will have success in America." They were both correct, for Jacob Joseph represented, to thousands of new immigrants, precisely what they had traveled a great distance to escape. A bearded, Yiddish- (and sometimes Hebrew-) speaking chief rabbi had little appeal to Jews breathing in the fresh air of North American religious voluntarism.[21]

Despite this unsuccessful attempt in New York City, many other communities did subsequently manage to elevate an Orthodox rabbi to the position, informally in most cases, of chief rabbi. They included Rabbis Jacob David Ridvaz (Willowsky), chief rabbi of Chicago; Moses S. Margolies of Boston; Judah Leib Levine of Detroit; Asher Lippman Zarchy of Louisville; Bernard Louis Levinthal of Philadelphia; Eliezer Silver of Cincinnati; and Solomon Scheinfeld of Milwaukee; men who supervised the necessary ritual preparations, presided over the court of Jewish law, and provided leadership to the emerging Orthodox communities of the twentieth century. Levinthal was typical; elected to the pulpit of B'nai Abraham in 1891, he was subsequently elected by several other congregations as well and gained recognition as "the chief of the Russian rabbinate."[22]

Dr. Mendes (1852–1937), who supported Jacob Joseph even as he expressed pessimism about his chances for success, received his medical degree at the University of the City of New York and served as *hazzan* and minister of Shearith Israel from 1877–1920, has been called a "modern orthodox" leader by one of his biographers. This term has been used by many observers of Orthodoxy to describe a largely post–World War II North American phenomenon, to be discussed later, of Orthodox Jews, knowledgeable and observant of Jewish law and yet involved in modern intellectual, cultural, and social life.[23]

Mendes represented an early model for the modern Orthodox Jew. Steeped in tradition in his father's London home, he satisfied the Orthodox of Shearith Israel that he had the piety of an observant East European Jew. Yet he took a degree in medicine at a secular institution, worked actively with non-Orthodox Jews and non-Jewish clergy, and participated vigorously in multifarious communal and public activities in the general New York community.[24]

But men such as Mendes, whose role was much like the rabbi (Mendes was not an ordained rabbi), were quite rare in the Orthodox rabbinate early in the twentieth century. Most Orthodox rabbis in North America, even as late as World War I, were European born and educated, and far more comfortable studying, preaching (increasingly, but still in Yiddish), and resolving ritual questions for their congregants than shaping the worship of their synagogue to parallel Western notions of decorum, joining the communal board of rabbis and clergymen, or heading a mayor's commission. Rabbi Abraham Jacob Gershon Lesser (1834–1925), the first president of the Union of Orthodox Rabbis and the head of the Cincinnati Orthodox community from the time this native of Poland left Chicago in 1898, "never learned to talk English and the only words in English that he could write comprised his name; as a result, he did not take part in the civic life of the community." In fact, rabbi and scholars were not plentiful at all among the immigrants; the Rabbi of Slutsk (David Willowski) spoke for many when he visited the United States and chastised the rabbis of the Union of Orthodox Jewish Congregations for "having emigrated to this *trefa* [impure] land."[25]

Chaos and confusion, rather than order and decorum, more properly characterized Orthodoxy at the end of the nineteenth century. Synagogues were frequently nothing more than a small cell or room somewhere, and laymen often handled all "rabbinic" and administrative duties, except for those tasks performed by paid functionaries such as those discussed earlier. The level of religious education was very low, the conditions for learning poor, and the teachers poorly (if at all) trained. Perhaps the only functionary held in esteem was the *hazzan,* no longer the jack-of-all-trades but now, if he could really sing, the major attraction; advertisements of the time rarely announced who would preach but emphasized who would sing. This situation, however, began to change as North American Orthodoxy developed institutions and trained leaders.

7. Institutions and Organizations: 1898–1983:

The Union of Orthodox Jewish Congregations of America

Henry Pereira Mendes, "minister" of Shearith Israel, gave shape to, and served as the first president of, the Union of Orthodox Jewish Congregations of America (1898–1913), or UOJCA. After an unsuccessful attempt to launch an Orthodox rabbinical council in New York City in 1896, Mendes, together with several rabbis such as Bernard Drachman, convened the association on 8 June 1898 with fifty delegates present at Shearith Israel. Its purpose, much like the impetus behind the Jewish Theological Seminary Association, was the Reform movement. Mendes himself pointed out, a couple of years after the UOJCA's founding, that the UOJCA was formed to protest against "declarations of reform rabbis not in accord with the teachings of our Torah . . . and the accepted rulings of recognized sages of Israel."[1]

This emphasis on Torah, Talmud, and Codes ("authoritative interpretations of our rabbis") is codified in the UOJCA's constitution, and explicit in its earliest activities. The constitution protests the reformers' neglect of ritual, their rejection of a personal messiah and of Zionism, underscores that the UOJCA is not merely a religious sect (as was Reform) but a "nation," and announces the organization's purpose: to "advance the interests of . . . Rabbinical and Historical Judaism."[2]

Initially, the UOJCA's sought not only to coordinate political (such as opposing immigration restriction legislation in Congress) and philanthropic (aiding the Galveston flood victims) efforts among a number of Orthodox synagogues, but to vigorously propagandize (albeit without much sophistication, as the business was done from Mendes's office and the conventions met at his synagogue) for its version of "positive, Biblical, rabbinical, traditional and historical Judaism." The UOJCA, in its first five years of existence, sought to support *kashrut* observance wherever possible, urged college boards and boards of examiners to accommodate Sabbath observers, vigorously supported Zionism, encouraged state and local employers to provide leaves of absence to Jewish workers on Jewish holidays, made traditional Jewish ceremonial objects more easily available, battled conversionist programs, missionaries, and unsanitary *mohalim* (ritual circumcizers), and emphasized Sabbath observance. In its own words, the UOJCA sought to inculcate "loyalty to Jewish law and custom."[3]

Most of the Orthodox congregations that founded the UOJCA were small, poorly organized and in desperate need of secular and religious leadership, and they represented only a minority of Orthodox congregations in the country. Temple Mishkan Tefilah of Boston, "an orthodox *shul* of the day," was described by an early rabbi, a JTS graduate, as in need of a patient ministry. The religious instruction of the girls was "completely neglected," while that of the boys "was conducted in dark and dingy synagogue vestries or by itinerant rabbis"; the younger members "mostly congregated on the side walk outside" during the high holidays; the worship services were "utterly devoid of decorum"; and the synagogue "became the arena for unseemly squabbles of shyster politicians."[4]

Lest one suspect that the new rabbi exaggerated the confusion to boost his own role in changing the synagogue's direction, we are able to confirm most of what was said of the Boston synagogue by studying the minutes of other synagogues affiliated in the early twentieth century with the UOJCA.[5] Tifereth Israel, in Greenport, Long Island, had the same problems, as well as others that had plagued eighteenth-century congregations.

The congregation in Greenport was poor; dues ranged from $6 per year in 1902 to $18 per year in 1908, and this amount, plus fines and the sale of seats (as everywhere, one could purchase a permanent seat or pay a yearly rental fee), left the congregation with just enough money to provide minimal services such as hiring a man, in 1908, for $500 a year, to lead services two Sabbaths a month, teach the children three hours a day after school, and read the Torah. Fines were imposed for attending a *yahrzeit* (anniversary of a loved one's death) of a nonmember without the congregation's permission ($3), for an officer who failed to attend worship services two consecutive weeks (25¢), and for attending a *simcha* (celebration) of a nonmember ($5). The *shochet,* who "will come every Friday between 7:00 and 9:00 in the morning to *schecht* chickens," received 10¢ from each member and 25¢ for each *yahrzeit;* the congregation raised $5.16 in 1903 for victims of the Kishinev pogroms; the trustees, from time to time, served as judges in secular disputes between members; and the congregation did not hesitate to enforce observance, study, and worship. Members who would not use the *shochet*, "disturbed divine worship," or who refused to send their children "to learn" were expelled. Unless an Orthodox congregation sought an English-speaking, American-trained JTS graduate, this situation in Greenport was repeated nearly everywhere.[6]

The Union of Orthodox Jewish Congregations of America (initially its name was the Orthodox Jewish Congregational Union) grew rather rapidly, although its own figures, especially after World War II, were frequently inflated. Its founders represented 50 congregations; the first biennial convention (1900) represented 96 or 104 (reports vary) synagogues; and the UOJCA at its conventions issued periodic (and usually exaggerated) claims of membership, including 2,303 congregations in 1935, 3,100 in 1956, 2,500 in 1960, 3,900 in 1962, 3,100 in 1964, 3,000 in 1965 and 1969. The most reliable figures suggest that there were 180 congregations in the UOJCA in 1925, 200 in 1927, 300 in 1942, 500 in 1950 (and a $92,000 budget for 1950–1951), 700 in 1955, 720 in 1957, and about 1,000 in 1983.[7]

These congregations were located in the largest metropolitan areas of the United States, and especially the New York area, to a much greater extent than Reform or Conservative synagogues. In 1947, 93 of the 310 (30 percent) UOJCA synagogues were to be found in Long Island, Manhattan, the Bronx, and Brooklyn, while in the same year more than half of all the congregations in the UOJCA were located in New York, New Jersey, and Philadelphia.[8]

Such distribution helps to explain the UOJCA's continual efforts to help Jews remain in large urban centers; in September 1966 the UOJCA held a special conference to discuss ways in which New York Jews could be encouraged to remain in, or move back to, the East Side of Manhattan, the Bronx, and Brooklyn, for scores of abandoned synagogues were to be found in New York City neighborhoods where blacks and Puerto Ricans had taken over. At the 1970 convention, a report noted that in the past ten years the number of Brownsville synagogues had dropped from fifty to two.

At the same time, the UOJCA tried to remain sensitive to the needs of Orthodox Jews far removed from such centers; in 1967 the UOJCA announced it would send twenty-five rabbis from large urban centers to spend four weeks in "religiously undeveloped areas" in the Far West, the South, and Canada. By the 1980s such outreach efforts yielded generous rewards, as vigorous Orthodox congregations were scattered throughout North America.[9]

The UOJCA regularly launched fundraising campaigns to support the Orthodox movement, for it had no automatic dues plan as did the Union of American Hebrew Congregations (UAHC) and United Synagogue. Campaigns, such as that of 1933, urged each seatholder in a member congregation to contribute $1 for the UOJCA religious programs; that of 1938 launched a $1 million campaign (a million members each contributing $1), coordinated by the National Orthodox Board of Education, to support Yeshiva College, Hebrew Theological College, Talmud Torahs, and even fifty small, rural programs of Hebrew education; and the $300,000 campaign, launched in 1955, hoped to provide support to newly forming suburban congregations. Such campaigns rarely did very well.[10]

The UOJCA brought together a heterogeneous Orthodoxy, and it is hard to judge its success. It made a strong commitment to the New World and to Americanization, refusing to conduct its business or take minutes in Yiddish, as did every organization of the immigrant Jews, and choosing young, Americanized Jews for leadership positions of various kinds. This had the disadvantage, however, of closing the UOJCA off from many potential members; at the 1903 convention, an observer commented on the large number of Orthodox congregations that had not joined the UOJCA. It was clearly an organization of Orthodox synagogues strongly eager to acculturate Orthodoxy in a North American idiom.[11]

One of the UOJCA's central activities for years, and perhaps its most notable achievement, continued to be the supervision of *kashrut* and the elimination of infamous scandals connected with its administration. Various editions of the *Kosher Directory* provided lists of kosher products and services and served as a guide to the relatively unobtrusive "U" symbol on thousands of products. The UOJCA also supervised consumer, industry, and institutional products, on a fee basis, and in 1925 signed an agreement with the Union of Orthodox Rabbis (UOR) to jointly issue *heksherim* (*kashrut* approvals) under the auspices of the Va'ad Ha-Horaah (appointed by the rabbis) and an advisory committee (appointed by the UOJCA). To solve the nagging problem of accusations about profiteering, a finance committee on *heksherim* (40 percent from the Union of Orthodox Rabbis; 60 percent from the UOJCA) controlled the proceeds and distributed them to the poor. Several Orthodox publications, such as *Jewish Life,* regularly listed all the food products and detergents eligible to display the "U," while the Kashrut Division of the UOJCA kept busy trying to convince Jewish leaders to serve kosher meals at all public functions. By 1954, 139 rabbis supervised 405 products in 181 plants in 129 firms; in 1955 alone, 113 products, manufactured by thirty-four companies, were added to the list; in 1963 more than 2,000 kosher products were produced by over 400 companies; and the list continued to expand through the following decades, until in 1983 it listed 10,000 products.[12]

In addition to *kashrut* discussions, the UOJCA devoted considerable time at its conventions, especially during the 1930s, 1960s, and 1970s, to issues of social justice. During the Depression, the major concerns included efforts to achieve a five-day work week (and thus encourage Sabbath observance), slum clearance, and social security legislation, while in the more recent decades the issues were religion in the public schools, federal civil rights legislation, fair housing, freedom of religious expression and exit for endangered communities abroad, nuclear disarmament or freeze, single-parent families, the Vietnam War and Israeli settlements on the West Bank of the Jordan River (endorsing, in February 1983, Karnei Shomron in Samaria, founded by North American Orthodox Jews). The UOJCA even entered the low-cost housing field; in June 1963 the executive board announced its plan to erect two nonprofit "middle-class" twenty-story apartment buildings on 4.3 acres of land in Newark, New Jersey, at the cost of $12 million.[13]

The Women's Branch of the UOJCA, which celebrated its sixtieth anniversary in 1982, claimed 35,000 members representing more than two thousand sisterhoods in 1952 and 20,000 members from 600 sisterhoods in 1982. Its activities paralleled, to a great extent, those of similar organizations among Reform and Conservative women, with one exception—fundraising. The Women's Branch, more so than the Reform and Conservative women who primarily supported the HUC and JTS respectively, raised money in endless ways for numerous Orthodox concerns, not just for Yeshiva University.[14]

In the early 1950s the first convention of the National Conference of Synagogue Youth (NCSY) took place (its predecessor, the National Union of Orthodox Jewish Youth, had already convened in 1942), and while much of the social and cultural life of the Orthodox youth movement paralleled Reform and Conservative programs, there was one significant area of difference. The NCSY ran *Shabbatonim* (weekend retreats), as did the NFTY (National Federation of Temple Youth) and USY groups, but among the Orthodox youth there was a much more determined effort not only to serve members of UOJCA synagogues but also to acquaint unaffiliated Jewish high school and junior high school youth with their heritage. For the NCSY, as well as many of their parents, all Jews not affiliated with either Reform or Conservative synagogues were potential (if not actual) Orthodox Jews. By 1982, the twenty-eighth annual convention had youth representing 200 chapters in fifteen regions of the country.[15]

These UOJCA-NCSY regions paralleled, more or less, the divisions of the Reform and Conservative national organizations. Nearly every region had a director or coordinator who administered and developed programs, trained NCSY advisors, offered assistance to congregations, and coordinated the work of the regional office and national organizations. The union's major services were provided by the Department of Synagogue

Activities, the Department of Publications, and the Kashrut Division.

For the first twenty years (1898–1918), and for ten more years shortly thereafter (1924–1933), the UOJCA was directed by rabbis. This domination came to an end, for the most part, with the election of William Weiss (1887–1958) in 1933, and when he left office after serving for a decade, an agreement between the UOJCA's rabbinic supporters and the congregational leaders stipulated that the UOJCA would be a "strictly lay organization composed of lay representatives of all the congregations affiliated with the Union." This did not prohibit a rabbi from leading the UOJCA—indeed, Rabbi Joseph Karasick served as president from 1966–1972—but to a very great extent, ever since the early 1930s, the UOJCA has been a lay organization much like the UAHC and the USA.

Rabbi Isaac Elchanan Theological Seminary and Yeshiva University

Despite the surge of Jewish immigration in the 1880s, only a very few afternoon Hebrew, or Talmud Torah, schools were established—in Baltimore, Philadelphia, New York and elsewhere—to provide religious education "for the children." In New York the Machzike Talmud Torah (1883) flourished—in 1888 it had 690 boys and eight teachers—but it was the *only* afternoon Hebrew school serving East European Jews in New York for several years. Indeed, at the end of World War I there would only be one high school- and college-level *yeshiva* in the United States, and the first day school outside New York City was not established until 1917 in Baltimore.[14]

More numerous than formal institutions was the *cheder,* or one-room "school," generally undertaken as a purely private enterprise and whose negative impact on thousands of young immigrant Jews has become a staple of countless memoirs and popular literature. Orthodox synagogues, unlike those of the reformers, simply did not sponsor Hebrew schools.[16]

In September 1886, some New York Jews established an elementary *yeshiva,* Etz Chaim, designed to teach Hebrew language and literature (some Bible but mostly Talmud) as well as secular studies, "according to the strict orthodox and Talmudical law," to Lower East Side boys aged nine to fifteen. (Its most renowned student would be Mordecai M. Kaplan.) The school provided seven hours of Hebrew text instruction until 4 P.M., and then two hours of Hebrew and English language instruction followed by one hour of Yiddish. Somewhere during the day Etz Chaim introduced a very modest amount of secular studies; they were always an appendage to the Talmud studies, however, as Abraham Cahan, a teacher and future newspaper editor, recalled vividly.[17]

By 1900 there were eighty students and a building on Henry Street; by

1905 at least 150 students in six classes. During this decade parental reports and public records indicate that not only did young boys, eight to twelve, learn the Pentateuch and Talmud, but they also completed the public school curriculum sufficiently to enter the City College of New York (CCNY).

In 1897, with the establishment of the Rabbi Isaac Elchanan Theological Seminary (RIETS) on the Lower East Side, graduates of the Etz Chaim could continue Talmudic studies on an advanced level for the first time in the United States, and, if successful and desirous, could enter the "Hebrew Orthodox Ministry." The rabbinate was secondary, however; the primary *raison d'être* of RIETS was *torah lishmah*—study for its own sake. Of eleven students studying at RIETS in 1901, only two became Hebrew school-teachers and one a rabbi. The school memorialized the distinguished Talmudist and spiritual leader of Kovno Jewry, Rabbi Isaac Elchanan Spector, who died in 1896. Secular subjects, as in the Etz Chaim, were soon included, however minimally, thus sparing students contact with a secular institution yet preparing them, if necessary, for possible careers, and within five years there were at least sixty-five to seventy students enrolled. By 1908, in a new facility on Henry Street, 125 students—primarily East European Jewish boys and men from the ages of thirteen to thirty—were enrolled in four levels.[18]

When the Union of Orthodox Rabbis, at its 1903 convention in Philadelphia, recognized the RIETS as the only legitimate *yeshiva* in the United States, that act boosted enrollment dramatically, although the school met, at that time, in the Ladies' Gallery of the Sons of Israel (Kalvarier) synagogue. But poor secular studies (the 1908 student strike demanded improvements here), a miserable facility, an ill-defined Judaica curriculum, poor management, an inflexible administration, and a single permanent faculty member prevented significant maturation.[19]

The rabbinical school, unlike either JTS or HUC, was not precisely a professional rabbinical school and did not, initially, ordain rabbis. If a student wished ordination *(semicha),* an agreement with the Union of Orthodox Rabbis (1904) stipulated that it would examine potential candidates and, if a candidate passed the rigorous oral exams of the Semicha Board he would receive ordination, signed by an individual (or several) rabbi (or rabbis), in full keeping with Orthodox tradition.[20]

Not until 1915, with the merger of two institutions, Etz Chaim and RIETS, was the Rabbinical College of America created, and RIETS became solely an advanced *yeshiva* for training Orthodox rabbis. Bernard Revel (1885–1940), who was to head the seminary for twenty-five years, made the school into a distinguished institution. He structured the curriculum; hired a respected faculty (overwhelmingly Talmudists); required Bible, history, and Hebrew literature; and established a high school program immediately. Then, in 1928, Yeshiva College, an institution combining secular and Judaic studies, and finally, in 1937, a graduate school, completed Revel's ambitious building and development program.[21]

Revel also vigorously built the school's endowment; from less than $50,000 in 1919, it had $100,000 by 1923, $400,000 by 1925, $600,000 by 1927 (a $5 million campaign for a building and an endowment was launched in 1925) and more than $2 million when Yeshiva College opened. Although the Depression presented serious financial problems for Revel, and the institution nearly had to close, Revel's considerable fundraising skills were abundantly evident.[22]

With the college established, and overtures from JTS for a merger firmly rejected, the purpose of the institution was not only, as it had been for some years, "to train rabbis and teachers," but also "to disseminate Jewish knowledge" and to offer bachelor's degrees in arts and in science. Like Revel, who himself had abundant secular as well as rabbinical education, the school sought to introduce students to both the secular and Jewish world of learning.[23]

When RIETS began to ordain its own rabbis (over 130 by 1930) rather than continue the traditional method of individual *semicha,* tensions between the Union of Orthodox Rabbis and the school developed, despite Revel's vigorous pursuit and hiring of leading European Talmudists, including Rabbi Solomon Polachek (1877–1928), an important disciple of the famed Rabbi Chaim Soloveitchik, and Soloveitchik's son Moshe (1876–1941). These arguments were further sparked with the opening of Yeshiva College, for although some Orthodox leaders not only advocated but pursued secular studies, and *yeshivot* in Europe (especially western Europe) had included secular studies in their curricula and used the vernacular as the language of instruction, others (and some faculty too), felt that modernity—that is, secular society and its values—should be kept completely out of the Talmudic academy. When Revel died in 1940, the president of the Union of Orthodox Rabbis, Rabbi Eliezer Silver (1882–1968), of Cincinnati's B'nei Israel, informed the directors of RIETS that he had appointed a committee to run RIETS and Yeshiva College. The chairman of the board, Samuel Levy (1876–1953), firmly but politely rejected Silver's ploy.[24]

The attempted takeover by the right (UOR) in 1940 highlighted the tightrope Revel was forced to walk for many years. The left wing of Orthodoxy urged RIETS to produce Americanized graduates who spoke, in the words of Rabbi Bernard Drachman, one of their leading spokesmen, "an able, eloquent and spiritual-minded English," would cooperate with non-

Orthodox rabbis in communal affairs, and had shed Old European manner-isms, personal habits, and speech—in short, to produce rabbis who would Americanize Orthodoxy, that is, maintain "tradition" punctiliously but also easily relate to an Americanized laity. The left wing appreciated Revel's own blending of Lithuanian Orthodoxy and secular studies (he possessed a doctorate from Dropsie College), his deep commitment to combining secular and traditional studies, and his willingness to allow a RIETS gradu-ate—although the school officially forbade its graduates from occupying pulpits with mixed pews—to serve a few years in a congregation with mixed seating in the hope he would convince the worshippers to erect a *mechitza*. To assuage the rightists, however (for the approval of RIETS graduates by the UOR gave legitimacy to the school), Revel would remove the rabbi if he was unsuccessful, and, if the rabbi balked, threaten to have RIETS revoke his *semicha* and to publicize the revocation in the press.

Revel's successor, Samuel Belkin, discovered that the tightrope on which Revel so delicately balanced had not become wider with the passing years. When the Synagogue Council of America honored him—together with the heads of the Reform and Conservative rabbinical seminaries—at its fortieth anniversary dinner, in November 1966, the heads of four sectar-ian Orthodox seminaries denounced Belkin's participation. Their ad in the New York *Times* accused Belkin of providing a "tacit endorsement" of "alien and dangerous ideologies" (Reform and Conservative Judaism) that "destroy belief in the Divine origin of Torah." On behalf of Yeshiva Univer-sity, Rabbi Joseph Lookstein (1902–1979), a former Rabbinical Council of America (RCA) president and senior rabbi of New York's Kehilath Je-shurun, accused the sectarians, out of jealousy of Belkin and Yeshiva Uni-versity, of seeking to "smash" Jewish unity and "shatter" Jewish solidar-ity.[25]

Under Belkin (1911–1976), who joined the Yeshiva College faculty in 1935 after taking his doctorate at Brown University, as an instructor in Greek, and who served as president of Yeshiva University (Yeshiva College became Yeshiva University in 1945) from 1943 (when he was only thirty-two years old) to 1975, the programs continued to expand and mature. Enrollment was 850 when he assumed the presidency and over 8,000 when he retired; the faculty grew from 94 to 1,600 in the same period, while the budget skyrock-eted from $440,000 to $93 million. More than 2,600 men were enrolled in courses at RIETS in 1954–1955; periodically, a sizable group of men would receive ordination. In April 1950, the RIETS of Yeshiva University or-dained a hundred rabbis who had completed a three-year postgraduate rabbinical program during the previous three years, and in June 1964, twenty-eight rabbis were ordained; in March 1956, 131; and in March 1983, seventy-seven. The 1950 ordination was the thirteenth exercise in RIETS's history, as, unlike HUC and JTS, the RIETS did not ordain annually, and by June 1968 RIETS had ordained more than a thousand rabbis.[26]

In 1957 Yeshiva revised its rabbinic curriculum, which had overwhelmingly emphasized Talmud and Law Codes, in an attempt not only to broaden learning but also to introduce Orthodox rabbinical students, many of whom had never studied at a secular institution nor concerned themselves with Bible, philosophy, or Hebrew literature, to carefully controlled non-Talmud courses. Henceforth, all students seeking *semicha* would need to complete ninety credits in the Bernard Revel Graduate School (Master of Hebrew Literature) and, if so wishing, could receive some practical rabbinic experience by "interning" with a pulpit rabbi while he conducted various life ceremonies.[27]

These rabbinical students were not recruited in the same manner as those as HUC or JTS, where recruitment officers actively pursued potential rabbis at colleges, universities, summer camps, and youth institutes and seminars. Most of the rabbinical students at RIETS came ready-made, that is, from Yeshiva's high school system and undergraduate college and, prior to that, from small *yeshivot* or Orthodox day schools. While the RCA and UOJCA jointly sponsored programs to bring young men and women to Yeshiva University for weekend seminars or week-long sessions with the hope that they might choose to attend, the RIETS student body itself came from highly predictable institutions.

By the early 1960s Yeshiva University had grown considerably, and tens of millions of dollars were about to be spent to develop the Washington Heights campus overlooking the Harlem River as well as to expand the Midtown Center. During the 1961–1962 academic year there were 630 men at Yeshivah College, 300 women at its Stern College for Women campus (founded in 1954), and the student body of 5,075 included 2,100 graduate and 2,975 undergraduate students. In addition, the Albert Einstein Medical School had been opened in the Bronx in 1953 and by the 1970s was supplying 80 percent of all the health care in that borough; the Gustav Wurzweiler School of Social Work opened in 1957; the 1962–1963 school year saw a West Coast "branch" launched in Los Angeles with Leon Stitskin (1911–1978), a professor of philosophy at Yeshiva, acting director; in 1975 Belkin named Dr. Haym Soloveitchik (1937–   ), the son of Joseph and the recipient of ordination from RIETS (1963) and a doctorate from the Hebrew University, to the deanship of the Bernard Revel Graduate School for Advanced Jewish Studies; and in 1976 the Benjamin Cardozo School of Law opened. The June 1982 graduation, Yeshiva's fifty-first, included the awarding of 1,381 degrees.[28]

Yeshiva, as did so many other universities, expanded too rapidly in the 1960s for its long-term financial security. Ground was broken, late in 1965, for the $15-million twenty-story Belfer Science Center, which by 1980 would be virtually empty, as the generous federal funding of science during the 1960s did not continue. Already in 1970 Yeshiva faced a $4.5-million deficit (a figure ten times the 1945 operating budget) in the school's $75-million current budget, and Belkin pleaded for more government aid. Yeshiva was eligible for an extra $1 million in New York State aid under the Bundy law if it could claim it was not a religious institution, and Belkin, despite student protests against what some termed "secularization," redesignated RIETS as an "affiliate" of Yeshiva to qualify for the funds.

Early in 1980 New York City banks filed multimillion-dollar claims against the university. Rabbi Norman Lamm (1927–   ), Yeshivah's first North American-born president (1977–   ), a professor of Jewish philosophy and the recipient of three degrees from its schools (bachelor of arts, 1949; ordination, 1951; doctorate, 1966), used the financial acumen he developed as the junior colleague of Joseph Lookstein at Kehilath Jeshurun and Leo Jung's successor at New York's Jewish Center for eighteen years, to stave off closing. Negotiating a debt-restructuring plan that called for the banks forgiving $61 million, he paid off $35 million by early 1982 to free the university of debts that nearly drove it to bankruptcy. Lamm did this by securing thirty-one pledges of $1 million each from Yeshiva supporters (mostly trustees)—a sign not only of his considerable skills but also of North American Orthodoxy's financial coming of age. Late in 1979 Lamm announced a six-year, $100-million fundraising campaign to conclude at the school's centenary anniversary in 1986.[29]

Hebrew Theological College

The Chicago Hebrew Theological College (HTC) was founded in 1922 with Rabbi Saul Silber (1881–1946), who served for a quarter-century, as its first president. HTC, during Silver's presidency, was the largest Orthodox seminary outside New York City, and had ordained 132 rabbis, beginning in 1925, in its first twenty-five years. In addition, 200 teachers of Hebrew had been trained, more than 1,500 men had studied at the college for two or more years, and numerous women had been certified as Hebrew school-teachers in the Teacher's Institute for Women.

Prior to 1922, Orthodox young men could study at Chicago's Yeshivath Etz Chaim (established in 1912) and then go east to pursue a rabbinic education. By absorbing Etz Chaim in 1921–1922 into the HTC, Chicago could provide a complete Jewish and rabbinic education for those in the Midwest.

Oscar Z. Fasman (1908–   ), who succeeded Silber as president (1946–1964), was the first North American-born person to head an Orthodox rabbinic institution. Despite a small budget ($200,000 in 1947) and small faculty, Fasman appointed the college's most well-known scholar—Eliezer Berkovits—and worked tirelessly to build the institution. The School of Graduate Studies, where ordained rabbis pursued advanced degrees in Hebrew literature, religious education, or pastoral counseling, was opened in 1950, and a liberal arts college was added in 1959. By the time this Division of Liberal Arts and Sciences was established, the school had relocated to a sixteen-acre campus in suburban Skokie.

For several years in the early 1960s the college operated not only as the HTC but also as the Jewish University of America, a symbol of its hopes for further expansion, and in 1961 the Yeshiva High School was opened on the Skokie campus as a preparatory school. By the mid-1960s, although now without Fasman, it resumed its programs of Jewish Studies, Teachers Institute for Women, and rabbinical education simply as the Hebrew Theological College, and continuously struggled to recapture its fame of old. In 1977 Irving Rosenbaum (1922–   ), a graduate of the HTC who had served as rabbi of Chicago's Loop Synagogue for fourteen years, took over the presidency. Despite the inability to realize its dream of university status, by 1982 the HTC had ordained over 400 rabbis and made a large contribution to Orthodox Jewish life in the United States and Canada.[30]

Union of Orthodox Rabbis (Agudat HaRabbanim)

The Union of Orthodox Rabbis (Agudat HaRabbanim) was founded by fifty-nine men (thirteen of whom came from New York City) in July 1902 in New York City with Rabbi Abraham Jacob Gerson Lesser of Cincinnati's Beth Tephila Congregation as president.[31] It followed efforts by Rabbis Levine (Detroit) and Zarchy (Des Moines), beginning in August 1900, as well as those of Rabbis Margolies (Boston), Silber (Worcester), Israelite (Chelsea), and Levinthal (Philadelphia) in 1901, and culminating in strong appeals to the East European rabbis, attending the Federation of American Zionists convention in May 1902, to attend the founding session.

Its goals, at the outset, were to improve religious instruction and seek only observant teachers in the *cheder,* organize careful records of marriages and divorces, war against "orthodox" Sabbath violators in the marketplace, and establish an inspection system of *kashrut* and *mikvaot.* All its members (sixty-five by the second annual convention in 1903) studied in European *yeshivot,* were ordained by European rabbis, and served congregations in North America.[32]

The leaders of the Union of Orthodox Rabbis (UOR), at its inception, were almost all from Kovno, largely ordained by Rabbi Isaac Elchanan Spector (whose name RIETS memorialized), and frequently served more than one congregation in a community in order to eke out a meager living. Six of the nine executive board members in 1903 came from Kovno, and a seventh was educated there. And Rabbis Levinthal, Sivitz, and Zarchy, in that same year, served six, three, and three congregations, respectively, in Philadelphia, Pittsburgh, and Louisville.[33]

The emphasis on Jewish education for youth and ritual observance for all Jews—a much different agenda from either the Reform or Conservative rabbinical organizations—dominated the early conventions of the UOR (known as the United Orthodox Rabbis until about 1920). The UOR sought to construct a uniform curriculum for all the Talmud Torah and *cheder* programs in America, to help financially in establishing Hebrew school programs for girls and Hebrew high school programs for advanced students, and to establish schools—in larger cities—that would combine Judaica and secular subjects during the course of a school day. Although this latter would be slow to develop, it would eventually be one of Orthodoxy's most significant (if not the most important) contributions to American Jewish life.[34]

The other area of great concern to these Orthodox rabbis—all of whom were themselves European immigrants—was the conflict between the Orthodox Jewish immigrant's need for sustenance and the demands of the Sabbath. The organization sought to put immigrants in touch with Sabbath-keeping employers, to urge its members' congregations to patronize such employers and manufacturers, to lobby with labor unions for Sabbath observance to be included in their platforms, to eliminate college examinations on the Sabbath, and to pressure Yiddish newspapers to cease Sabbath publication. For many years too the UOR lobbied the New York State legislature to support legislation permitting Sabbath observers to do business on Sunday, with the hope that New York City would then exempt these people from provisions of the state's Sunday-closing statues. In this area the UOR successes were few and it was to be, ironically, neither the immigrants or their children but, as we shall see in Chapter 9, their grandchildren, who would, in significant numbers, and in part because of their greater affluence, vigorously lobby for and observe a day of rest.

The UOR affirmed Zionism, albeit in its religious form, from nearly its

inception. Although Israel Levinthal, then a teenage leader of Ozrei Zion (Aids to Zion), recalled petitioning the UOR to adopt the Zionist platform and the rabbis tabling the motion, at the 1903 convention Zionism was unanimously accepted as part of the conference program. At the 1904 convention there were memorial services at a local synagogue for Theodore Herzl; and subsequent conventions discussed, debated, and resolved how to bring Torah and *mitzvot* to Palestine Jewry and how to ensure Palestine Jewry's survival—for it was not just Zionism but religious Zionism to which the Union of Orthodox Rabbis was committed.[35]

The UOR grew steadily. There were 80 members in 1904, 120 in 1913, 200 in 1920, over 350 by 1930, 450 in 1940, 500 in 1945, and 650 in 1955— by which point the organization's peak of influence had been reached. The UOR established a close relationship with the RIETS very early by recognizing the seminary (1903) and accepting its graduates, steeped in Talmud with commentaries and properly ordained, into the UOR. Nevertheless, both of these positive facts disguise underlying problems: significant numbers of Orthodox rabbis did not join the UOR at all, and there was much tension in the relationship between the UOR and the RIETS.

The UOR admission requirements were exceedingly strict, that is, beyond the course of study offered by RIETS, and this had the effect of closing membership to a growing number of North American-born and -educated Orthodox rabbis. Eventually (1935) they would form their own rabbinic organization—the Rabbinical Council of America (RCA).

In addition, the growing program of secular studies at Yeshiva College irritated the UOR's more separatist members, even if, in reality, the Judaica and the secular spheres never really mixed, as the *yeshiva* was the *yeshiva,* and the college was the college, and each, by and large, taught its subjects independently of the other. As early as 1904 the UOR questioned whether the *yeshiva* was really "orthodox" since the professors apparently believed in biblical "Higher Criticism," were not all qualified (according to the UOR) as teachers of Talmud, and the students received improper and insufficient learning for rabbis.[36]

In addition, internal squabbles weakened the UOR. By 1925 there was no longer a president but a "presidium" of four or five men, representing different positions among the Orthodox, who governed the group. Having poorly supervised (unlike the UOJCA) the operation of *kashrut,* the UOR's reputation had sunk considerably, and the agreement with the UOJCA in 1925 to jointly administer *kashrut* approval was an attempt to regain credibility in this area.

UOR conventions addressed a diversity of concerns, but many had in common increasing levels of education and observance among American

Jews. These included the resolve to oppose the building of new Orthodox synagogues without a *mechitza,* periodic campaigns to promote *mechitzot* in Orthodox congregations without them, and support of court suits in which one side argues that the synagogue constitution required *mechitzot.* [37] The issues also included support for periodic "self-tax" campaigns among Orthodox Jews for education (such as the $5 "self-tax" in 1931 to keep the Hebrew Theological College afloat), a boycott of the Yiddish *Day-Jewish Journal* because it was published on the Sabbath, and vigorous opposition to the attempt of the Conservative movement in the 1930s to liberalize the laws affecting the *agunah* (abandoned wife). [38] And finally, the conventions considered the demand that all Jewish community centers be closed on the Sabbath and Jewish holidays; and approved "Torah Tours" (initiated in 1949), jointly sponsored with the Rabbinical Council of America, which covered dozens of cities in the United States and Canada and concentrated on bringing Orthodox Judaism to Jewish college students.

The rabbis also discussed political issues, including opposition to socialism, Bolshevism, and radicalism (1919); a *cherem* (excommunication) against any Jew who handled or traded with German goods (1933); an Emergency Religious Relief and Rehabilitation Department; and the launching of a $2.5-million campaign to rescue Jewish orphans and refugee children, repair and reconstruct synagogues, restore Jewish cemeteries, reunite separated families and provide Torah scrolls and prayer books for European Jewish survivors of the Holocaust (1945).

In addition the UOR's conventions devoted considerable time to similar rabbinic welfare concerns, as did the Reform and Conservative rabbis, including meager salaries, uncertain tenure, unpleasant relations with lay leaders, lack of pensions or medical support, and the annual disbursement of charitable funds donated by UOR members to support indigent European and Palestinian rabbis and scholars. [39] It was, at its peak of influence among the Orthodox rabbinate, a busy and constructive professional organization.

The Rabbinical Council of America

The Rabbinical Council of America was formed by thirty-five to forty English-speaking rabbis in early July 1935, at a convention in Belmar, New Jersey. It grew out of two organizations: (1) the Rabbinical Association of Yeshiva (Histadrut HaRabbanim), an alumni organization for RIETS graduates not accepted by the Union of Orthodox Rabbis, which had served, mostly, to help RIETS raise money during the Depression years and find synagogue positions for RIETS graduates; and (2) the Rabbinical Council of the UOJCA, a group formed by Rabbi Leo Jung in 1925 to assume the rabbinic functions of the UOR.[40]

For the first two years a presidium governed the RCA, but at the 1937 convention Rabbi Herbert S. Goldstein (1890–1970), of New York's West Side Institutional Synagogue, was elected president and the organization began to assume a structure. Its energies, to its dismay, were directed mostly to conflicts with the senior rabbinic group (UOR) in the early years. The UOR, with its mostly East European *yeshiva* educated membership, looked down on those members of the RCA who had only received RIETS's *Yoreh Yoreh* (ordination that restricted a rabbi's decisions to ritual matters) rather than the more advanced (and restricted to a handful of rabbis) *Yadin Yadin*, required for full membership in the UOR. Most of all it resented the growing popularity and strength of this new competition (especially after the RCA merged with the 100-member alumni association of the Hebrew Theological College of Chicago), and failed in every attempt to either co-opt or dissolve the Rabbinical Council, which, by the 1950s at the latest, dominated Orthodox Jewry.[41]

The RCA grew rapidly; from about 100 members in 1936 it claimed 145 in 1940, 250 in 1942 (after the merger)—a figure that the RCA said represented "the entire English-speaking orthodox rabbinate of the country"— 294 in 1947, 435 in 1951 (with a $20,000 budget), 475 in 1952, 608 in 1954, 660 in 1955, 702 in 1957, 750 in 1958, 800 in 1962, 830 in 1964, 900 in 1965, and more than 1,000 by the 1980s.[42]

Its involvement in Jewish communal affairs grew steadily too, from internal recordkeeping (especially on Jewish marriages and divorces), publications (including *Tradition,* a quarterly journal of Orthodox Jewish thought) and welfare activities in support of its members, to activities on behalf of Israel, Jewish education, civil rights, social justice, overseas Jewries (its Ezra Fund regularly dispatched Passover food packages to needy Jews), federal aid to private schools, and much else, including a very active Political Action Committee. A social justice commission was established in 1946, and it made its first report to the 1947 convention. This convention resulted in the first pronouncement by North American Orthodox rabbis on economic problems ("labor-management relations"). The commission reported regularly on its efforts; in 1969 it organized meetings with black and Puerto Rican leaders to discuss ways to keep Jews in changing neighborhoods, as a RCA survey revealed 75 abandoned synagogues in New York City and 250 in other cities around the country.[43]

The RCA, unlike other Orthodox rabbinical associations, generally sought rapprochement, when possible, with non-Orthodox rabbis. This was well illustrated by a lengthy controversy between the RCA and two other Orthodox rabbinical organizations, the Union of Orthodox Rabbis (UOR) and the Rabbinical Alliance of America (RAA). Late in 1954 the UOR unanimously prohibited Jews from using a Conservative Beth Din (Law Court), calling Conservative Judaism "heresy." The Rabbinical Alliance (established in 1944), claiming 300 members and consisting mostly of rabbis, who rejected secular higher education, from sectarian Brooklyn *yeshivot* transplanted from Eastern Europe (such as Yeshivat Torah Vodath and Yeshivat Chaim Berlin), pressed hard in 1955 for Orthodox rabbis to disassociate themselves entirely from "coordinated activity"—that is, boards of rabbis—with Reform and Conservative colleagues. This culminated on 6 March 1956 when the Rabbinical Alliance—represented by eleven *yeshiva* heads and their extremist spokesman Rabbi Aaron Kotler (1891–1962)—released an interdiction *(issur)*. It forbade Orthodox rabbis to participate in both the 600-member New York Board of Rabbis (established in 1881) and the Synagogue Council of America (the Jewish religious spokesman for Orthodox, Conservative, and Reform Judaism in their relations with secular and Christian agencies)—on the grounds that joint action with liberal rabbis was "prohibited by Torah law"—and all Rabbinical Alliance members immediately resigned.[44]

The RCA president, David Hollander (1913–   ), rabbi of the Mt. Eden Jewish Center in the Bronx, agreed that Orthodox rabbis should follow the RAA order, but he did not, on this occasion, represent the membership. Emanuel Rackman, the vice-president, argued that much of the progress Orthodoxy had made in convincing non-Orthodox rabbis to adopt rules and values, in communal matters, sensitive to Orthodox practices, owed its origins to organizations and boards, especially of rabbis, where all rabbis joined together. The RCA executive council agreed, voting in March 1956 to remain in the Synagogue Council of America (SCA) and to urge RCA members of the New York Board of Rabbis (NYBR) not to follow the lead of the Rabbinical Alliance. This position was supported by the RCA membership, too, as it strongly denounced the RAA ban at its July 1958 convention.[45]

Two years later the UOR, at its December convention, affirmed the old RAA *issur* against membership in the NYBR by publishing the *issur* and the names of several hundred Orthodox rabbis who agreed not to join the board. The RCA again rejected this proposal, as it did a motion to withdraw from the Synagogue Council, arguing that "whereas we will never recognize the religious legitimacy or authority of the reform and conservative movements," we must try to work with them. The RCA stood firmly in the camp of intra-Jewish cooperation, at least on the external religious issues, despite the occasional lack of sensibilities on the part of Reform and Conservative colleagues and the practice of many Reform rabbis to officiate at intermarriages. At the same time, however, the RCA continued its formal refusal to recognize the legitimacy of non-Orthodox wings of Judaism.[46]

Before this controversy made coordination all but impossible, the RCA and RAA had discussed the possibility of a merger in the late 1940s. But the RAA demand that all rabbis serving congregations with mixed seating —a sizable minority of RCA members—be barred from the new organization doomed the merger discussions. Despite numerous pleas for unity over the years—especially in presidential addresses at RCA conventions—Orthodoxy has remained divided into numerous synagogue, rabbinical, seminary, and educational organizations frequently at odds with each other.[47]

In addition to its annual meetings, the RCA frequently sponsored special "convocations" to address specific concerns such as alienated youth (1969), Christian campus missionizing (1973), Jewish education (1974), rising divorce rates (1977), family life (1978), and nuclear freeze (1983). These sessions frequently attracted hundreds of Orthodox rabbis (500 attended the 1977 sessions in Hasbrouck Heights) and provided those in attendance the opportunity to hear from experts how to better address, from the perspective of Jewish tradition, generally secular concerns.[48]

Young Israel

Young Israel, organized in 1912 on the Lower East Side by fifteen or so Americanized Orthodox Jewish men and women with a single purpose— Friday evening lectures in English—alternated synagogues every two weeks until, by 1915, it conducted its own services. These services were marked, in 1915 as well as six decades later, by decorum, spirit, abundant congregational singing, and English lectures. In 1918 the organization and the synagogue combined into Young Israel Synagogue, purchased the old Hebrew Immigrant Aid and Shelter building on Lower Broadway, and energetically began to establish more Young Israel synagogues around New York. By 1924 these Young Israel synagogues had formed the Council of Young Israel, held their first convention (Brooklyn), and were soon (1928) to require a full-time executive director.[49]

Today, Young Israel consists mainly of college-educated, American-born, middle-class young men and women whose Orthodox synagogues have decorous services, a rich variety of adult and youth programs, intensive adult education, *mechitzot* (unlike many UOJCA member congregations), officers who must be Sabbath observers, and rabbis (since World War II) who have replaced laypeople as leaders. The Council of Young Israel Rabbis, the rabbinical organization of Young Israel congregational rabbis, has increasingly dominated the movement, and hardly a branch of Young Israel today is without rabbinic leadership. The ninety-five synagogues and 23,000 families reported in 1965 belie the militancy, outspokenness, and *halachic* rigor with which Young Israel followers spread their own Orthodoxy and criticize that of others. Hence there are many Orthodox leaders who feel that Young Israel basks in the self-righteous glow of splendid isolation and must be incorporated into the "mainline" Orthodox institutional apparatus.[50]

8. Beliefs

Emanuel Rackman (1910–   ), rabbi of Far Rockaway's Shaarey Tefilah and professor at Yeshiva University before becoming president of Bar Ilan University in Israel, noted "the existence of different orthodox approaches" and found Orthodoxy "no more monolithic than the non-orthodox movements." This comment suggests that it is not as easy as one would suspect to describe "Orthodox" ideology, doctrine, or belief, for Orthodoxy is as complex and diverse, if not more than, as the other sectors of Judaism. First, to whom do we listen? Virtually every Reform rabbi has been ordained at the HUC and, if in the pulpit rabbinate, serves a UAHC congregation, and nearly every Conservative rabbi has been ordained at the JTS and serves a United Synagogue congregation. But Orthodox rabbis and congregations are far more heterogeneous; an "orthodox" synagogue may belong to the UOJCA, the National Council of Young Israel, or the Yeshiva University Synagogue Council, while "orthodox" rabbis may be members of the UOR, RCA, RAA, Hithadut Harabbonim Haredim, Agudat Haadmorim, or Council of Refugee Rabbis.[1]

Furthermore, only a portion of synagogues that are referred to as *orthodox* actually can be identified as *orthodox*, i.e., rigorously observant; Charles Liebman, in 1965, estimated that only 1,607 of the 3,100 "orthodox" synagogues actually claimed by the Union of Orthodox Jewish Congregations of America were orthodox. But even among those synagogues designated as orthodox, there are enormous differences. In many communities one may find an Orthodox synagogue with a large sanctuary, mixed seating, prayers and sermons characterized by abundant decorum and English, and a rabbi and/or cantor who "leads" the service much as do Reform and Conservative officiants. Such a milieu would take seriously the advice of Rabbi Bernard Drachman, one of the earliest presidents of the Union of Orthodox Jewish Congregations of America, that "services must be genuinely refined and reverential and all the surroundings of worship should be such as to offer no offense to aesthetic natures." Another Orthodox synagogue, occasionally on the same street, might be quite small, with a rigidly demarcated woman's section not observable by the men, congregational members informally "leading" the worship,[2] a service of spontaneity, individuality, and even, to some, cacophonous voices in prayer ("davening"), as frequently, while the cantor repeats the prayers that have already been said by the congregation, people will walk around and talk with each other. How does one find unity of doctrine in such dissimilarity?[3]

Moreover, dozens of academies of advanced Talmudic study exist in the United States, and major ideological differences exist among rabbis and institutions labeled, far too simply, *orthodox*. Some, to cite but two examples, argue that there is no intrinsic value in any knowledge outside of Torah, that Torah is totally self-sufficient for a Jew's intellectual needs, that study or enjoyment of secular studies and culture is a waste of time, for all knowledge—religious and secular—is to be found in the Talmud. As Rabbi Aaron Kotler, the founder of the Beth Medrash Gevoha in Lakewood, New Jersey, put it, those who receive a secular education cannot express authentic Torah views.

Other rabbinic authorities, in contrast, urge their followers to acquire the best knowledge their age has to offer, confident that secular knowledge, in the words of Emanuel Feldman (1927–   ), rabbi of Atlanta's Beth Jacob, "increases our appreciation of God's unfolding will in nature and history, [and] can be an instrument in the understanding of Divine truths," or that, as David Berger (1943–   ), an Orthodox historian at Brooklyn College expressed it, "Torah combined with secular learning . . . is one road to human perfection."[4]

Some, especially among the Orthodox sectarians such as the Satmar Hasidim, explain that even the *idea* of a Jewish state either before or without the Messiah is a heresy, and that the intimidation of, and violence against, Zionist sympathizers is (paradoxically) based on an intense love for the Jewish people and the land of Israel. Others among the Orthodox (the vast majority) worked vigorously for the Jewish state's creation and development. Such differences make a discussion of Orthodoxy riddled with exceptions, no less than in our attempt to describe Reform or Conservative ideology.

The Union of Orthodox Jewish Congregations of America, at its first meeting in 1898, articulated a "platform" of Orthodoxy; the following UOJCA statement can serve as an introduction to Orthodox doctrine: "We believe in the Divine revelation of the Bible."[5]

Divine Revelation of the Bible

Likewise, Rabbi Marc D. Angel (1945–   ), of New York's Shearith Israel, feels that "what unites all orthodox groups is a belief in the Divine authority of the Torah," and although there is some disagreement about precisely how encompassing the word *Torah* is (Pentateuch? all of the Hebrew Bible? the Hebrew Bible and the Oral Law, i.e., Talmud?), there is quite widespread agreement about Torah's divine nature, that is, all Orthodox Jews regard the Pentateuch as divinely revealed.[6]

Leo Jung (1892–   ), who served as rabbi of New York City's Jewish Center from 1922 until his retirement, stated that "a true Jew believes in revelation and the divine origins of the Torah," while Samuel Belkin wrote that "the essence of traditional Judaism is the indisputable faith that the Torah, the revealed word of God, is . . . the law of God" and that "it represents divine authority." Eliezer Berkovits (1900–   ), a former professor of Jewish philosophy at the Hebrew Theological College, affirms that "God did indeed speak to Moses, as the Bible says." Marvin Fox (1922–   ), who teaches at Brandeis University, believes "in the traditional doctrine . . . that the Torah is divine," while Emanuel Rackman feels that "Moses wrote it while in direct communion with God." Norman Lamm (1927–   ), former rabbi of New York's Jewish Center (1958–1976) and now president of Yeshiva University, accepts "unapologetically the idea of the verbal revelation of the Torah," while M. D. Tendler (1926–   ), a teacher of Talmudic law at Yeshiva's seminary, notes that "the literal interpretation" of God speaking unto Moses is the "foundation of our faith," and "differentiates Torah Judaism from the organized faith communities that have arisen as deviants from the traditional form."[7]

Orthodox thinkers, by acknowledging the divine origin of Torah, thus reject modern biblical criticism. For them, the text of the Torah we have today is the text given to Moses by God, and this view of a literal, direct, verbal revelation—the single most striking and important distinction between the Orthodox and non-Orthodox—is articulated in the *yeshivot,* is explicit in Orthodox writings of various kinds (including the contemporary multivolume *Artscroll* biblical commentary series), and explains much about Orthodox beliefs, attitudes, and values.[8]

The Obligatory Nature of Ceremonial Law

"Ceremonial Law Is . . . Obligatory," states the 1898 Platform. Although an isolated Orthodox thinker, such as Emanuel Rackman, acknowledges that much of the Pentateuch "may have been written by people in different times" and that some of the divine commandments are more important than others, nearly all Orthodox ideologues affirm the equal importance of all the commandments, for they all come from the same "author." For a believing Jew, therefore, all the commandments have equal force, all are binding, and no hierarchical division is valid. Reform Judaism divided the hundreds of commandments in the Torah into ethical (those between the human being and his or her fellow) and ritual (those between man or woman and God); for Orthodoxy, even to fulfill the ritual commandments, as Eliezer Berkovits observed, "is to do the will of God." As Norman Lamm succinctly expressed it, "I regard all of the Torah as binding on the Jew."[9]

Reform Judaism, of course, placed greater emphasis on the ethical rather than on the ceremonial legislation of scriptures, arguing that only the latter, if anything at all, was binding on Jews, while Conservative Judaism has continually hesitated to define a Conservative Jew, at least on the lay level, in terms of ritual or ceremonial observances. The actual practice of the overwhelming number of Reform and Conservative Jews is clearly discontinuous with the emphasis on ritual and ceremony in earlier forms of Judaic expression.

Few, however, are those who would define an Orthodox Jew merely in institutional terms, that is, as one who belongs to an Orthodox synagogue; most would insist that an Orthodox Jew affirms the binding nature of Jewish law *(halacha)* and makes an effort to observe that law. True, numerous unobservant "Orthodox" Jews—members of Orthodox synagogues—have no commitment to the details of Jewish law, but Orthodoxy feels uncomfortable about them in a way unparalleled among Reform and Conservative Jews. The synagogue leaders, and ideologists, act as if all Orthodox Jews were either observant or were desirous of being so.

The very essence of Orthodox Judaism rests on the acceptance of a spiritual-historical event during which God conveyed to Moses the Torah (written down by Moses) and the Oral Law (taught by Moses to disciples). The former has been carefully preserved, the Orthodox believe, since the time of Moses, while the latter eventually developed into the Talmud.

The Torah was given to Moses not only to understand but also to interpret, and the process of Torah analysis by qualified men over the past two millenia is known as *Torah she-b'al peh* (Oral Law), and the legal decisions based upon them are the *halacha* (literally, "norm" or "practice"). The rabbis who analyze the Torah, in ancient times as well as our own time, are considered to employ principles that ultimately derive from God's revelation to Moses at Mt. Sinai, and hence whatever a *halachic* scholar might propound at any time was already revealed to Moses at Sinai.

As Marvin Fox explained it, "I conceive of revelation as including *Torah she-b'al peh,* the oral tradition [which] continues to unfold through all the generations of Jewish history."[10]

It follows, of course, that because the oral tradition, both what is recorded in the Talmud and what has been added since then, is also the result of divine revelation, the Torah and the Oral Law are of equal authority. "Every traditional Jew," M. D. Tendler pointed out, "accepts these rabbinic laws as no less obligatory than the biblical laws." Or, as Emanuel Rackman noted, "Orthodoxy regards any rejection of the revealed character of both the Written and Oral Law as a negation of the very essence of the *halacha.* "[11]

The interpretation of the Torah by *halachic* scholars, all attempting to discover its timeless message, is not, however, monolithic. In fact, there have been, according to Eliezer Berkovits, "vast differences between them in the understanding of the *halacha.* " Some, in the American Orthodox community, have determined to transport the Orthodoxy of Eastern Europe to American soil and to interpret the Torah without particular concern for the contemporary situation. Others, such as Berkovits, argued that *halacha*'s purpose is to "humanize" the Torah, to render it practically feasible, economically viable, ethically significant, and spiritually meaningful, and if its practitioners fail to do so they are not representative of "authentic, *halachic* Judaism."[12]

Berkovits had special sensitivity to those areas of Jewish law that were interpreted differently by the Orthodox and by the non-Orthodox, and urged that the "unity of the Jewish people" and "the love for the people of Israel" become so paramount that the Orthodox, albeit possessing an interpretation with divine authority, should compromise with non-Orthodox. Berkovits would reject Rackman's contention "that there is but one authentic Judaism" and his argument that "other approaches are error, distortion, heresy, or even pretense," and seek a meeting ground on behalf of *k'lal yisrael,* the Jewish people.[13]

An observant Jew needs a variety of institutions, within the neighborhood, to make his or her observance possible. This explains why Orthodox Jews are usually found close to each other, within walking distance of the synagogue (driving is prohibited according to Jewish law on the Sabbath and certain holidays), and within reasonable proximity of a kosher butcher, kosher baker, and ritual bath *(mikveh).* Increasingly, too, observant Orthodox use the growing network of day schools, including the studying of Torah under the obligatory "ceremonies" of Judaism.

The obligatory nature of the ceremonial law, of course, separates committed Orthodox from non-Orthodox Jews. Some Conservative and Reform Jews in every community observe *kashrut,* celebrate Jewish festivals, cease work on the Sabbath, buy kosher meat, and worship with covered head—but their decision to observe a particular ceremony, or several ceremonies, is rarely made with a sense of obligation. Their reasons vary widely, but they usually are able to provide them; for example, to refrain from eating pork or to say grace before eating may bring sanctity to the mundane and be solitary exercises. Orthodox Jews, on the other hand, need no "reasons" for observing a particular commandment, for they are divine injunctions. As Samuel Belkin, president of Yeshiva University for more than a quarter of a century, explained, "the divine reason behind certain laws of the Torah . . . may be valid as philosophic explanations of the divine cause, [but] they can in no way effect man's duty to practice the divine law." God gave all of the more than 600 mitzvot in the Torah, as well as their rabbinic or Talmudic interpretations, and hence the obligation for the committed Jew to observe all the commandments—those others call "minor" as well as "major." They represent, in short, the will of God.[14]

However, among the Orthodox, there are different interpretations about the rigor and exactness with which the abundant commandments are to be observed. Some, usually designated as "right-wing" Orthodox in liberal Orthodox publications, take pride in the strictness with which they observe the commandments, arguing that the greater the degree of ritual exactitude, the greater one's religiosity, while others, usually termed "modern" Orthodox or "centrists" in their own publications, see no special value in finding ways to go beyond simple observance. The right-wing Orthodox, so-called, will often refuse to attend a worship service at any synagogue that does not have a formal separation (mechitza) between men and women—and some of the most strict of their number will insist not only on separation but also on a divider that makes eye contact impossible—thus preventing their participation in Conservative or Reform worship services as well as those of numerous Orthodox congregations. Others, however, while worshipping with separate sections in their own synagogues, will place "love of fellow Jews" (ahavat yisrael) as a high priority, and, when invited, worship with non-Orthodox.

The issue of whether to use microphones on the Sabbath also divides the Orthodox. Some congregations are so large as to necessitate them, but disputes exist as to whether the prohibition is biblical or only rabbinic, or a prohibition at all. It is not only a question of activating electrical charges and discharges on the Sabbath, whether hidden microphones are prohibited and visible ones not, but of how one ought to respond to the technology of modernity.[15]

Halachic Authority

The obligatory nature of Jewish ceremonial law also touches on another theme that unites all the Orthodox—a common approach to *halachic* authority and even a belief in the divine nature of this process of interpreting God's will. Indeed, Orthodox scholars write about Jewish law much more than any other subject and some even make extraordinary claims for it; in the 1898 Platform, for example, "There is not a single theoretical or technological discovery, from new psychological insights into the human personality to man's attempt to reach out among the planets, with which the *halachah* is not concerned." This view, articulated by the spiritual leader of the 1,000-member Rabbinical Council of America, Rabbi Joseph B. Soloveitchick (1903–   ), a professor of Talmud at RIETS ever since 1949, suggests the breadth of concerns of Jewish law and the conviction that the Orthodox Jew has a body of teaching *(halacha),* stretching back to Sinai, that anticipates every phenomenon, event, or thing—every human problem.[16]

Soloveitchick, as others, insists that the *halachic* process is an objective one, needing no external validation and unmoved by economic, social, or psychological factors. But many Orthodox scholars feel the *halachists* have not shown sufficient flexibility or creativity in applying Jewish law to new situations, that practical as well as economic, social, humanitarian, and esthetic considerations have been integral to *halachic* decisions in every age, and that a number of issues could be handled with a more liberal interpretation.

Correct Observance

"We protest against the admission of proselytes into the fold of Judaism without *milah* [circumcision] and *tebillah* [ritual immersion]." According to this excerpt from the 1898 Platform, the Orthodox feel that they have an exclusive claim to truth, to the correct or authentic manner of observance, and hence, in numerous areas of ritual, ceremony, and worship, the practices of Reform and Conservative Jews are viewed as false and even dangerous. For this reason the Orthodox leaders refuse to recognize many of the practices of the non-Orthodox, fearing that such recognition would legitimate such "aberrations" as officiating at intermarriages, marrying a divorcee who has not had a valid Jewish divorce *(get),* or converting a non-Jew to Judaism without circumcision and ritual bath for a male or a ritual bath for a female. This means, to be more specific, that the "marriage" of a Jew and non-Jew, even if blessed by a Reform or a Conservative rabbi, has no validity, according to the Orthodox, under Jewish religious law and is not, therefore, religiously valid, and that a conversion, without the appropriate rites *(milah* and *tebillah),* is invalid. There are, however, differing interpretations among the Orthodox as to how to respond to their erring co-religionists who have their own understanding of what constitutes genuine conversion (this act rarely includes either ritual in the case of Reform Judaism and often includes only one ritual in Conservative Judaism).[17]

A Nation, not a Sect

"We protest against the idea that we are merely a religious sect and maintain that we are a nation." This quote from the 1898 Platform is an obvious reference to Reform Judaism and its rather widespread attempt to become, in most ways, much like a Protestant confessional faith. Reform Jews had been attempting to eradicate any of the particularities of a "nation" that might distinguish them from other Americans—language, dress, rituals, dietary prohibitions, culture—and, to a large extent, what distinguished a Reform Jew from a Lutheran in 1900 was only a private matter —synagogue versus church—and even in the private sphere, as already noted, the differences were becoming less and less definable.

The Orthodox, in 1898 and subsequently, affirm what today we refer to as *ethnicity*—all the characteristics that help to define a religious or national group. This would have included, for the Orthodox in North America, a distinctive language (Hebrew and Yiddish) and manner of worship, and a particularity of observance and ceremony *(kashrut, mikvaot,* Sabbath observance, *kippot,* and so on).

Zionism

"The restoration of Zion is the legitimate aspiration of scattered Israel, in no way conflicting with our loyalty to the land in which we dwell." Again, in response to the reformers who rejected Zion, in part because of the fear of "dual-loyalty" accusations, the Orthodox in the 1898 Platform affirm a commitment to a central tenet of the Judaic tradition. The issue of the state of Israel finds the Orthodox Jews of North America united except for a small and fanatical fringe, and their commitment extends beyond that of the non-Orthodox because of their desire to build an observant nation committed to Torah and Jewish law. North American Orthodox Jews have contributed to Israel far out of proportion to their numbers: by contributing financially to Zionist appeals, ever since 1898, out of proportion to their means; by settling permanently in Israel *(aliyah)* in greater numbers then non-Orthodox; and by studying in Israeli institutions in greater numbers too. The high reverence for Israel among Orthodox Jewry cannot be doubted.

There are, however, some significant differences among North American Orthodox, differences that go back to events early in the twentieth century. Mizrachi, a religious Zionist movement, was founded in Vilna in 1902 and within a decade or so was firmly entrenched in the United States. Early chapters were organized in New York, St. Louis, and Pittsburgh, and when Rabbi Meyer Berlin, secretary of the World Mizrachi movement, came to the United States in 1913 he immediately began to coordinate the movement. He called a national convention for Cincinnati in 1914, attended by thirty-nine delegates, and by 1915 there were 48 affiliated chapters, and by 1916, 101. In this way, hundreds of Orthodox Jewish men and women were drawn to religious Zionism.[18]

Mizrachi's most vigorous supporters included Rabbis Bernard Levinthal (Philadelphia), honorary vice-president of the federation of American Zionists and vice-president of the Union of Orthodox Rabbis, Schepshel Schaffer (Baltimore), honorary vice-president of the FAZ and president of the Baltimore Zionist Association, Aaron Ashinsky (Pittsburgh), David Ginsburg (Rochester), Solomon Scheinfeld (Milwaukee), Isaac Estersohn (New York), A. A. Weinberger (New York), A. S. Gross (New York), Abraham Jacob Gerson Lesser (Cincinnati), and Nathan Isaacs (Cincinnati). Their enthusiasm, and that of others, made Orthodox synagogues into centers of Zionist fundraising activities, lectures, club meetings, and cultural events for several decades.[19]

There was, however, a small group of Orthodox anti-Zionists, organized in Kattowitz, a Polish city in Silesia, in 1912. The Agudath Israel (League of Israel) rejected secular nationalism (territory, culture, language, sovereignty), but saw Zion (Palestine), nevertheless, as the proper place to carry out God's will. Their Zion-centered ideology ("to animate and sustain Israel's collective body by Torah") rejected nationalism and found them often at odds with Mizrachi over goals and specific programs. When several Agudah leaders (mostly Hasidic) settled in the United States on the eve of World War II, they immediately clashed with the Mizrachi. At their second North American convention, in Cincinnati, in 1940 (the first was held in 1939 in Far Rockaway, New York, although Agudath Israel dates its origins in America to 1922), the Agudah urged the Mizrachi to abandon Zionism and return to the "true faith" of the past, and counseled against cooperation with Zionist organizations on the grounds that such cooperation constituted a legitimation of secular nationalism as a definition of Jewishness. The

Mizrachi, on the other hand, had always been willing to work with non-Orthodox Zionists, in the hope that it could convey its religious sensibilities to the irreligious and on the grounds that a spiritual center in the Holy Land was an important and necessary first step to a Jewish state.[20]

This brief summary of Orthodox Jewish beliefs has emphasized several essentials of its faith: that God revealed or communicated commandments *(mitzvot)* to the Jewish people at Mount Sinai; that the oral tradition as well as the written Torah has its origin there; that Jewish law *(halacha)*, which applies these *mitzvot* to every situation a Jew faces, has its origin in the divine and must be the guide to a Jewish way of life; that Judaism is more than merely a faith—it is a people too; and that aspirations to establish and return to Zion have been built into the Jewish faith and are taken seriously by Orthodox Jews.

9. Postwar Revival: 1940s–1980s:

The revival of a somewhat dormant North American Orthodoxy in the 1940s and 1950s, and its continual growth, renewed vitality, vigor, and increasing adherents in the 1960s, 1970s, and 1980s has been noted by many students of North American religion. It has generally been attributed to a variety of factors, including the influx of militant Orthodox immigrants (especially distinguished rabbis and heads of famous European *yeshivot*) before and after World War II, the general religious revival of the late 1940s and 1950s discussed earlier, the shift to the right across a broad spectrum of North American religion, the increasing organizational sophistication of Orthodox institutions both national and local, and the emergence of a new generation of Orthodox rabbis able to compete successfully for followers with their Conservative and Reform colleagues.

Among the major Orthodox leaders who arrived in the United States before the end of World War II were Elijah M. Bloch of Telshe (1894–1955), Joseph Breuer (1882–1980), Moses Feinstein (1895–   ), Aaron Kotler, Joseph Isaac Schneerson, the Lubavitch *rebbe* (1880–1950), Joseph Soloveitchik (1903–   ) and Joel Teitelbaum, the Satmar *rebbe* (1887–1979). Although in some cases the impact of their arrival was not immediate, each of them was destined to attract innumerable followers and indelibly stamp American Orthodoxy.

Elijah M. Bloch arrived in Cleveland in 1941 where he transferred—via Shanghai—the famous Telz (Telshe) Yeshiva when the Russians occupied Lithuania. Maintaining and developing the celebrated "Telshe method" of Talmud study—graded classes, designated curriculum, fixed places of study, compulsory attendance, regular exams, and, especially, inductive reasoning—the Rabbinical Academy of Telshe, with its full-time advanced study of Talmud, became, together with R. Kotler's academy in New Jersey, the leaders of the postwar growth of Talmud study.

Joseph Breuer, who arrived in the United States in 1939 and served

Congregation Khal Adath Jeshurun in New York City, led the *Torah Im Derech Eretz* movement for four decades. Emulating the founder of "modern" Orthodoxy in Germany, Samson Raphael Hirsch, who firmly believed that Jews did not have to choose between a commitment to the Jewish tradition and modernity and that classical Judaism itself mandated a creative synthesis between Torah and secular knowledge *(Torah im Derech Eretz),* Breuer also founded the Yeshiva Samson Raphael Hirsch in 1944 and provided direction and inspiration to a generation of Orthodox Jews.

Moses (Moshe) Feinstein arrived in the United States in 1937/1938 and quickly established himself as one of the most distinguished experts in applied *halacha.* A strongly sectarian Orthodox leader who eventually became *rosh yeshiva* (Talmud instructor) at Mesivta Tifereth Jerusalem in New York City, he has served as one of the *gedolim* (masters of the Jewish tradition) on the Agudath Israel's ruling body, the Council of Torah Authorities. His decisions on issues of Jewish law are given the same authority by sectarian Orthodox as Joseph Soloveitchik's decisions are given by "centrist" Orthodox.

Joseph Isaac Schneerson, the sixth Lubavitch *rebbe* and the great-great-great grandson of the founder of Habad Hasidism, Rabbi Schneur Zalman (1745–1813), arrived in Brooklyn in 1940/1941 and in the decade of life left to him vigorously organized the Lubavitch wing of Hasidism—named for the town in which Schneur Zalman's son settled. Menachem Mendel Schneerson (1902–   ; Schneur Zalman's grandson took the name Schneersohn, with the "h"), the son-in-law of Joseph Isaac and also the great-great-great-great grandson of the founder, even more energetically promoted the Lubavitcher movement. He further stimulated the renaissance of Orthodoxy in the United States begun under Joseph Isaac, through his writings, marathon lectures at *farbrengen* (get-togethers), and the development of "Habad Houses" on college campuses and weekend "Encounters with Habad" at the Brooklyn headquarters of the worldwide movement.

Joseph Soloveitchik, also known as "J. B." and simply as "The Rav" (rabbi of rabbis), held no elective office and occupied no pulpit. Nevertheless, by the depth of his learning and the breadth of his piety his authority in matters of Jewish law was enormous. He came to the United States in 1932/1933, already distinguished as a Talmudist and the recipient of a doctorate from the University of Berlin, dominated Talmudic studies at RIETS as well as the RCA for more than four decades, and is widely recognized by most RIETS alumni as their spiritual mentor and the personification of Orthodox piety and scholarship and modern Orthodoxy's greatest intellectual. He lived in Brookline, Massachusetts, but spent several days each week at Yeshiva University, where he delivered four lectures in

Talmud (until the late 1950s in Yiddish) and taught a graduate seminar; he spoke almost weekly in Brookline's Maimonides School or at the Moriah Synagogue in Manhattan; and he delivered three "major" lectures (several hours in length) each year to his followers.

Joel Teitelbaum, the leader of the Satmar Hasidim of Williamsburg and a descendant of the first Satmar leader Moshe Teitelbaum, died in 1979 in Monroe, New York's Kiryas Joel, a community he founded. He was born in 1887 in Sigut, Rumania, and founded the Satmar *yeshiva* movement in Satu Mare in 1906 (the Satmar movement began in 1871); at seventeen he became the chief rabbi of Hungary's Satmar Hasidim (succeeding his father); and he came to Brooklyn from Palestine at the end of the war. He failed in his efforts to create a colony for his Williamsburg congregation in New Jersey's Mt. Olive Township in the early 1960s, and after many legal problems he established Kiryas Joel in 1976 by compromising his original requests with local authorities. The 100,000 or so mourners who attended his funeral attest to his enormous impact on Orthodox Jewry.

A significant number of the Orthodox newcomers to North America around the time of World War II established or became involved with *yeshivot*—schools for advanced (post–high school) Talmudic study. Aaron Kotler, as noted earlier, with twenty students founded the Beth Medrash Gevoha in Lakewood, New Jersey—an attempt to virtually duplicate the academy he headed for twenty years in Kletzk. By 1946 there were 100, in 1964, 200, and by the early 1980s close to 1,000 students were "learning [*vos lernen*] in Lakewood." This "learning," as enshrined in the Lithuanian *yeshivot* tradition, consisted exclusively of Talmud (and its commentaries).[1]

Numerous Orthodox commentators would agree with Rabbi Shlomo Riskin (1940–   ) of New York's Lincoln Square Synagogue that "orthodoxy's greatest achievement on the American scene has been the *yeshiva* movement." Charles Liebman found 4,000 students studying in Talmudic academies of various sizes in 1964, and a study fifteen or so years later noted forty academies with a total enrollment of 6,500 students. These included numerous *kolelim,* where students (many married) spent the entire day studying Talmud (for no practical purpose) while receiving a modest subvention from the *yeshiva.*[2]

The growth of the Orthodox Jewish day school movement in North America after World War II testified to the depth of the Orthodox revival. This growth can be measured in the number of schools, the number of students, and the number of communities with day schools, for in each of these areas there was significant, even spectacular, growth. Although precise figures vary, one study claims that between 1917–1938 twenty-eight day schools were founded (including two post–high school *yeshivot,* Torah Vadaat in Brooklyn and Tifereth Jerusalem in Manhattan), another claims that in 1935 there were sixteen day schools in New York and only one outside the city, and in 1945 thirty-three in New York and twelve outside.

The expansion in the following years was more accurately measured, especially by Torah Umesorah, the National Society for Hebrew Day Schools. Although contradictory figures were still released by various organizations, the dramatic growth in enrollment cannot be doubted.

Torah Umesorah reported, in 1960–1961, that there were 278 day schools in the United States and Canada (90 of them in New York City) with thirty-five thousand students in New York and fifteen thousand elsewhere. The following year the Union of Orthodox Jewish Congregations of America reported 290 schools with 54,000 students; in 1963–1964, according to Torah Umesorah, there were 306 Orthodox day schools with sixty-five thousand students in thirty-four states and provinces of the U.S. and Canada; while in 1964–1965 Torah Umesorah pointed out that the day school movement had grown from five thousand to fifty thousand in the past twenty years.

In 1968 the organization reported 310 Orthodox day schools with seventy-five thousand students and twenty-six Conservative day schools with five thousand students. By 1970 the number of schools reached 400, with eighty-three thousand students; in 1973, 448 schools were identified in 140 communities, and in 1976 Torah Umesorah reported 446 Hebrew day schools in the United States and 32 in Canada, with an enrollment of ninety-two thousand students—302 elementary and 144 high schools. By 1981, the same organization announced, North America had 546 schools in thirty-six states and five Canadian provinces (489 and 57 respectively).[3]

Torah Umesorah held regular conferences of day school administrators and teachers to improve the quality of instruction, pushed hard in several communities for generous financial assistance (and scholarships) from the federation of Jewish philanthropies, and continually sought to establish day schools in communities without them.

Orthodox groups vigorously lobbied, despite the opposition of secular Jewish organizations, for federal funding of nonpublic schools. Torah Umesorah leaders frequently testified before congressional subcommittees, the Agudath Israel lobbied extensively for federal and state aid to parochial Jewish education, the leadership of the Rabbinical Council of America appealed regularly for federal aid to private schools, and the UOJCA supported these efforts in varying ways.

The Agudath Israel, early in the 1970s, launched an active political action campaign to urge passage of the Parent-Aid (Speno-Lerner) bill in the New York State legislature—a bill to provide grants to parents of children in nonpublic elementary and high schools. It also censured the American Jewish Congress and American Jewish Committee for "smearing the *yeshivos*" by supporting a challenge to the constitutionality of a state law that reimbursed religious schools for certain expenses. And the Agudath Israel congratulated Governor Shapp of Pennsylvania when he signed a private school aid bill immediately after the U.S. Supreme Court had ruled it unconstitutional.[4]

Despite many failures in these areas, the day school movement gained increasing acceptance among non-Orthodox leaders in local communities and began, in the mid-1970s, to receive larger allocations from communal philanthropic drives.

The general renewal of religious sectarianism and fundmentalism in the 1970s and early 1980s gave a boost to this wing of Orthodoxy, too. The Agudah Israel noted in 1982 that its "greatest growth has come in the last decade and the trend is clearly upward." While it exaggerated in its claim that the slogan of the 1920s, "My son the doctor, my son the lawyer" had given way to "My son the *Talmid Chochom* [brilliant Talmud student], my son the Torah Activist," the vigor of Agudah activities was quite apparent.[5]

The Agudath Israel Women of America maintained many social action and welfare programs; Project COPE (Career Opportunities and Preparation for Employment) and Project RISE (Russian Immigrant Services and Education) were accomplishing much; and Agudath Israel's Jewish Education Program (JEP), Commission on Legislation and Civic Action, neighborhood revival, and senior citizen centers busied themselves in dozens of projects. In 1980, Agudath Israel's Southern Brooklyn Community Organization (SBCO) won federal approval for a private- and government-financed $5-million condominium park in Brooklyn's Borough Park neighborhood, while in 1983 the Commission on Legislation and Civic Action successfully lobbied bills in Ohio (a comprehensive package of *kashrut* legislation), Illinois (forcing cemetery authorities and workers to perform burials on Sundays), and New York (restrictions on medical examiners performing autopsies without the consent of next of kin).[6]

With respect to Torah, in addition to communal involvement, the Daf Yomi program continued to attract thousands of Orthodox Jews. Conceived by Rabbi Meir Shapiro at the 1923 Agudath Israel assembly, it demanded that a Jew study one page of Talmud daily (all Jews in the world studying the same folio leaf). The program began on Rosh Hashana of 1923, and is now celebrated with an enormous *siyum* (completion) celebration when, every few years, the entire Talmud (2,720 folios) is completed. The sixth *siyum* was celebrated in 1967, the seventh (at Madison Square Garden in New York City) in 1975, and the eighth, in New York, in 1983.

Signs of "centrist," or "modern," or mainline[7] Orthodoxy's revival in the 1980s are everywhere apparent, especially in its rising birthrate, expanding interest in intensive Jewish education for girls (as well as boys), and abundant use of kosher meat and other specialty food items. In religion, too, Orthodoxy's vitality is apparent. A visitor to Atlanta's Congregation Beth Jacob in early 1983, a relatively small congregation by Atlanta's standards, noted several hundred "young" adults worshipping on two consecutive Sabbath mornings, and at least two hundred men, women, and children in attendance at late Saturday afternoon services and *shalosh seudot* (concluding Sabbath "snack"). In Beverly Hills, California, a short distance from a kosher pizza shop, hundreds of young Jews attended Sabbath morning worship services at Congregation Beth Jacob, the largest Orthodox synagogue in the West.

In Los Angeles, a few weeks later, a visitor noticed that a neighborhood whose non-Orthodox Jewish children of the 1940s and 1950s had all moved away was now dominated by young Orthodox Jews whose stores, though closed on Saturdays, provided the focal point for a lively street life on Sunday. The pizza parlor just mentioned had chefs with *yarmulkas* (head covering) and outside its doors several mothers pushed strollers with baby boys also wearing these hats.

In yet other cities, in the Far West, Pacific Northwest, and South as well as surburban New Jersey and New York, a resurgent Orthodoxy was revealed in the 1970s and early 1980s by the opening of a *mikveh*—a symbolic bath required for all married Orthodox women after their menstrual period —in numerous quiet, surburban, residential neighborhoods.

Still another sign of Orthodox vigor was the increasing number of communities in the 1970s and early 1980s that "erected" an *eruv* as a result, over and over, of pressure applied by a steady stream of younger Orthodox Jews, especially professionals. As Orthodox Jews demonstrated a strong interest in Sabbath observance, the verse in Exodus 17:19, which had been interpreted to permit walking on the Sabbath but banned carrying any object (such as a prayer book or prayer shawl, or even pushing a stroller), proved irksome to the wives of Jewish men whose husbands walked to the synagogue for Sabbath worship. Women with infants could not leave their "private" domain (house) where carrying was permitted and enter the "public" domain where the ban applied, unless an *eruv*—a symbolic boundary to form a large nonpublic area—was established. This change required considerable help from the utility companies, whose poles and wires, when adjusted, would form a continuous "boundary," and a symbolic purchase from town authorities. Despite the complexity and, often, expense, numerous *eruvin* were established in the 1970s and early 1980s, including one in

Highland Park (New Jersey's first), and in Baltimore (a sixteen-mile unbroken line of fences, telephone wires, fish line, and wire) in 1978, and one in New York's North Woodmere, in 1982. In a great many places, especially in New York State, the push for the *eruv* came from Young Israel synagogues of upwardly mobile Jewish professionals, and was usually followed by the arrival of numerous additional Orthodox Jews. Kew Garden Hills (Queens) set up an *eruv* in 1974, and within two years hundreds of middle-class Jews had returned to the area.[8]

Among these Jews in Queens, as elsewhere, especially in the larger cities, are a sizable number of *baale teshuvot* (literally, "repenters")—Jews who have adopted the lifestyle of Orthodoxy after a lengthy period (even a lifetime) of nonobservance or even assimilation. Conversations with rabbis in New York, Los Angeles, Cleveland and Atlanta suggest that a sizable number of Jews, perhaps in the thousands, have found their way to Orthodoxy. Some sought an anchor for chaotic lives, others an attachment to a charismatic rabbinic personality, and for many the sense of acceptance offered by similar souls in search of meaning and commitment proved most attractive. In nearly every community during the 1970s and early 1980s, Orthodox individuals (and not just militantly missionizing [among Jews only] Lubavitch activists) have been eagerly seeking out wayward Jews and enticing them to participate in a synagogue or community class especially organized for those Jews discovering Orthodox Judaism for the first time. Every Orthodox congregation has some of these folk, nearly every Orthodox rabbi boasts of his ability to attract and nurture them, and they constitute an increasingly interesting phenomenon for those interested in studying the "return to religion."[9]

There is yet another sign of Orthodoxy's resurgence. Only a generation ago, Orthodox synagogues—in their simplicity, starkness, and small size—stood out dramatically in contrast to the large and elegant Conservative and Reform temples, often designed by distinguished architects, all over the United States and Canada. In the past two decades, however, with the increased prosperity and greater acculturation of Orthodox Jews, they too have erected imposing structures in affluent suburbs indistinguishable in appearance from local Reform and Conservative synagogues.

More and more, too, the calendar of events at Orthodox congregations resembles that which is found in most Reform and Conservative congregations—an abundance of social, cultural, and recreational (i.e., secular) activities, with no obvious Jewish identification, held within the synagogue. At Richmond's Keneseth Beth Israel, the Noar, or youth program, in 1982–1983, had a hobo day (September), kite making (October), bowling tournament (November), marionette making (January), bingo (February), softball game (April), and miniature golf outing (May) for its activities during the year. In addition to worship services and modest adult education forums, Orthodox congregational bulletins—like their counterparts in other wings—are dominated by activities that parallel those to be found at every Jewish community center.

The Hasidim

Hasidism originally represented, in the eighteenth century, a sectarian element in Jewish life, and the Hasidim have continued to be the most sectarian of all Orthodox groups in North America. The Lubavitch and Satmar Hasidim are the best-known, but smaller Hasidic groups exist and flourish too in relatively compact and tightly knit communities largely in the New York area. They range from the mildly sectarian Lubavitch to the fiercely sectarian Satmar Hasidim, both of whom began to attract attention in the years following the destruction of European Jewry as their surviving leaders struck permanent roots in the United States.

Each of the Hasidic groups looks to a *rebbe* (leader) for guidance, employs a special dress (beards; *peyes,* or side locks; *shtreymel,* fur-rimmed hats; long black coats; *shetyl,* wigs for women), language, and self-ghettoization to isolate itself from what it considers the contaminations of both the general Jewish and North American societies. These sectarians also shave off the hair and put wigs on married women so they are not considered a temptation. And they totally reject (except for Lubavitch, whose "Habad Houses" dot and interact with U.S. and Canadian secular university campuses) the modern secular world.

The Hasidim, who lived almost exclusively in the narrow confines of Williamsburg and Crown Heights, where they first settled in groups of 50 to 1,000 families in the 1940s and 1950s, began in the late 1950s to leave these areas, largely in response to the "invasion" of blacks and Puerto Ricans, and to move to Borough Park as well as to establish self-contained communities outside the New York metropolitan area. By the early 1980s, in fact, 90 percent of Borough Park's 100,000 residents were Jewish (most Orthodox, and a great many Hasidic) and there were at least two hundred synagogues.

The congestion, lack of adequate housing, and changing racial mix in the neighborhoods of first settlement, as well as the opportunity to control their own municipalities, led to these efforts at autonomous village life. With the opening of the Brooklyn (1883) and the Williamsburg (1903) bridges, Jews had flocked from the Lower East Side to the brownstones of Williamsburg, but by the time the Hasidim, displaced by World War II, were drawn to this section of Brooklyn it had become a slum, locked in by a river and a black ghetto.[10]

The first to plan a move were the Satmar of Williamsburg (formerly of Satmar in Hungary) as the 1,260 families of Congregation Yetev Lev D'Satmar, led by Rabbi Joel Teitelbaum, bought a 250-acre dairy farm in Franklin, New Jersey, in June 1959. They planned to break ground in December for a self-contained village of their own, and to move the first 500 families there in 1960. This effort was unsuccessful, and three years later the congregation acquired a 500-acre tract in New Jersey's Mt. Olive Township, for a reported $850,000, hoping to settle nearly 400 families in split-level homes, initially, and another 400 at a later date. The Township Committee, however, successfully blocked Teitelbaum's plans in and out of court for years. A third attempt, this time in Monroe, New York, was successful, as a 1976 compromise with the Monroe Town Council (in Federal Court) permitted the Satmar incorporation of 350 acres (as opposed to the intended 450) as Kiryas Joel (Joel's town). By that time five-hundred Satmar had settled in twenty-five homes (eighteen of which became multiple-family units) and eighty garden apartments (especially constructed for Hasidic living, i.e., twin kitchen sinks and stoves for guaranteeing separation of meat and milk) in this Satmar town just outside Monroe in Orange County.[11]

In 1961, after a long court battle, seventy families of the Skvirer Hasidim, led by Rabbi Jacob Joseph Twersky, won New York State Supreme Court endorsement for a separate village in New York's Rockland County town of Ramapo, to be known as New Square (after Skvir, the Russian town near Kiev where the group originated). First settling the 130-acre village farm in Ramapo with twenty families in 1956, Twersky's congregation, Zemach David, numbered 530 in 1961, including 250 children among the Skvirer who, as all Hasidim, took literally God's injunction in Genesis "to be fruitful and multiply" by rejecting birth control.

By 1971 New Square had 1,200 residents who rejected television, rock and roll music, comic books, chewing gum, and other standard ingredients of contemporary North American culture. They explained once, to a visitor, that Jewish youth have been mangled by the banality of television and the nonsense of child psychologists, spoiled by a godless materialistic existence, alienated from their traditions, and corrupted by American society's decadence.

Two light industries in the town employed a score of Skvirer; others either worked in nearby towns or commuted to New York City on a village-owned bus ("synagogue on wheels") specially equipped with an ark, Torah scrolls, and separate seating for men and women so the Hasidim could worship on their way to work. Their schools were not accredited, as secular studies were minimal, but the Skvirer, who shunned colleges and universities, did not seem to care. All knowledge resided in the Talmud, and their hope was that after spending a number of years in a *yeshiva* studying rabbinic wisdom a man would become sufficiently knowledgeable to lead a truly religious existence for the rest of his life.[12]

In a great many ways, despite embracing modern cooperative housing as well as commercial and industrial enterprises, New Square resembled an East European village of the nineteenth century—including its position as the town with the lowest per capita income in New York State. More than a hundred married young men, in the mid-1970s, lived rent-free in one-third of the town's homes and studied Talmud for long hours six days a week, young boys began their Judaica studies at the age of three, and all marriages were arranged. New Square's Hasidim remain a highly insular community.[13]

Several of the Hasidic groups, but especially the Lubavitch, reached out into the community and engaged in aggressive programs of religious education, ceremonial observance, and social service work among the unaffiliated and especially the "alienated" younger Jews via the distribution of Hasidic literature produced by their presses. Lubavitch families regularly hosted hundreds of high school and especially college students eager to experience a Hasidic Sabbath of music, study, and prayer.

Lubavitch institutes and seminaries, such as the Lubavitch Rabbinical College of America in Newark (founded by Rabbi Moshe Herzon in 1957) and the Crown Heights Hadar Hatorah Rabbinical Seminary and Institute (founded by Rabbi Israel Jacobson in 1963), aggressively recruited, especially through Habad Houses and the Lubavitch "New Direction" program, young Jews for study and indoctrination. One year twenty vans distributed tens of thousands of Chanuka Kits to New York City Jews, while frequently "synagogues on wheels" (also known as "tanks against assimilation" and *"mitzvah* mobiles," small trucks adorned with religious slogans) traveled all over New York City and other larger Jewish centers with Lubavitch students eager to explain the use of sacred religious objects to any Jew who would listen (i.e., "Put on Tefillin [phylacteries] Campaign"). In addition, fifty Habad Houses, first established on University of California campuses in 1969, brought thousands of university-age Jews into contact with Habad-Lubavitch teachings. The Habad House in West Los Angeles, a $2-million storefront operation for the rehabilitation of drug addicts and Jewish college students who have had too much of secular good life, gained great visibility among Los Angeles Jews of all types during the 1970s.[14]

The Hasidic groups in Brooklyn, early in the 1970s, began to realize the political clout they possessed by virtual bloc voting. On Yom Kippur of

1972, 4,000 Satmar Hasidic worshippers in Williamsburg were urged by their leader to vote for a particular Catholic candidate (who supported federal and state aid to parochial schools), and the following day he defeated his Jewish competitor, in a special Democratic primary, by double the margin he achieved in the June primary. In Crown Heights, the Lubavitch vote went almost exclusively to one candidate who, although second in the June primary, won by 200 votes.[15]

As the Hasidim struggled (and sometimes cooperated) politically with hispanics and blacks for control of their neighborhoods, especially in Crown Heights, and, in particular, control of funds for subsidized housing, aid to schools, retraining unemployed Hasidim, small business loan assistance, bilingual signs (Yiddish-English), bilingual federal, state, and city directives as well as Civil Service exams, and much more, they developed increasing political sophistication.

The Hasidim filed suit (unsuccessfully) in Federal District Court in 1974 to protest being divided into two Assembly Districts (15,000 in the Fifty-sixth; 20,000 in the Fifty-seventh) in New York's attempt to respond to a federal order to give blacks and Puerto Ricans more voting power. And in 1982 their American Friends of Lubavitch lobby in Washington urged all 500,000 Lubavitch followers in thirty states to deluge U.S. congressmen with appeals to declare 4 April, Menachem M. Schneerson's eightieth birthday, "A National Day of Reflection."[17]

The Hasidic sects, actually poles apart from each other theologically, contended not only with non-Hasidic, non-Jewish neighbors but also with each other, often on ideological issues in addition to political control of their neighborhoods, much like the Hasidic rabbinic feuds of eighteenth- and nineteenth-century Poland and Russia. Physical struggles often erupted: in spring 1975 the Satmar hung an effigy of the Lubavitch *Rebbe* from a telephone pole. In the summer of 1977 and 1978, physical conflict arose between Lubavitch (Crown Heights) and Satmar (Williamsburg) Hasidim over turf, over differing views of involvement in North American society, and over attitudes toward the state of Israel. And Belzer and Satmar Hasidim, two years later, clashed in the synagogue of the Congregation Belz over a similar ideological issue.[18]

In the spring of 1981 hundreds of Satmar, who fiercely oppose Zionism and a Zionist state not established by the Messiah, again pelted a Belz synagogue in Williamsburg with eggs and bottles, and threatened to harm the Grand Rebbe of the Belz if he came for a visit from Israel to celebrate the thirtieth anniversary of the Belz's arrival in North America. Rabbi Rokeach, whose followers, like the Lubavitcher Hasidim, supported the Israeli government, came anyway. And in the summer of 1983 Lubavitch leaders accused the Satmar of abducting a Hasidic rabbi of the Borough Park Lubavitch sect (who had left the Satmar community), forcing him into a van, assaulting him, and then shaving off his beard (an Orthodox sign of piety) before dumping him in the street. Such sporadic tensions will likely continue among sectarian Jews who care passionately about their faith and its demands.[19]

PART IV

RECONSTRUCTIONIST JUDAISM

10. Origins and Ideology: 1934–1983

No individual—including Israel Jacobson and Isaac Mayer Wise (Reform Judaism) as well as Zacharias Frankel and Solomon Schechter (Conservative Judaism)—played as crucial a role in the development of a modern branch of Judaism as did Mordecai M. Kaplan for the Reconstructionist movement. He provided its ideology, both at the time he created the movement and for several decades thereafter, sanctioned its rabbinic and congregational institutions, and vigorously missionized, especially among Conservative and Reform rabbis, educators, and Jewish lay people. While he never met much success, quantitatively, his efforts left a significant mark on the contours of American Judaism and, eventually, resulted in a fourth branch of Judaism in the United States.

Kaplan was born in Lithuania in 1881, studied Talmud as a child in Vilna, and came with his family to New York in 1889/1890. He graduated from the City College of New York in 1900 and the Jewish Theological Seminary in 1902, received a master's degree from Columbia in 1902, and, on his graduation from the seminary, became an associate ("minister") of Rabbi Moses S. Margolies at New York's Orthodox Kehilath Jeshurun where, among other tasks, he preached in English. Although personally observant, and in fact, ordained (during his honeymoon) by the distinguished Isaac Reines in Russia in 1908, Kaplan's growing inability to "conscientiously preach and teach according to orthodox doctrine," especially with respect to divine revelation, led him to eagerly accept Schechter's invitation (1909) to direct the emerging Teachers Institute of the seminary (a position recently endowed by Jacob Schiff), and to leave the pulpit. In 1910 he became a professor of homiletics at the seminary's rabbinical school —a relationship that would endure for more than a half-century—and later taught philosophies of religions as well. He was not, one student recalled, just "a great scholar and a great teacher; he was, in his prime, a titanic force, reshaping the landscape around him."[1]

In the 1910s and 1920s, however, it was less his seminary teaching than his organizational work that was to have the greatest impact on Judaism in North America, for he developed, experimented with, and refined his ideas in two congregational laboratories. In the spring of 1915 Kaplan, together with several former Kehilath Jeshurun members who had moved to the Upper West Side, organized the New York Jewish Center and, for the first time, Kaplan experimented with his developing notion that Judaism was not just a religion but a civilization. In 1917 the first story of a $1-million synagogue-center was completed on West 86th Street, and Kaplan officially became the rabbi. He implemented a program of worship, study, and "meeting," and the latter included drama, song, dance, basketball, and calisthenics. Increasingly, however, the board of directors found his strong support for controversial sociopolitical and economic issues a nuisance and his challenge to the fundamental tenets of Orthodoxy more and more apparent—and more objectionable.

When, in 1921, the board demanded strict Orthodoxy, Kaplan's future was in doubt, and he resigned in January 1922, despite a vote of support. He quickly led away two dozen or so members of the center, and they created the Society for the Advancement of Judaism (SAJ) down on 86th Street—a synagogue (though called a "society") that would offer its rabbi (though called a "leader") an opportunity to expound and actualize his philosophy of Judaism. Kaplan led the SAJ for more than two decades, preserved his complete freedom of speech and action by never accepting remuneration, and resigned as its leader early in 1945. He was named Leader Emeritus.[2]

Some students of Reconstructionist Judaism date its origin to 1922 when Kaplan, via his rabbinate at the SAJ, began to programmatically "reconstruct" Judaism. One historian of the movement argues that the founding of Reconstructionism occurred in 1940 with the establishment of the Jewish Reconstructionist Foundation. Others, including the founder's disciples, suggest that the movement dates from 1934, when Kaplan's *Judaism as a Civilization: Toward a Reconstruction of American Jewish Life* appeared. Kaplan himself stated that the Reconstructionist movement began in January 1935 when, as a result of publishing *Judaism as a Civilization,* he and some friends launched the Reconstructionist magazine.[3]

In *Judaism as a Civilization,* his most important work, Kaplan delineated both the "illness" and "prescription" for Judaism in North America. He analyzed the "reformist," Conservative, and "neo-orthodox" versions of Judaism especially and concluded that they failed—not only in doctrine, which he subjects to scathing criticism, but in attracting adherents as well. They failed because half of North America's Jews, more or less, remained uninterested in any of the branches. And it was to these Jews that Kaplan wished to speak.[4]

He proposed a "reconstructed" historical Judaism (thus its linkage to the Conservative Jewish wing) without supernatural revelation or supernatural "choosing" of the Jews, but with an abundance of customs, ceremonies, rituals, holidays, and festivals from the rich storehouse of Jewish tradition —all to be celebrated and observed for reasons other than that they were divinely revealed.[5]

What Kaplan called "the cultural residium of the Jewish past" was to be given a "revaluation . . . in terms of present-day thought," for the foundation on which Judaism rested for centuries—supernaturalism, or what Kaplan called the "astrology and alchemy of religion"—had been thoroughly discredited in the modern world. "We can no longer believe," he wrote, "that God is a mighty Sovereign, or that the universe is the work of his hands."[6]

Kaplan spoke to Jews who, he assumed, had ceased to believe in divine revelation and found Conservatism too vague and Reform too sterile. He offered them an alternative concept of God and a new explanation of what Judaism means—all under the assumption that men and women used their minds, overwhelmingly, in satisfying their religious needs. Unlike his philosophical-theological arguments, which have never been widely acclaimed, Kaplan's sociological analysis of post–World War I Judaism was powerful and on the mark. The book is so comprehensive that the reader who reads only it, and none of Kaplan's other voluminous writings, will know almost everything there is to know about Reconstructionist Judaism.

In this same volume Kaplan developed his notion of Jewish civilization or "organic community." As he had already written and preached, in numerous essays and sermons at both the New York Jewish Center and SAJ, all parts of the Jewish community and the Jewish religion must be systematically correlated and interact together: "The organic character is maintained so long as all the elements that constitute the civilization play a role in the life of the Jew." This goal meant, for Kaplan, that the life of each Jew, each synagogue, each community, and each national group must be organic. Religious and secular organizations as well as the individual Jew's history, prayer, language, singing, dancing, social hopes, spiritual ideal, land, art, and literature must be part of the mosaic that constitutes Jewish "civilization."[7]

On the national or communal level Kaplan called for an organic community—one in which democratically organized secular and religious organizations, often at odds with each other's ideology, interact constructively. On the personal level it meant that participation in the totality of modern Jewish life—religious, Zionist, and secular—ought to be each Jew's goal. For Kaplan, "modern" Judaism was Judaism without supernaturalism, that is, without revelation, divine commandments, miracles, and chosenness. Such a Judaism is, essentially, classical Judaism "reconstructed" in consonance with modernity, for Kaplan refuses to discard either Jewish rituals or the Jewish religion and, in fact, urges that they find their rightful place as the underpinning of Judaism as a civilization.[8]

Perhaps influenced by John Dewey, the North American philosopher, and Emile Durkheim, the French Jewish sociologist, Kaplan saw the function of religion (Judaism) as primarily social—it revolved around the Jewish people. The people became the source of authority and "one's chief source of salvation," and each individual Jew was urged to link him- or herself to the destiny of the Jewish people, to the group.[9]

Kaplan argued that the modern Jewish denominations had neglected or rejected every opportunity to substitute for the traditional but discredited notion of salvation (the world to come), and he was offering a humanistic conception whose "pragmatic functionalism" would make possible group solidarity. This solidarity was desperately needed, Kaplan argued all through his writings and sermons of the 1920s and 1930s, as talented and valuable Jews, finding little commonality between their own interests and the interests of the group, have been seeking "salvation"—that is, group associations—outside Judaism. To maintain the Jewish group, or "salvation," Kaplan proposed a Judaism that would encompass synagogue groups, center groups, and Zionist groups—the religious and secular activities of a Jewish civilization. All these activities would function, as the otherworldly values of Judaism once did, to provide group survival. And the "sancta" of the group—heroes, events, places, books, values—would constitute the sacred or holy aspects of Judaism that, together with the group, must be preserved.[10]

Kaplan's indebtedness to the anthropological and sociological studies of the late nineteenth and early twentieth centuries is immense. The Jewish people articulated their destiny by "reconstructing" God, that is, shaping or constructing a "new" God to fit their particular "sancta." God become a projection of the people or group, which, eagerly seeking "survival," grounded its survival values in the deity. God served as the grounding, the guarantor, the "transcendent source," the ultimate triumph of the values of the "sancta." Kaplan thus defined God "as the power that endorses what we believe ought to be, and that guarantees that it will be." God operated both through individuals but especially through social institutions, and in subsequent Kaplan writings God is described as "trans-natural"—a "force" or "process" or a "presence" or "power" that regenerates the Jewish people;

makes for goodness, justice, and mercy; and provides the possibility of reaching toward greater creativity and greater unity.[11]

In this first book, *Judaism as a Civilization,* God is more carefully restricted to the "God-idea" and/or the "power that makes for salvation" —a phrase that seems to indicate the deity's intimate connections with the processes of the universe that make for "health, goodness, order, reason, beauty and meaning in the world" as well as with all the components of Jewish civilization that have become valued or even sacred to the Jewish people. By the word *process,* Kaplan meant that we discover God through men and women interacting with a universe that is an organic totality. Most of all, Kaplan attempts to clearly disengage the "God-idea" from super-naturalism, from a personification of the deity as a superhuman being, and from any connection with *creatio ex nihilo.*[12]

Most of these ideas, germinating after World War I and emerging in book form in the 1930s, were to become embodied in a corpus of creative religious literature that began to appear in published form in the 1930s. These liturgical works included Kaplan's *Supplementary Prayers and Readings for the High Holidays* (1934), a *New Haggadah* (1941), a reconstructed *Sabbath Prayer Book* (1945), a *High Holy Day Prayer Book* (1948), and a *Festival Prayerbook* (1958). Most of these were published by the Reconstructionist Press, which was established in 1945.

The *New Haggadah,* edited by Kaplan, Eugene Kohn (1887–1977), and Ira Eisenstein, systematically applied Kaplan's theology to a liturgical text for the first time. It subordinated the supernatural miracles and plagues of the traditional Passover text to the story of Israel's redemption from Egypt and its meaning for both contemporary Jews and a humanity struggling for freedom. It also added rich but hitherto unused material in an attempt, according to the editors, to make an "interesting, beautiful and meaningful Haggadah." Kaplan had suggested this very thing in *The Meaning of God* a few years earlier, and had pointed out the excessive discussion of outdated legal matters, miracles, and uninspiring texts in the traditional *Haggadah.* The appearance of the new volume created a storm of controversy, but it seemed to be a ripple compared to the hurricane of opposition that buffeted Kaplan when the Reconstructionist movement issued its *Sabbath Prayer Book* in 1945 and used it, for the first time, at Sabbath services on 5 May.[13]

The *Sabbath Prayer Book* was compiled primarily for those "who do not find themselves at home in the synagogues and temples as constituted at present." It hoped to arouse religious emotion in those who felt services provided little emotional impact, to eliminate passages to which a worshipper could not conscientiously subscribe, to add scores of pages of inspiration drawn from the rich religious literature of Jewish creativity, and to restore in modern Jews who had lost it the sense of need for worship and prayer.[14]

The new prayer book eliminated all references to supernaturalism, that is, to a literal revelation of the Torah at Sinai. This meant the omission of passages on God's "choosing" the Jewish people, God's revealing the Torah to Moses, bodily resurrection or other miraculous deeds, and a personal messiah. Various additional prayers, central to the traditional liturgy but deemed by Kaplan and his fellow editors as "untenable," were excised, while others, with which the editors felt uncomfortable, were provided with commentaries and "modern" interpretations.[15]

Some of Kaplan's colleagues at the Jewish Theological Seminary, where he had taught for thirty-five years, denounced him, while the Orthodox rabbinate went even further. At an emergency session at the Hotel McAlpin in New York in June 1945, the Union of Orthodox Rabbis (to which Kaplan did *not* belong) excommunicated him for "expressing atheism, heresy and disbelief in the basic tenets of Judaism" and burned a copy of the *Sabbath Prayer Book*. The UOR's president Rabbi Israel Rosenberg (the New York *Times* reported) objected particularly to the *Sabbath Prayer Book's* introduction, which he alleged to be "contrary to the spirit and law of Judaism."[16]

In all probability, the Orthodox rabbinate was most alarmed by Kaplan's naturalist theology; specifically, the introduction suggested that the editors hoped to "preserve the authority of Jewish tradition" and "retain the classical framework of the service" and "adhere to the fundamental teachings of that tradition concerning God," while simultaneously feeling the need to "eliminate from the traditional text statements of belief that are untenable." While intimating that the *Sabbath Prayer Book* was a "traditional" prayer book, it omitted, revised, and modified traditional prayers concerning chosenness, revelation, messianism, sacrifices, resurrection, reward, and punishment. Hence its danger—purporting to be traditional and yet destroying the heart of the traditional *siddur*. More succinctly, Kaplan clearly did not believe in a personal God, in revelation, or in the doctrine of chosenness.[17]

Kaplan expressed great outrage and shame at the behavior of the rabbis. To him it was the worst possible example of "moral degeneracy on the part of men who call themselves rabbis," and he was especially saddened by what he called "rabbinical gangsters resorting to Nazi methods in order to retain their authority." He could only take solace in the fact that the controversy produced an unprecedented demand for the *Sabbath Prayer Book* and introduced a larger number of Jews to Reconstructionism than anything previously had been able to do.[18]

Despite the publications of the 1940s and 1950s, all the Reconstructionist leaders continued to insist that they were not attempting to create a new branch or wing of Judaism—Kaplan loudest and most sincerely of all. Ever since November 1936, when Kaplan told two hundred supporters that Reconstructionism ought not to become another religious denomination but remain a way of thinking, and that they ought, thus, to maintain membership in existing synagogues, the leaders of the movement rejected further denominationalism.[19]

"Reconstructionism," a 1945 editorial in the movement's official organ trumpeted, "is *not* a new denomination," while Kaplan often reminded his readers and listeners that Reconstructionism was a "state of mind." By this he meant that it was not a wing or branch or denomination but an ideology seeking to be supportive of the existing branches of North American Judaism. As Jacob Agus, rabbi of Chicago's North Shore Agudas Achim expressed it, Reconstructionism is "not a sect but a movement to concentrate and give organizational form to the elements of strength within all sections of American Judaism."[20]

The movement, throughout the 1920s, 1930s, 1940s, and 1950s, viewed its objective as infusing the three wings of North American Judaism with its message: democratizing the Jewish community, intensifying Jewish education, cultivating the Jewish arts, re-Judaizing the Jewish home, rebuilding the Jewish homeland in Palestine, enriching the content of Jewish worship, and raising the ethical standards of the Jewish community. Reconstructionism sought, in Kaplan's words, "to provide a rationale and a program . . . of Jewish unity which might enable Jews to transcend the differences that divide them."[21]

As noted later, by the end of the 1960s the Reconstructionist movement had become a fourth denomination in the North American Jewish community. It had a seminary to train Reconstructionist rabbis, a congregational organization to recruit new members and sustain old ones, and would shortly have a rabbinical organization of its seminary graduates. The 1970s, as the movement consolidated itself, were years of modest growth, but the 1980s opened with a flurry of activity and promise.

At the twenty-first annual convention of the movement in June 1981 a five-year expansion plan—including publication of a new prayer book, new educational programs, the founding of a camp, and the pursuit of new congregations and fellowships—was approved. A nearly $1-million budget for 1981–1982 was announced; the Jewish Reconstructionist Foundation (JRF), Reconstructionist Rabbinical College, and Federation of Reconstructionist Congregations and Havurot (FRCH) undertook to raise $1 million during the 1981–1982 fiscal year; and the president of the JRF, Rabbi Ludwig Nadelman (1928–   ), noted that the movement had raised $1.5

million during Mordecai Kaplan's centennial. Strongly worded resolutions on political, social, economic, and religious issues were passed (the 1983 conference theme was "Social Justice: A Fading Jewish Concern?"), and reports indicated abundant activity and some growth in every area of Jewish concentration in the country.[22]

In addition, at the 1981 and 1983 conferences both the JRF and FRCH hammered out new by-laws. The JRF would still serve as the coordinating body of the federation, Reconstructionist Rabbinical College, and Reconstructionist Rabbinical Association, but it clarified in great detail overriding organizational policies concerning membership, the executive board (fifteen members) and national advisory board (thirty–five), and the duties of officers. At the same time, the federation's by-laws revised numerous organizational matters and delineated a detailed set of responsibilities and purposes. By 1983 the JRF and FRCH—with a $1-million budget for the fiscal year and nearly fifty congregations and fellowships, respectively—gave every appearance of being at least as carefully organized as each of the other three denominations of North American Judaism.[23]

Ideologically, Reconstructionism also matured in the 1980s. At its 1980 convention, the Reconstructionist Rabbinical Association (RRA) issued a statement on *halacha* that placed its authority in the Jewish people (versus the rabbis) and established a process whereby each congregation, after "a thorough study of . . . Jewish tradition," would "evolve its *minhag* (local custom) democratically." Thus, unlike the Reform (who rejected *halacha*), the Orthodox (who did not place authority in the Jewish community but in rabbinic scholars), or the Conservative (whose *halacha* decisions were made by rabbis and were, usually, binding) movements, the Reconstructionist position was that congregational committees, under rabbinic leadership, should determine *halacha* for themselves alone and with as much input as possible.[24]

Three years later, again at the RRA convention, guidelines on intermarriage were approved. In contrast to the Conservative and Orthodox movements, the rabbis encouraged their colleagues to welcome "mixed" couples (a Jew and non-Jew) who sought rabbinic counseling when contemplating marriage and, if preparing to officiate at such a marriage, maximize the chance that the non-Jew will convert to Judaism and that the couple will establish a Jewish home and raise their children as Jews. But, should the couple be resistant to or uninterested in conversion, or should the rabbi meet them after they have already been married, the Reconstructionist movement (as the Reform) encourages their participation in synagogue life and recognizes the children of a mixed marriage (as does the Reform movement) as Jewish when raised as Jews. Finally, if the Reconstructionist rabbi chooses to sanctify an intermarriage, the RRA urged her or him to do so with a civil ceremony, reserving the traditional rites of the Jewish wedding ceremony *(kiddushin)* for a marriage of Jew and Jew. The Reconstructionist movement thus joined with Reform in permitting a rabbi to decide whether he or she wished to officiate at an intermarriage (Orthodox and Conservative rabbis are prohibited from doing so), joined reformers in rejecting claims to Jewishness being established only through conversion or matrilineal descent, and became the only movement to urge its rabbis to create two wedding ceremonies in the hope of preserving "the essential integrity of Jewish sancta through their authentic application." Reconstructionism's flurry of ideological activity in the early 1980s focused attention on a movement with new vigor and growth.[25]

11. Institutions and Organizations: 1922–1983

The Society for the Advancement of Judaism

Mordecai Kaplan and several supporters founded the Society for the Advancement of Judaism (SAJ) in 1922 in order to "advance Judaism as a modern religious civilization." Its activities, from the very start, emphasized both the religious nature of the organization and an attempt to extend beyond the parameters of most synagogues and encompass Jewish civilization.[1]

In addition to regular religious celebrations of festivals and holidays, brief worship took place on Friday afternoons about 5:30 P.M. and on Sunday mornings about 9:30 A.M. The primary service, which included Kaplan's "lecture," was held on Saturday morning beginning at 9:30. From the start, men and women had complete equality in worship; in fact, on several occasions during the 1920s a Bat Mitzvah took place at the SAJ (Kaplan's eldest daughter Judith celebrated her Bat Mitzvah at the SAJ in September 1922), possibly the earliest such ceremonies in the United States. The SAJ described its worship as "vital, inspiring, fresh and spontaneous" and used traditional prayer books, with loose-leaf inserts of songs and readings, for many years. Eventually, of course, the SAJ switched to the *Supplementary Prayers and Readings for the High Holidays* (1934), *Shir Hadash: New Prayers and Meditations for Rosh Hashanah and Yom Kippur* (1939) and the *Sabbath Prayer Book* (1945).[2]

In addition to divine worship, a panoply of activities took place at the SAJ, where current Jewish magazines and books greeted a visitor on entrance and Palestinian and Jewish art covered the walls. During the 1920s alone, the SAJ encompassed cultural, Palestine, "extra-mural," and educational programs, and all were held within the buildings. The cultural activities included concerts of Jewish music and performances of Jewish plays, Friday evening and Monday morning lectures, a Saturday afternoon history hour, a Sunday and a Wednesday evening forum (the latter to discuss Kaplan's sermon of the previous Sabbath), study circles, Jewish music programs, current events discussions, and youth (Junior League) education.

Among the Palestine activities were very large and successful fundraising programs, a Zionism study group, illustrated lectures about Palestine, and service projects to benefit Palestine's Jewish community. The most common "extra-mural" activities involved the SAJ Sewing Circle, college groups, and a library foundation—the latter placed Judaica books in New York public libraries—while the SAJ served as an educational center not only for the society's own three-days-per-week Hebrew school and Sunday school but also for many Jewish groups in Manhattan. In sum, the SAJ, with its approximately 100 members in 1923, 150 in 1927, and perhaps 300 in 1928, functioned as a center and synagogue, although—unlike the center movement of the 1920s and 1930s—nearly all its recreational and cultural activities included Jewish content.[3]

The striking exception to this pattern of Judaica programming was the "athletic department." Very early in its existence the SAJ had a director of athletics (who doubled as the director of the Hebrew School), and the top story of the SAJ House at 13–15 West 86th Street (the SAJ acquired this property in 1925) rocked with basketball, volleyball, and other recreational programs for Jewish members of varying ages. The sports program took literally Kaplan's claim that "Judaism . . . is the sum of *everything* about the Jewish people," not just "a synonym for Jewish religion."[4]

The SAJ had no central organization for some years yet represented a movement that sought to encourage other congregations to emulate its program of Judaism as a total civilization. Since it explicitly rejected "Reformism" and Orthodoxy in its literature, but did not mention Conservative Judaism, the SAJ immediately realized its close bond with the Conservative movement. Nearly all the synagogues that "affiliated" with the SAJ also belonged to the United Synagogue, while most of the rabbis who pledged support of the SAJ and its principles had been students of Kaplan and graduates of the Jewish Theological Seminary. Rabbi Max Arzt, for example, when establishing a "branch" of the SAJ at his Conservative synagogue in Scranton, noted that he was consciously combining the twin programs of Conservative Judaism and the Jewish Center movement into his congregational setting. Most of those who followed Kaplan's lead made similar observations, and the SAJ, as well as, later, the Reconstructionist "movement," became commonly viewed as a left-wing tendency within Conservative Judaism.[5]

Rabbi Ira Eisenstein, a JTS graduate, served the SAJ as Kaplan's assistant during the 1930s (and married one of his daughters), a decade in which the SAJ, because of the impact of the Depression on its most generous supporters, struggled for survival. When Kaplan retired in 1945 as "leader" of the society, Eisenstein accepted the position, having been promoted from assistant leader (1931) to associate leader (1933) and, finally, acting leader. Eisenstein guided the SAJ in the 1930s during Kaplan's several leaves of absence (to finish his first book and to teach in Jerusalem) and then in the decade after World War II, until he left to develop a Reconstructionist base in Chicago (1954–1959), to preside over the Jewish Reconstructionist Foundation, direct the Fellowship of Reconstructionist Congregations and Havurot, and edit the *Reconstructionist* Magazine. Alan W. Miller (1926–) has served as the SAJ rabbi ever since 1961.

The Jewish Reconstructionist Foundation and the Federation of Reconstructionist Congregations and Havurot

The Jewish Reconstructionist Foundation (JRF) was organized in 1940 to carry on the Reconstructionist program, which for several years had been sustained, almost exclusively, by the SAJ. It was the successor to the Friends of Reconstructionism, a group of generous SAJ and Park Avenue Synagogue supporters organized in the 1930s by the latter congregation's rabbi, Milton Steinberg. The JRF assumed responsibility for the publication of the bi-weekly *Reconstructionist* magazine, books, pamphlets, and general educational and informational materials, as well as for the coordination of the movement's activities and institutions. Thus the JRF began, almost immediately after its creation, to sponsor a Reconstructionist Youth Institute of study and activity for young men and women in their twenties and, for the institute, to publish a bi-monthly periodical *(Tehiyah, "Renascence")*. The formal emergence of the JRF was a recognition of the contradiction inherent in the Reconstructionist philosophy: Reconstructionism presented a broad program under which all of North American Judaism ought to unite; it also presented a very specific platform of ideology and practice; and it demonstrated great reluctance in establishing an organizational apparatus to complement the SAJ.[6]

One of the most constructive ways to convey Reconstructionist ideology, Kaplan and his associates argued throughout the 1940s, was to create small fellowships or *havurot* within congregations that would, in Eugene Kohn's words, "intensify Jewish lives." These fellowships, formally initiated in 1943 and later coordinated by the Jewish Reconstructionist Fellowship, would serve as the vehicle or instrumentality through which the Reconstructionist ideology would be translated into a way of living, and would resolve the problem of how to be both an ideology and movement yet not "compete" with the three organized branches of North American Judaism. In 1945 there were four Reconstructionist fellowship chapters, each under the direction of a local rabbi, and forty-one active study groups. All the members were encouraged to belong to an existing congregation.[7]

Most of the fellowships consisted of a rabbi and laypeople and met for discussions of Reconstructionist literature. The laypeople usually included a mixture of men and women affiliated with Reform, Conservative, and Orthodox congregations as well as those Jews who were not attracted to any denomination but who found the study groups and various programs of interest. An exception to this pattern during the 1940s was the Reconstructionist Fellowship of Chicago, under the leadership of Rabbi Solomon Goldman. More than twenty rabbis, many employed by very large Reform and Conservative congregations, participated in the study groups.[8]

As the number of fellowships grew, and three congregations (Buffalo, West Los Angeles, Skokie) in addition to the SAJ declared themselves Reconstructionist, a formal congregational organization—Reconstructionist Federation of Congregations—was created in 1955. Unique in its inclusion of both synagogues and fellowships and in its insistence that the congregations retain or acquire membership in the UAHC or United Synagogue, it became the Federation of Reconstructionist Congregations and Fellowships in 1961. This change of name was a signal that the movement was moving toward denominationalism; in addition, the FRCH no longer required members to belong to another movement, and Rabbi Ira Eisenstein, the leader of the JRF, announced his intention to move Reconstructionism from a "school of thought" to another "wing" of North American Judaism.[9]

With the approval of Kaplan, at about the time Kaplan became Professor Emeritus at the JTS at the age of eighty-two, and the creation of the Reconstructionist Rabbinical College (RRC) in the late 1960s, what Kaplan had once called a "state of mind" and had insisted over and over should not replace or compete with existing denominations became, formally, the fourth branch of Judaism in North America. By 1983 the federation, no longer a financial subsidiary of the JRF, could list forty-six member units, or about 10,000 members, in the United States and Canada. The synagogues and fellowships included twelve in New York, six each in California and Pennsylvania, and Reconstructionist synagogues in both Montreal and Toronto.[10]

Reconstructionist Rabbinical College

As more and more Reconstructionist leaders during the 1970s became convinced that the "school of thought" needed institutionalization, discussions at Reconstructionist conferences centered around the lack of rabbis trained in Reconstructionist ideology available to the small but growing number of Reconstructionist congregations. By 1967, at the Montreal conference, the leaders of the movement were ready to charge the JRF with establishing a rabbinical school. Although some leaders favored continuing the Kaplan approach of not formally creating a new branch of North American Judaism, enough leaders were inspired by Ira Eisenstein's vision of a new type of school that would attempt to provide rabbis—who had studied Reform, Conservative, Orthodox, and Reconstructionist Judaism—for all of North American Jewry. This vision convinced the Reconstructionist leadership to vote to move Reconstructionism in a new direction and to open the Reconstructionist Rabbinical College in Philadelphia in the fall of 1968.[11]

The formal dedication and opening, under the presidency of Ira Eisenstein (1968–1981), was 13 October 1968, with an address by the nearly ninety-year-old Kaplan highlighting the occasion. The first class was offered what one scholar called "an *aggiornamento* in clerical training"—a combined program with Temple University leading to both a doctoral degree from the university and a doctorate of Hebrew literature, with the title "rabbi," from the RRC. Women were accepted equally with men (the first seminary to do so), and by 1983 about seventy rabbis (including a dozen women) had been ordained by the school (the first in 1973). They served primarily in Reconstructionist as well as in Reform and Conservative congregations as rabbis and/or educators, and in Hillel Foundations, and they included a husband and wife, Dennis and Sandy Sasso, who served together at Indianapolis's Congregation Beth El Zedek.[12]

The RRC, whose second president, Ira Silverman (1945–   ), succeeded Eisenstein in 1981, offered a unique curriculum for its five years of graduate study, as the students spent one full year on each of five major periods of Jewish civilization: biblical, rabbinic, medieval, modern, and contemporary. This cycle of study attempted to translate into a program of studies Kaplan's notion of Judaism as "an evolving religious civilization," so that both the comprehensiveness and the evolutionary character of Judaism would be understood. Together with the graduate study of religion (or another appropriate discipline) at Temple University, Kaplan's hope that rabbinic students would understand the history and philosophy of the world's major religions in the most objective and scientific sense was being realized.

Reconstructionist Rabbinical Association

The antecedents of the Reconstructionist Rabbinical Association extend back to December 1950 when the Reconstructionist Rabbinical Fellowship (RRF), with nearly a hundred Conservative and Reform rabbis, sympathetic to the Reconstructionist philosophy, was formed. Its concerns included encouraging creative synagogue worship and education, intensifying Hebrew education, building democratically constituted local and national "organic" communities, and initiating cooperative programs among religious and secular Jewish organizations and individuals. The rabbis felt no contradiction in retaining their memberships in the Central Conference of American Rabbis and Rabbinical Assembly. In fact, in concert with other statements of the movement prior to the 1960s, the rabbis assured their fellow Jews that they had "no intention of creating a new and competing denomination."[13]

The very large number of Reform and Conservative rabbis that belonged to the RRF was direct evidence of the generous impact of Reconstructionist ideology on non-Orthodox branches of North American Judaism. I have already noted the intimate relationship between the Reconstructionist leadership (especially Kaplan and Eisenstein) and both the Conservative movement and the Jewish Theological Seminary (and every intimate relationship contains conflict). Conservative rabbis continuously acknowledged their indebtedness to their former teacher, Kaplan, and to Reconstructionism for stimulating their thinking on numerous issues. In addition, Reconstructionism played a major role in shaping the ideas of Reform Judaism, especially the notion that Judaism includes a cultural component, that naturalist theology is legitimate, and that Jewish communal democracy must be continuously affirmed and implemented.[14]

This influence, albeit unofficial and indirect, was largely communicated from Reconstructionist rabbis to Reform rabbis on an individual basis, for Kaplan had only a very few identifiable followers. This was, of course, precisely what Reconstructionism wished to do; it sought, for several decades, to be a "school of thought" influencing North American Judaism rather than a fourth denomination. It may have hoped that its ideas, when communicated by Reform and Conservative rabbis to their congregants, would much more often than was the case be conveyed as Reconstructionist rather than as "genuine" Reform or Conservative Judaism. Nevertheless, Reconstructionists rejoiced at the extent to which the writings of Kaplan and Milton Steinberg, especially, were quoted, studied, and internalized by a generation of Reform and Conservative rabbis.[15]

With the establishment of the Reconstructionist Rabbinical College, a Reconstructionist rabbinical association of Conservative and Reform rabbis seemed incongruous and even disloyal, and as the RRC began to ordain rabbis a rabbinic association of RRC alumni naturally formed. It met for the first time in 1975, and by 1981 began to publish its own journal, *Raayonot* *("Ideas")*, and, together with laypeople, to study the possibility of producing a new prayer book for the movement.

The 1945 Reconstructionist prayer book, as Charles Silberman has noted, responded to the problem of a group of first- and second-generation Jews finding Orthodoxy a burden, struggling with how to be both Jewish and American, and desperately seeking something in which to believe. A new Reconstructionist prayer book would respond to a third, fourth, and even fifth generation of Jews, at home in North America, comfortable with their Judaism, and no longer from Orthodox homes. Today's Reconstructionists are concerned with a new agenda of issues, still wary of ethnic triumphalism or "chosenness," but more easily able to affirm uniqueness, increasingly sensitive to the matter of gender and God imagery in prayer, and open to the symbolism and mythology of what their parents and grandparents rejected as outrageous literalism or anthropomorphism. The 1980s, it seems quite clear, will witness the first new Reconstructionist liturgical publications in a generation or more.[16]

PART V

TABLES

Table 1: UAHC Congregations, 1873–1980

Year	Number of Congregations	Members
1873	34	NA[a]
1874	55	1,966
1875	72	NA
1879	105	NA
1887	86	[b]
1893	90	7,831
1894	95	9,302
1895	95	8,053
1896	90	9,072
1897	90	8,888
1898	90	8,418
1900	99	9,845
1902	107	10,037
1903	115	11,176
1904	125	13,083
1905	134	13,336
1906	167	14,774
1907	184	16,127
1908	198	17,401
1909	193	17,997
1910	185	17,457
1915	191	21,706
1916	198	NA
1917	200	23,105
1920	208	NA
1922	262	NA
1924	278	47,294
1925	279	53,960
1926	279	56,860
1927	283	60,006
1928	279	58,844
1930	285	60,006
1931	285	58,844
1932	286	NA
1934	282	54,089
1935	286	52,568
1936	289	53,436
1937	293	55,000
1938	293[c]	55,000
1940	265[d]	59,000
1943	303	NA
1947	364	100,000+
1949	400	NA
1951	442	NA
1952	450	NA
1953	461	NA
1954 (March)	483	NA
1954 (December)	497	NA
1955	520	255,000

Table 1: UAHC Congregations, 1873–1980 (cont.)

Year	Number of Congregations	Members
1956	536	700,000 (161,000 member units)
1958	565	NA
1959	585	NA
1960	605	NA
1961	629	NA
1962	640	NA
1963	646	NA
1964	660	1,000,000 (210,000 member units)
1966	664	NA
1970	700	NA
1980	750	NA

SOURCE: UAHC, *Annual Reports.* Union of American Hebrew Congregations, 838 Fifth Avenue, New York NY 10021
[a]Not available
[b]Of the 86, 77 reported 6,096 members.
[c]Sixty congregations didn't contribute dues because of the "effects of the Depression."
[d]Of the 305 congregations belonging to the UAHC, only 265 pay dues.

Table 2: UAHC Chairmen, 1873 to the Present

Moritz Loth	1873–1889
Julius Freiberg	1889–1903
Samuel Woolner	1903–1907
Louis J. Goldman	1907–1911
J. Walter Freiberg	1911–1921
Charles Shohl	1921–1925
Ludwig Vogelstein	1925–1934
Jacob W. Mack	1934–1937
Robert P. Goldman	1937–1943
Adolph Rosenberg	1941–1946
Jacob Aronson	1947–1951
Dr. S. S. Hollender	1951–1955
Judge Solomon Elsner	1955–1959
Judge Emil N. Baar	1959–1963
Irvin Fane	1963–1967
Earl Morse	1967–1971
Sidney I. Cole	1971–1972
Harry Guttman	1972–1974
Matthew H. Ross	1974–1979
Donald S. Day	1979–1983
Charles J. Rothschild, Jr.	1983–

Table 3: Hebrew Union College Presidents, 1875 to the Present

Isaac Mayer Wise	1875–1900
Moses Mielziner	1900–1903
Gotthard Deutsch	1903
Kaufmann Kohler	1903–1921
Julian Morgenstern	1921–1947
Stephen S. Wise	1922–1948[a]
Nelson Glueck	1947–1971
Alfred Gottschalk	1971–

[a]Jewish Institute of Religion.

Table 4: United Synagoge of America Presidents, 1913 to the Present

Solomon Schechter	1913–1915
Cyrus Adler	1915–1917
Louis Ginzberg	1917–1918
Elias L. Solomon	1918–1926
Herman Abramowitz	1926–1927
S. Herbert Golden	1927–1929
Nathan Levy	1929–1931
Jacob Kohn	February–April 1931
Louis J. Moss	1931–1944
Samuel Rothstein	1944–1950
Maxwell Abbell	1950–1953
Charles Rosengarten	1953–1957
Bernath L. Jacobs	1957–1961
George Maislen	1961–1965
Henry N. Rapaport	1965–1969
Jacob Stein	1969–1973
Arthur J. Levine	1973–1977
Simon Schwartz	1977–1981
Marshall Wolke	1981–

Table 5: Jewish Theological Seminary Presidents

Sabato Morais	1886–1897
Solomon Schechter	1902–1915
Cyrus Adler	1915–1940
Louis Finkelstein	1940–1972
Gerson Cohen	1972–

Table 6: Union of Orthodox Jewish Congregations of American Presidents, 1898 to the Present

Dr. H. Pereira Mendes	1898–1913
Dr. Bernard Drachman	1913–1918
Charles H. Shapiro	1918–1920
Julius J. Dukas	1920–1924
Rabbi Herbert S. Goldstein	1924–1933
William Weiss	1933–1942
Dr. Samuel Nirenstein	1942–1949
William B. Herlands	1949–1951
Max J. Etra	1951–1954
Moses I. Feuerstein	1954–1966
Rabbi Joseph Karasick	1966–1972
Harold M. Jacobs	1972–1978
Julius Berman	1978–1984

Table 7: Yeshiva University Presidents, 1915 to the Present

Bernard Revel	1915–1940
Samuel Belkin	1943–1975
Norman Lamm	1977–

Table 8: Federation of Reconstructionist Congregations and Havurot Presidents, 1960 to the Present

Benjamin Wm. Mehlman	1960–1962
Arthur C. Kellman	1962–1966
Lavy M. Becker	1966–1972
Herman Levin	1972–1974
Leroy C. Shuster	1974–1976
Leonard Leveton	1976–1978
Herbert I. Winer	1978–1980
Jacob M. Snyder	1980–1982
Samuel Blumenthal	1982–

Notes

CHAPTER 1

1. Jacob S. Raisin, "Reform Judaism Prior to Abraham Geiger, or the Conflict Between Rationalism and Traditionalism in Ancient Judaism," *Year Book of the Central Conference of American Rabbis (YBCCAR)* 20 (1910): 197, 229. Abraham Cronbach, *Reform Movements in Judaism* (New York: Bookman Association, 1963), pp. 45, 59. Jacob Neusner, *From Politics to Piety: The Emergence of Pharisaic Judaism* (Englewood Cliffs, N.J.: Prentice-Hall, 1973), pp. 13–19.

2. S. D. Goitein, *Jews and Arabs: Their Contacts Through the Ages* (New York: Schocken, 1955), pp. 182–184. Hyman G. Enelow, "The Theoretical Foundations of Reform Judaism," *YBCCAR* 34 (1924): 230–46. Fred Rosenbaum, *Architects of Reform: Congregational and Community Leadership—Emanu-El of San Francisco, 1849–1980* (Berkeley, Calif.: Western Jewish History Center, 1980), pp. 93–98.

3. N. Wieder, "Islamic Influences on the Hebrew Cults" (Hebrew), *Melilah* 2 (1946): 37–120.

4. Michael Meyer, *The Origins of the Modern Jew* (Detroit: Wayne State University Press, 1967), p. 41. Alexander Altmann, *Moses Mendelssohn: A Biographical Study* (University, AL.: University of Alabama Press, 1973), p. 289. Felix A. Levy, "Moses Mendelssohn's Ideals of Religion and Their Relation to Reform Judaism," *YBCCAR* 39 (1929): 351–367. One scholar places the origins of Reform in Italy in the sixteenth century; see Gotthard Deutsch, "The Jewish Reform Movement Historically Considered," *Hebrew Union College Monthly* 6, no. 5 (March–April 1920): 131–41.

5. Carl Becker, *The Heavenly City of the Eighteenth-Century Philosophers* (New Haven, Conn.: Yale University Press, 1932). Ernst Cassirer, *The Philosophy of the Enlightenment* (Boston: Beacon Press, 1955). Walter H. Bruford, *Culture and Society in Classical Weimar 1775–1806* (London, England: Cambridge University Press, 1962). Charles Vereker, *Eighteenth-Century Optimism* (Liverpool, England: Liverpool University Press, 1967). Samuel H. Goldenson, "Present Status and Future Outlook of Reform Judaism," *YBCCAR* 34 (1924): 288–89.

6. Heinrich Graetz, *History of the Jews*, vol. 5 (Philadelphia: Jewish Publication Society, 1895), pp. 560–61, 587. Ismar Freund, *Die Emanzipation der Juden in Preussen . . .*, vol. 1 (Berlin: M. Poppelauer, 1912), pp. 214–19.

7. Michael A. Meyer, "The Religious Reform Controversy in the Berlin Jewish Community 1814–1823," *Leo Baeck Institute Year Book* 24 (1979): 139–42.

8. Jacob R. Marcus, *Israel Jacobson: The Founder of the Reform Movement in Judaism* (Cincinnati: Hebrew Union College Press, 1972). W. Gunther Plaut, ed., *The Rise of Reform Judaism: A Sourcebook of its European Origins* (New York: World Union for Progressive Judaism, 1963), pp. 27–31. Meyer, "The Religious Reform Controversy"; Julian Morgenstern, "Achievements of Reform Judaism," *YBCCAR* 34 (1924), pp. 252–56. For an interesting parallel to Jacobson's emphasis on reason, see the suggestions

of Albert S. Goldstein (born 1908), of Brookline's Ohabei Shalom, to eliminate "the un-couth gesture" of the breaking of a glass at weddings because it is "absurd" and "pure superstition"—"Don't Break the Glass," *American Judaism*, 7, no. 3 (January 1958): 12–13.

9. Plaut, *Rise*, pp. 31–42. Jakob Petuchowski, *Prayerbook Reform in Europe: The Liturgy of European Liberal and Reform Judaism* (New York: World Union for Progressive Judaism, 1968), pp. 49–58, 84–104. For an interesting example of the impact of decorum on a traditional congregation, see the regulations at New York's Bene Jeshurun, which ordered the *kaddish* (prayer for the dead) to be read in unison and the congregation to refrain from walking around during its recitation, in Israel Goldstein, *A Century of Judaism in New York: Bene Jeshurun 1825–1925, New York's Oldest Ashkenazic Congre-gation* (New York: Bene Jeshurun, 1930), p. 127. For an example of the traditionalists' opposition to the Hamburg Temple *Prayer Book*, see Chatam Sofer, *"Responsa by Moses Sofer,"* in Alexander Guttmann, *The Struggle over Reform in Rabbinic Literature During the Last Century and a Half* (New York: World Union for Progressive Judaism, 1977), pp. 242–51.

10. Joseph Krauskopf, "Fifty Years of Judaism in America," in *American Jews' Annual* (Cincinnati: Bloch Pub. Co., 1888), p. 73.

11. L. C. Moise, *Biography of Isaac Harby* (Macon, Ga.: CCAR, 1931), pp. 52–59. Charles Reznikoff and Uriah Z. Engelman, *The Jews of Charleston* (Philadelphia: Jewish Publica-tion Society, 1950), pp. 115–26. David Philipson, *The Reform Movement in Judaism* (New York: C. J. Krehbiel, 1931), pp. 329–34.

12. W. Gunther Plaut, ed., *The Growth of Reform Judaism: American and European Sources until 1948* (New York: World Union for Progressive Judaism, 1965), pp. 8–9. Lee M. Friedman, *Pilgrims in a New Land* (New York: Jewish Publication Society, 1948), pp. 151–62. Reznikoff and Engelman, *Jews of Charleston*, pp. 138–46.

13. C. A. Rubenstein, *A History of Har Sinai Congregation of the City of Baltimore* (Balti-more: Press of Kohn and Pollock, 1918), pp. 8–10, 21. Isaac M. Fein, *The Making of an American Jewish Community: The History of Baltimore Jewry from 1773 to 1920* (Phila-delphia: Jewish Publication Society, 1971), pp. 56, 62–66, 113.

14. Myer Stern, *The Rise and Progress of Reform Judaism, Embracing a History Made from the Official Records of Temple Emanu-El of New York . . .* (New York: M. Stern, 1895), pp. 16–41. Hyman B. Grinstein, "Reforms at Temple Emanuel of New York 1860–1890," *Historia Judaica*, 6, no. 1 (April 1944): 163–74. David Philipson, *The Oldest Jewish Congregation in the West (Bene Israel, Cincinnati)*, (Cincinnati: C. J.Krehbiel and Co., 1894), pp. 49–50. James G. Heller, *As Yesterday When It Is Past: A History of the Isaac M. Wise Temple—K. K. B'nai Yeshurun—of Cincinnati . . .* (Cincinnati: n.p., 1942), pp. 69–72. Emma Felsenthal, *Bernhard Felsenthal: Teacher in Israel* (New York: Oxford University Press, 1924), pp. 25–28. Bernhard Felsenthal, *The Beginnings of the Chicago Sinai Congregation* (Chicago: S. Ettlinger, 1898), pp. 9–38.

15. Leon Jick, *The Americanization of the Synagogue, 1820–1870* (Hanover, N.H., University Press of New England, 1976), p. 120. David Philipson, *Max Lilienthal, American Rabbi: Life and Writings* (New York: Bloch Pub. Co., 1915). *The Israelite* 23, no. 2 (1876), quoted in Philipson, *Max Lilienthal*, p. 63. Francis M. Perko, "A Time to Favor Zion: A Case Study of Religion as a Force in American Educational Development," unpublished doctoral dissertation, Stanford University, 1981 (on the Cincinnati controversy of 1869 and the struggle between the evangelicals, on the one hand, and Catholics, Jews, and liberals on the other). Lilienthal's interpretation of the destruction of the second Jewish Commonwealth by the Romans as a blessing rather than a tragedy paralleled the inter-pretation given this event by Wise, Einhorn, Kohler, Felsenthal, and the others who met at Philadelphia in 1869; see David Philipson, "Authority and the Individual Spirit," *YBCCAR 39* (1929): 207.

16. Isaac M. Wise, *Reminiscences*, trans. and ed. by David Philipson (Cincinnati: L. Wise and Co., 1901), pp. 52–54, 73 (these reminiscences first appeared in *Die Deborah*, from 3 July 1874 to 11 August 1875. Letter, Isaac M. Wise to Isaac Leeser, 1 December 1849,

quoted in Maxwell Whiteman, "Isaac Leeser and the Jews of Philadelphia," *Publications of the American Jewish Historical Society* 48 (1959): 223. By 1854 Wise had mastered English sufficiently to publish *A History of the Israelitish Nation* (Albany: J. Munsell, 1854).

17. Naphtali J. Rubinger, "Dismissal in Albany," *American Jewish Archives* 24, no. 2 (November 1972): 160–83. Heller, *As Yesterday,* pp. 82–95. Wise, *Reminiscences,* pp. 165–66, 281. I. J. Benjamin, *Three Years in America,* vol. 1 (Philadelphia: Jewish Publication Society, 1956, 1975), p. 310. For a provocative discussion of Wise's thought, and the argument that his rationalist, deistlike statements represented his true opinions, see Aryeh Rubenstein, "Isaac Mayer Wise: A New Appraisal," *Jewish Social Studies* 39, no. 1–2 (Winter—Spring 1977): 53–74.

18. Felsenthal, *Bernhard Felsenthal,* pp. 125–28, 250, 260–63. Bernhard Felsenthal, "Kol Kore Bamidbar" (Chicago, 1859), in Bernhard Felsenthal, *The Beginnings of the Chicago Sinai Congregation,* pp. 41–74.

19. Kaufmann Kohler, "David Einhorn, the Uncompromising Champion of Reform Judaism," *YBCCAR* 19 (1909): 215–67. *YBCCAR* 34 (1924): 226. Some evidence indicates that Einhorn left Har Sinai with a deep hatred for Baltimore Jewry and that he was suspended from his post in Philadelphia—Gershon Greenberg, "The Messianic Foundations of American Jewish Thought: David Einhorn and Samuel Hirsch," in *Proceedings of the Sixth World Congress of Jewish Studies,* vol. 2 (Jerusalem, 1975), p. 218.

20. Plaut, *Rise,* pp. 93–94, 138.

21. Barnett A. Elzas, "A Memoir of Alexander Kohut," *YBCCAR* 35 (1925): 263. Central Conference of American Rabbis (CCAR), *Sermons by American Rabbis* (Chicago: Central Conference Publication Committee, 1896), pp. 260–61. Philipson, *The Reform Movement,* p. 355. Plaut, *Growth,* pp. 31–35. Kaufmann Kohler's lectures on Reform Judaism, delivered in June and July of 1885 and published as *Backwards or Forwards? A Series of Discourses on Reform Judaism* (New York: Press of Stettiner, Lambert and Co., 1885), served as an important ideological statement for the rabbis at Pittsburgh.

22. On Philadelphia and its crucial decisions in the area of marriage, divorce, and circumcision, see Sefton D. Temkin, ed., *The New World of Reform* (Bridgeport, CT.: Hartmore House, 1971). And on Cincinnati and the vigorous opposition to its results, see Krauskopf, "Fifty Years," pp. 81–85.

23. *YBCCAR* 5651 (1890–1891): 120–22. David Einhorn, ("Services for the Afternoon of the Day of Atonement"), *Olat Tamid* (Baltimore: Har Sinai, 1856), p. 198. One of the most interesting accounts of the causes and the accomplishments of the Pittsburgh conference is that of Solomon Schindler, *Messianic Expectations and Modern Judaism* (Boston: S. E. Cassino and Co., 1886), pp. 170–205.

24. Heller, *As Yesterday,* p. 68. Plaut, *Growth,* pp. 27–28. Union of American Hebrew Congregations (UAHC), *Proceedings,* 5 vols. (Cincinnati, 1873–1903), vol. 1: pp. i–ii, vii–xiii, 3–5, 7–9, 11, 22–24; vol. 2: p. 1073. There were actually twenty-nine accredited congregations, and delegates from five more, at the 1873 convention; see UAHC, *Proceedings of the First General Convention and Preamble, Constitution and By-Laws, 8–10 July 1873,* vol. I, pp. 7–9.

25. UAHC, *Proceedings,* vol. 1: 242–43, 345–48, 421–33, 537. On the conflict between the radical and moderate reformers, see Martin Ryback, "The East-West Conflict in American Reform Judaism," *American Jewish Archives* 4 (January 1952): 1–18.

26. *The Asmonean,* 10 March 1854. UAHC, *Proceedings,* vol. 1: v–xi. *Israelite,* 1 (1854–55); 2 (1855–56), passim. Michael A. Meyer, "A Centennial History," in Samuel E. Karff, ed., *HUC-JIR at One Hundred Years* (Cincinnati: Hebrew Union College Press, 1976), pp. 17–18.

CHAPTER 2

1. Martin A. Meyer, *Western Jewry: An Account of the Achievements of the Jews and Judaism in California* (San Francisco: Emanu-El, 1916), p. 18.

2. *American Israelite,* 25 August 1876; 8 and 22 September, 1876. *Emanu El,* 20 May 1898, p. 5. *American Jewish Year Book* 5664 (Philadelphia, 1903): 104.

3. The scholars contributing to *Emanu El* included Moses Buttenweiser, Max Margolis, Israel Abrahams, Gotthard Deutsch, and Marcus Jastrow.

4. Bernhard N. Cohn, "Early German Preaching in America," *Historia Judaica* 15, no. 2 (October 1953): 100. Samuel Freuder, *Bellamy and Judaism: A Reply to Rev. Dr. Jacob Voorsanger's Criticism of Looking Backward* (San Francisco: Pacific Union Co., 1897 or 1898).

5. *YBCCAR* 5651 (1890–91): 120–22.

6. Isaac M. Wise, *The Cosmic God: A Fundamental Philosophy in Popular Lectures* (Cincinnati: Office American Israelite and Deborah, 1876), pp. 10, 181. Emil G. Hirsch, "The Doctrine of Evolution and Judaism," in Emil G. Hirsch, *My Religion* (New York: Macmillan, 1925), pp. 243–62. *Emanu El,* 10 April 1896, pp. 8–10; 17 April 1896, pp. 9–12; 14 October 1904, p. 7. For the impact of evolutionary theory on American religious thought, see Herbert W. Schneider, "The Influence of Darwin and Spencer on American Philosophical Theology," *Journal of the History of Ideas* 4 (1945): 3–18. Joseph Krauskopf, *Evolution and Judaism* (Kansas City: Berkowitz, 1887). Syndey E. Ahlstrom, *A Religious History of the American People,* vol. 2 (New Haven, Conn.: Yale University Press, 1975), pp. 229–34.

7. *Emanu El,* 14 October 1904, p. 7; 11 February 1898, p. 5; 10 December 1897, p. 7; 12 October 1900, p. 7; 13 March 1896, p. 6; 8 April 1898, p. 6; 28 October 1898, pp. 6–7. Jacob Voorsanger, *Sermons and Addresses* (New York: Bloch Pub. Co., 1913), p. 7.

8. *Emanu El,* 1 September 1899, p. 6; 11 December 1903, p. 5. Leon Harrison, *The Religion of a Modern Liberal: The Selected Sermons of Thirty-Five Years in the Jewish Ministry* (New York: Bloch Pub. Co., 1931), pp. 106, 282. *Emanu El,* 26 November 1897, pp. 7–8. For a fuller discussion of the "mission theory" and Reform Judaism, see Kaufmann Kohler, *Jewish Theology* (Cincinnati: Riverdale Press, 1943), Part 3.

9. *Emanu El,* 13 January 1899, pp. 7–8; 13 January 1905, p. 5; 22 April 1898, p. 7; 2 May 1901, p. 6; 11 December 1903, pp. 5–6; 25 December 1903, p. 7; 22 November 1895, p. 4.

10. *Emanu El,* 6 May 1898, p. 7; 3 February 1905, p. 5; 28 October 1898, p. 6. *Jewish Progress,* 26 January 1894, p. 1; 2 February 1894, p. 1.

11. *Emanu El,* 9 May 1901, p. 5; 11 December 1903, p. 6. Joseph Krauskopf, *Our Pulpit: Sunday Discourses* (Philadelphia: O. Klonower, 1906), p. 173, quoted in Jerrold Goldstein, "Reform Rabbis and the Progressive Movement," unpublished master's thesis, University of Minnesota, 1967. Krauskopf, *Evolution and Judaism.* David Philipson, "The Eternal Verities: A New Year's Sermon," in Central Conference of American Rabbis (CCAR), *Sermons by American Rabbis,* p. 8. *Jewish Progress,* 30 March 1894, p. 1. See Lyman Abbott, *The Evolution of Christianity* (Boston: Houghton, Mifflin, 1892), pp. 255–56. John Bascom, *The New Theology* (New York: G. P. Putnam, 1891), p. 22. Washington Gladden, *Ruling Ideas of the Present Age* (Boston: Houghton, Mifflin, 1896), pp. 290, 298. Walter Rauschenbush, *Christianity and the Social Crisis* (New York: Hodder and Stoughton, 1912), p. 90. Josiah Strong, *The New Era or the Coming Kingdom* (New York: The Baker and Taylor Co., 1893), pp. 1–40. Emil G. Hirsch, "The Concordance of Judaism and Americanism," in David Einhorn Hirsch, *Rabbi Emil G. Hirsch: The Reform Advocate* (Chicago: Whitehall Co., 1968), pp. 49–62. Kaufmann Kohler, *Evolution and Morality* (New York: Stettiner, Lambert and Co., 1887). Wise, *The Cosmic God.* Aaron Hahn, *History of the Arguments for the Existence of God* (Cincinnati: Bloch Pub. Co., 1885). For an account of how "this faith in an irresistible progress paralyzed the will and militated against the crusader's zeal" in the Reform movement prior to 1910, see Leonard J. Mervis, "The Social Justice Movement and the American Reform Rabbi," *American Jewish Archives* 7, no. 2 (June 1955): 171–230.

12. *Emanu El,* 12 November 1897, p. 9; 24 July 1896, p. 6.

13. *Emanu El,* 13 January 1899, p. 7; 29 July 1898, p. 7; 12 September 1902, p. 7.

14. *Emanu El,* 13 January 1899, p. 6; 28 April 1905, p. 6.

15. *Emanu El,* 25 November 1898, p. 8; 27 January 1899, p. 8. David Philipson, "The Eternal

Verities," p. 9. Adolph Moses, *Yahvism and Other Discourses,* ed. H. G. Enelow (Louisville: The Louisville Section of the Council of Jewish Women, 1903), pp. 22–23. *Emanu El,* 9 September 1904, p. 9; 13 January 1899, p. 9.

16. *Emanu El,* 10 June 1904, p. 5; 17 June 1904, pp. 5–6; 29 May 1896, pp. 6–7.
17. *Emanu El,* 17 June 1904, p. 6; 18 February 1898, pp. 6–7; 27 January 1899, p. 9.
18. *Emanu El,* 15 April 1904, p. 6; 21 January 1898, p. 7; 28 October 1904, p. 6; 2 December 1898, p. 7.
19. *Emanu El,* 27 January 1899, pp. 7–8; 3 March 1899, p. 5; 13 January 1899, pp. 6–7.
20. *Emanu El,* 17 June 1904, pp. 5–6; 6 December 1895, p. 6; 10 February 1905, p. 5; 20 January 1905.
21. See, for the economic argument and Shylock image, Oscar Handlin, "How United States Anti-Semitism Began," *Commentary* 11 (1951): 541–48. *Emanu El,* 4 December 1903, p. 7; 22 November 1906, p. 7. *American Hebrew,* 19 March 1886, pp. 81–82, and Voorsanger's communication to *AH.,* 5 June 1891, p. 107. *Jewish Messenger,* 3 February 1893, pp. 4–5. *American Israelite,* 4 August 1882, p. 56. *Emanu El,* 7 October 1904, p. 5; 1 July 1904, pp. 5–6; 30 September 1904, pp. 5–6; 28 October 1904, p. 5. Barbara Miller Solomon, *Ancestors and Immigrants* (Cambridge: Harvard University Press, 1956), pp. 17–18, 169.
22. *Emanu El,* 10 January 1908, p. 2; 6 December 1907, p. 3; 29 November 1907, pp. 3–4; 19 August 1904, p. 8. A similar program was supported equally vigorously by a number of leading Reform rabbis of Voorsanger's day: Wise and Philipson of Cincinnati, Joseph Stolz of Chicago, Kohler of New York, and Krauskopf of Philadelphia. Krauskopf, rabbi of Keneseth Israel from 1887 to 1923 and the author of more than five hundred extant sermons, demanded both distribution and occidentalization; see especially "What to Do with the Russian Refugee," 17 December 1905; "The Wail of the Modern Ghetto—The Diagnosis," 23 December 1900; and "The Wail of the Modern Ghetto, II. A Remedy," 6 January 1901, in Joseph Krauskopf, "Papers, 1887–1906," American Jewish Archives (3101 Clifton Avenue, Cincinnati, OH 45220).
23. *Emanu El,* 25 February 1898, p. 7; 17 July 1896, p. 5; 16 December 1898, p. 8. Jacob Voorsanger, *Zionism: Open Letters Written by Rev. Dr. Jacob Voorsanger of San Francisco, Cal. to Hon. Simon Wolf of Washington D.C.* (1903–1904), n.p. pp. 6, 12–13, 17–18, 41. See also Kaufmann Kohler, *Studies, Addresses and Personal Papers* (New York: Alumni Assoc. of the Hebrew Union College, 1931), pp. 457–58.
24. *YBCCAR* 7 (1898), pp. xi–xii, xli. Isaac Mayer Wise, "Zionism," *Hebrew Union College Journal* 4, no. 3 (December, 1899): 45–47. *American Israelite,* 2 May 1885; 29 July 1897; 18 November 1897; 10 March 1898; 7 July 1898; 3 November 1898; 26 January 1899.
25. *Emanu El,* 16 December 1898, p. 7; 9 June 1905, p. 13; 31 March 1905, p. 5. Voorsanger, *Zionism,* pp. 15–18.
26. *Emanu El,* 16 December 1898, p. 8; 8 July 1904, p. 5; 23 June 1905, p. 5; 13 September 1907, p. 2; 28 February 1908, p. 1; 18 August 1905, p. 5; 10 January 1896, pp. 6–7; 20 August 1897, p. 6. Voorsanger, *Zionism,* p. 33. UAHC, *Proceedings,* vol. 6 (1903–1907), p. 5317 (January 1905).
27. *Emanu El,* 2 December 1898, p. 5; 16 December 1898, p. 8; 29 July 1898, p. 7; 9 March 1906, p. 8; 15 July 1904, p. 5.
28. Voorsanger, *Zionism,* pp. 22–26. *Emanu El,* 24 February and 3, 10, 17, 31 March 1899; 7 April 1899 ("The Jewish Framework of Christianity: Palestine, From the Time of Ezra"); 28 April 1899 ("The Jewish Framework of Christianity: The Origin, Growth and Development of the Messianic Idea"); 5 May 1899 ("The Jewish Framework of Christianity: The Messianic Idea During the Babyonian [sic] Exile"). Parallel views are to be found in Isaac Mayer Wise's *A History of the Israelitish Nation.*
29. Minutes of Congregation Keneseth Israel, 13 September 1861, quoted in Jick, *Americanization of the Synagogue,* p. 166.
30. Philipson, *The Reform Movement,* pp. 65, 253–54, 375. Samuel Holdheim, *Neue Sammlung Jüdischer Predigten,* 3 vols. (Berlin: C. David, 1852–1855), vol. 1 pp. 70 ff., quoted in Plaut, *Rise,* p. 195. Kaufmann Kohler, *A Living Faith* (Cincinnati: Hebrew Union College Press, 1948), pp. 19–31.

31. *Jewish Tidings,* 2 May 1890.

32. *Jewish Chronicle,* 7 May 1897.

33. See especially Jacob Voorsanger, "The Sabbath Question," *YBCCAR* 12 (1902): 102–22. Hymen G. Enelow, "The Influence of the Sunday Services," *YBCCAR* 16 (1906): 87–113. "Continuation of Sabbath Discussion," and "The Sabbath Commission," *YBCCAR* 13 (1903): 96–101, 139–71. Beryl Harold Levy, *Reform Judaism in America: A Study in Religious Adaptation* (New York: Bloch Pub. Co., 1933), pp. 92–108.

34. The Hirsch quote comes from *Reform Judaism: Discourse at the Celebration of Dr. Samuel Hirsch's 70th Anniversary, Delivered by His Son, The Rabbi of Chicago Sinai Congregation* (Chicago: Sinai Congregation, 1885), and the discussion of his Torah-less ark is in Letter, Joseph Krauskopf to A. L. Fribourg, 1902, Joseph Krauskopf, "Papers, 1887–1906."

35. Ahlstrom, *A Religious History,* vol. 2, pp. 238–42.

36. Benny Kraut, *From Reform Judaism to Ethical Culture: The Religious Evolution of Felix Adler* (Cincinnati: Hebrew Union College Press, 1979). Levi A. Olan, *Felix Adler: Critic of Judaism and Founder of a Movement,* Union Anniversary Series (New York: Union of American Hebrew Congregations, 1951), p. 7.

37. Minot J. Savage, "Preface" to Schindler, *Messianic Expectations,* p. ix; Schindler, *Messianic Expectations,* p. 166. Solomon Schindler, *Dissolving Views in the History of Judaism* (Boston: Lee and Shepard, 1888), pp. 299–313. Arthur Mann, "Solomon Schindler: Boston Radical," *New England Quarterly* 23, no. 4 (December 1950): 453–76. Arthur Mann, ed. *Growth and Achievement: Temple Israel 1854–1964* (Cambridge: Riverside Press, 1954), pp. 45–62.

38. Joseph Krauskopf, *The Service Ritual* (Philadelphia: Edward Stern, 1888), pp. 3, 22, 59–60, 72–3, 105. Joseph Krauskopf, *Sunday Lectures,* 36 vols. (Philadelphia: n.p., 1887–1922). On Krauskopf as radical reformer, see "Joseph Krauskopf, 1887–1903," rabbinic thesis, Hebrew Union College, 1975, pp. 151–67.

39. Solomon B. Freehof and Vigdor W. Kavaler, *J. Leonard Levy: Prophetic Voice* (Pittsburgh: Rodef Shalom Congregation, 1970). J. Leonard Levy, *The Reform Pulpit: Sunday Lectures . . . Before Rodef Shalom of Pittsburgh, Penn.,* vol. 3 (Pittsburgh: C. H. Joseph, 1903–1904), pp. 13, 16, and vol. 4 (1904–1905), pp. 9–10.

40. Arthur Mann, "Charles Fleischer's Religion of Democracy: An Experiment in American Faith," *Commentary* 17 (1954): 557–65. Arthur Mann, *Growth and Achievement,* pp. 63–83.

41. *YBCCAR* 3 (1892–1893): 15–19, 33–39, 65–69. *Jewish Encyclopedia,* vol. 10, pp. 358–59. *YBCCAR* 28 (1918): 133–34.

42. *Jewish Encyclopedia,* volume 10, p. 180. Late Friday evening (about 8 P.M.) worship services, initiated by Isaac Mayer Wise in the 1860s, had already become popular, and perhaps even standard, in many Reform congregations by the late 1880s. See Krauskopf, "Fifty Years," p. 43.

43. Fred Rosenbaum, *Architects of Reform: Congregational and Community Leadership— Emanu-El of San Francisco, 1849–1980* (Berkeley: Western Jewish History Center, 1980), "Martin Meyer: Temple and Community," Ch. 4, pp. 67–85, "Louis Newman: The Renascent Twenties," Ch. 5, 87–105. Janice J. Feldstein, *Rabbi Jacob J. Weinstein: Advocate of the People* (New York: KTAV, 1980), p. 103. When Rabbi Weinstein arrived at Chicago's K.A.M. congregation, he found that the hymnal "scores showed the smudge marks where the word 'Christ' had been scratched out and the word 'Lord' substituted." *Jewish Comment,* 3 October 1913, cited in Fein, *Baltimore Jewry,* p. 185.

44. Henry Berkowitz, *Intimate Glimpses of the Rabbi's Career* (Cincinnati: Hebrew Union College Press, 1921), p. 121. See also Moses, "The Duty of the Pulpit," in *Yahvism,* pp. 320–30.

45. *YBCCAR* 44 (1934): 132.

46. At San Francisco's Emanu-El, for example, Rabbi Martin Meyer, who served the congregation from 1910–1923 and was very sympathetic to East European Jewry, refused to wear

either a *tallit* or *yarmulka* or to change the virtually all-English liturgy of the congregation. See Rosenbaum, *Architects*, p. 70.

47.   Rosenbaum, *Architects*, p. 72. Bernard J. Bamberger, "Mythology of Reform Judaism," *CCAR Journal* 22, no. 2 (Spring 1975): 8. *YBCCAR* 34 (1924): 300. Commission on Research, Union of American Hebrew Congregations, *Reform Judaism in the Large Cities: A Survey* (Cincinnati: UAHC, 1931), p. 47.

48.   Samuel H. Goldenson, "The Present Status and Future Outlook of Reform Judaism," *YBCCAR* 34 (1924): 290.

49.   D. Max Eichhorn, "The Student Body—Today [1930] and Yesterday [1900]," reprinted in Howard Greenstein, *Turning Point: Zionism and Reform Judaism*, Brown Judaic Studies no. 12 (Chico, Calif.: Scholars Press, 1981), pp. 173–76. Robert I. Kahn, "On the Centennial of the HUC-JIR," *CCAR Journal* 22, no. 3 (Summer 1975): 54. UAHC, *Reform Judaism in the Large Cities*, pp. 10, 13, 47–51, 73, 74.

50.   UAHC, *Sixth-Third Annual Report of the Union of American Hebrew Congregations, May 1937* (Cincinnati: UAHC, 1937), p. 158. *YBCCAR* 58 (1948): 319. Hyman G. Enelow, "Palestine and the Jews," in *The Allied Countries and the Jews: A Series of Addresses* (New York: Temple Emanu-El, p. 73. Isaac M. Wise, "Zionism," *Hebrew Union College Journal* 4, no. 3 (December 1899): 45–47. Henry Berkowitz, "Why I Am Not a Zionist," *YBCCAR* 9 (1899): 167–73. Moses, *Yahvism*, pp. 21, 27. UAHC, *Proceedings*, 1898–1903, vol. 5 (Cincinnati, 1903), p. 4002. Meyer, "A Centennial History," pp. 63, 77–78.

51.   Greenstein, *Turning Point*, pp. 15, 18–22.

52.   Norman Bentwich, *For Zion's Sake: A Biography of Judah L. Magnes* (Philadelphia: Jewish Publication Society, 1954). Rosenbaum, *Architects*, p. 103. Leon Feuer, "Abba Hillel Silver: A Personal Memoir," *American Jewish Archives* 19, no. 2 (November 1967): 118–24. Melvin Urofsky, *A Voice that Spoke for Justice: The Life and Times of Stephen S. Wise* (Albany: SUNY Press, 1982), chaps. 6, 7, 17. Wise attended a Zionist Congress (1898) with Herzl as chairman; see Stephen S. Wise, "The Beginning of American Zionism," *Jewish Frontier* (August 1947), p. 7.

53.   *YBCCAR* 45 (1935): 102–103; 53 (1943): 92–93; 56 (1946): 225; 58 (1948): 320. Lou H. Silberman discusses the impact of the "historicizing, psychologizing, sociologizing and religionizing" of the 1920s and 1930s on the Columbus Platform in "The Recent History of Reform Philosophy," *YBCCAR* 63 (1953): 282–89.

54.   *YBCCAR* 45 (1935): 208, 212, 232, 280, 330.

55.   *YBCCAR* 46 (1936): 88–107.

56.   *YBCCAR* 47 (1937): 418–22.

57.   *YBCCAR* 47 (1937): 94–114.

58.   For the "Guiding Principles," see *YBCCAR* 47 (1937): 97–100.

59.   Ethel and David Rosenberg, *To 120 Years! A Social History of the Indianapolis Hebrew Congregation, 1856–1976* (Indianapolis: Indianapolis Hebrew Congregation, 1979), p. 70. *American Judaism* 6, no. 2 (Hanukkah 1956): 4. Irving F. Reichert, *Judaism and the American Jew: Selected Sermons and Addresses* (San Francisco: Grabhorn Press, 1953), p. 9, "Getting Back to Fundamentals". Congregation Beth Israel, *A Hand Book of True Facts Concerning the "Basic Principles" of Cong. Beth Israel* (Houston: Beth Israel, n.d.).

60.   UAHC, *Proceedings* 1898–1903, vol. 4, pp. 3653–56; vol. 5, passim. Joseph Leiser, *American Judaism: The Religion and Religious Institutions of the Jewish People in the United States* (New York: Bloch Pub. Co., 1925), pp. 167–71, 191, 193–94. Joint Commission on Social Action of the UAHC and CCAR, *Social Justice: Resolutions Adopted by the UAHC* (New York: UAHC, 1954). Robert J. Wechman, "Emanuel Gamoran: Pioneer in Jewish Religious Education," unpublished doctoral dissertation, Syracuse University, 1970. *Fifty-Seventh Annual Report of the Union of American Hebrew Congregations, May 1931* (Cincinnati: UAHC 1931), p. 119.

61.   Julia Richman, "The Jewish Sunday School Movement in the United States," *Jewish Quarterly Review* 12 (1900): 563–601. UAHC, *Proceedings*, vol. 1, pp. 87, 142–44, 157, 236–37, 241–42, 251; vol. 3, pp. 1992, 1995, 2502; vol. 4, p. 6861; vol. 6, pp. 5020–24,

5098–5104. Emanuel Gamoran, *Methods of Teaching the Jewish Subjects* (Cincinnati: UAHC, 1950). Jacob B. Pollak, *Classroom Organization and Management* (Cincinnati: UAHC, 1927). Emanuel Gamoran, *A Study of 125 Religious Schools Affiliated with the Union of American Hebrew Congregations* (Cincinnati: UAHC, 1925), pp. 1–50. Emanuel Gamoran, "Jewish Education in the United States," in Philip H. Lotz, ed., *Studies in Religious Education* (Nashville: Cokesbury Press, 1931), pp. 490–514. *Thirty-Second Annual Report of the Union of American Hebrew Congregations, January 1906* (Cincinnati: UAHC 1906), pp. 5476–82.

62. Plaut, *Growth,* pp. 29, 31. Sefton Temkin, trans., *The New World of Reform,* pp. 80, 117.

63. *YBCCAR,* 1 (1890): 3–5, 12–17, 19–23.

64. Roland B. Gittelsohn, "The Conference Stance on Social Justice and Civil Rights," in Bertram Wallace Korn, ed., *Retrospect and Prospect: Essays in Commemoration of the Seventy-Fifth Anniversary of the Founding of the Central Conference of American Rabbis,* (New York: CCAR, 1965), p. 81.

65. *YBCCAR* 27 (1917): 112–13; 28 (1918), pp. 101–07. Ahlstrom, *A Religious History,* vol. 2, pp. 270–73.

66. *YBCCAR* 30 (1920): 87–90; 38 (1928): 80–86; 40 (1930), pp. 64, 78–79; 39 (1929), pp. 85–86.

67. Leonard Judah Mervis, "The Social Justice Movement of the American Reform Rabbis 1890–1940," unpublished doctoral dissertation, University of Pittsburgh, 1951.

68. Samuel S. Cohon, "Authority in Judaism," *Hebrew Union College Annual* 11 (1936): 601. *YBCCAR* 38 (1928): 81. See also Sidney E. Goldstein's description of the New York Free Synagogue Social Service Department in *YBCCAR* 24 (1914): 352–65, and the review, by Rabbi Horace J. Wolf, of Graham Taylor's *Religion in Social Action,* in the same volume, pp. 366–74.

69. Abba Hillel Silver, *Therefore Choose Life: Selected Sermons, Addresses, and Writings,* vol. 1 (Cleveland: World Pub. Co., 1967), pp. 117–18.

70. Samuel S. Mayerberg, *Chronicle of an American Crusader* (New York: Bloch Pub. Co., 1944), pp. 100, 122.

71. Feldstein, *Rabbi Jacob J. Weinstein,* pp. 48–49, 108–65, 186–95.

72. Hyman G. Enelow, *Selected Works,* vol. 3: *Collected Writings* (Kingsport, Tenn.: Kingsport Press, 1935), pp. 34, 127–28. Stephen Wise, *Challenging Years: The Autobiography of Stephen Wise* (New York: Putnam's Sons, 1949), pp. 72, 73.

73. Meyer, "A Centennial History," passim. I. Edward Kiev and John J. Tepfer, "Jewish Institute of Religion," *American Jewish Year Book* 49 (1947–1948): 91–100. "Hebrew Union College—Jewish Institute of Religion: A Centennial Documentary," *American Jewish Archives* 26, no. 2 (November 1974): 181–86. Samuel S. Cohon, "The History of the Hebrew Union College," *Publications of the American Jewish Historical Society* 40, no. 1 (September 1950): 17–55. David Philipson, "The History of the Hebrew Union College," *Hebrew Union College Jubilee Volume* (1875–1925), (Cincinnati, 1925), pp. 30–31, 34, 42. Mayerberg, *Chronicle,* pp. 6–8.

CHAPTER 3

1. Alvin J. Reines, "God and Jewish Theology," in Bernard Martin, ed., *Contemporary Reform Jewish Thought,* (Chicago: Quadrangle, 1968), p. 66. In the 1960s, Reines created a word to describe this way of thinking: *polydoxy.*

2. Jakob Petuchowski, "The Question of Jewish Theology," *Judaism* 7 (Fall 1958): 49–55.

3. Roland B. Gittelsohn, "A Naturalist View," in Jack Bemporad, ed. *The Theological Foundations of Prayer: A Reform Jewish Perspective* (New York: UAHC, 1967), p. 44.

4. Samuel S. Cohon, *The Jewish Idea of God,* UAHC Popular Studies no. 28. (Cincinnati: The Tract Commission, 1930), p. 30. Samuel S. Cohon, *What We Jews Believe* (Cincinnati: UAHC 1931), pp. 85–114. At the Cincinnati rabbinical conference (1871) a Dr. Mayer of Cleveland startled the rabbis, and caused American Jewry to be "all aflame," when he stated that he "did not belong to those who believed in a personal God." See Krauskopf, "Fifty Years," pp. 82–84.

5. Bernard Martin, "An Existentialist View," in Bemporad, ed. *The Theological Founda-tions of Prayer,* p. 36. Arnold Wolf, *Challenge to Confirmands* (New York: Scribe Publications, 1963), p. 43. Arthur J. Lelyveld, *Atheism Is Dead: A Jewish Response to Radical Theology* (Cleveland: World Pub. Co., 1968), pp. 121–23, 126.

6. Emil Fackenheim, *Paths to Jewish Belief* (New York: Behrman, 1960), pp. 55, 57. Robert I. Kahn, "This I Believe," *American Judaism* 5, no. 1 (Rosh Hashanah 1955): 4–5. Eugene Borowitz, *The Mask Jews Wear: The Self-Deceptions of American Jewry* (New York: Simon and Schuster, 1973), p. 195. Eugene Borowitz, *A New Jewish Theology in the Making* (Philadelphia: Westminster Press, 1968), pp. 63–68. Jakob J. Petuchowski, "The Dialectics of Reason and Revelation," in Arnold Jacob Wolf, ed., *Rediscovering Judaism: Reflection on a New Theology,* (Chicago, 1965), p. 49. Jakob J. Petuchowski, "Problems of Reform Halacha," in Bernard Martin, ed., *Contemporary Reform Jewish Thought* (Chicago, 1968), p. 119.

7. Roland B. Gittelsohn, *Wings of the Morning* (New York: UAHC, 1969), pp. 133, 135. Bemporad, *Theological Foundations,* pp. 29, 46–47. Roland B. Gittelsohn, "Where Religion and Science Meet," *Saturday Review* 23 (March 1963): 23–24, 79–80. Roland B. Gittelsohn, "Is Prayer a Waste of Time?" *American Judaism* 5, no. 1 (1955): 4. See also Roland B. Gittelsohn, *Man's Best Hope* (New York: Random House, 1961), pp. 164, 172. For the implications of Gittelsohn's theology on the nature of prayer, see Dudley Weinberg, *The Efficacy of Prayer,* UAHC Pamphlet Series no. 2 (New York: Jewish Chautauqua Society, 1965), and for a vocabulary and a theology similar to that of Gittelsohn, see Joseph R. Narot, of Miami's Temple Israel, "What do we mean when we say 'God gives and God takes away'?" and "Does God reward and punish?" in Joseph R. Narot, *Sermons* (Miami: Rostrum Books, 1978), especially pp. 180–81, 191. Gittelsohn too finds it hard to completely avoid "personal" language; in his *Fire in My Bones* (New York: Bloch Pub. Co., 1969, pp. 105–13), he speaks of "the voice of God."

8. Levi Olan, "An Organicist View," in Bemporad, *Theological Foundations,* p. 59. Levi Olan, "The Prophetic Faith in a Secular Age," *CCAR Journal* 26, no. 2 (Spring 1979): 1–9. Olan's theology is extensively discussed in the hundreds of radio broadcasts (KRLD and WFAA in Dallas), available from the Temple Emanu-El Brotherhood (Dallas), and in "New Resources for a Liberal Faith," in Martin, *Contemporary Reform Jewish Thought,* pp. 21–38.

9. Alvin Reines, "Reform Judaism," in Belden Menkus, ed., *Meet the American Jew* (Nashville: Broadmen, 1963), p. 36.

10. Emil Fackenheim, "Can There Be Judaism Without Revelation?" *Commentary* 12, no. 6 (December 1951): 566.

11. Roland B. Gittelsohn, "Covenant with God—Challenge to Man" (paper delivered at the National Federation of Temple Sisterhoods and UAHC Biennial Conventions New York, 10 November 1973), pp. 10, 12. Abraham J. Heschel, *God in Search of Man* (New York: Harper and Row, 1955), p. 168.

12. Maurice Eisendrath, *Can Faith Survive? The Thoughts and Afterthoughts of an American Rabbi* (New York: McGraw-Hill, 1964), pp. 243–44.

13. Solomon B. Freehof, "Reform Judaism and the Halacha," *YBCCAR* 56 (1946): 279.

14. Solomon B. Freehof, *Reform Jewish Practice and Its Rabbinic Background,* vol. 1 (Cincinnati: HUC Press, 1944), pp. 14, 15.

15. Plaut, *Rise,* pp. 260–65. *YBCCAR* 13 (1903): 139–171; 14 (1904): 22. Typical of the arguments against a guide are those of Abraham J. Klausner, in "The Forty-Fourth UAHC Biennial Assembly," *CCAR Journal* no. 18 (June 1957): 60. Also Max Schenk's comments in "Panel Discussion: A Guide for Reform Judaism," *YBCCAR* 69 (1959): 264–65. Also Joseph R. Narot, of Miami's Temple Israel, in his 1958 sermon "Does Reform Need a Ritual Guide?" in Narot, *Sermons,* p. 59. Also Beryl D. Cohon, "Code: Magic Wand or Hot Poker?" *Liberal Judaism* 18, no. 1 (June 1950): 46–47 ("a totalitarian iron curtain"). For the "wide-spread and increasing acceptance of ritual and ceremonial practices" in the postwar Reform movement, see the following: Max Arzt, "Conservative Judaism as a Unifying Force," *Conservative Judaism* 5, p. 4 (June 1949): 11. Morton M.

Berman, "Whither Trending?" *Liberal Judaism* 18, p. 3 (December 1950): 52–56, 59. Also Lou H. Silberman and Albert S. Goldstein, "More Ritual for Reform Judaism? Two Views," *American Judaism* 1, no. 3 (March 1952): 6–7. Also Lawrence Siegel, "The Neo-Reform Growth of American Reform Judaism as Reflected in the CCAR *Yearbook* 1942–59," rabbinic thesis, Hebrew Union College, 1961.

16.   *YBCCAR* 48 (1938): 64–65; 58 (1948): 289–98 ("A Code of Ceremonial and Ritual Practice"), 326. Frederick A. Doppelt, "Report on Change in Reform Jewish Practice," *YBCCAR* 64 (1954): 125–27. Bernard J. Bamberger, "Towards a Code," *YBCCAR* 68 (1958): 260–73. See also the views of Reform laypeople in *American Judaism* 6, no. 3 (January 1957): 10. Also David Polish, "The Case Against Anarchy," *American Judaism* 16, no. 2 (Winter 1966–1967): 9–10. Also Samuel S. Cohon, "The Contemporary Mood in Reform Judaism," *Liberal Judaism* 18, no. 1 (June 1950): 35–39.

17.   Frederick A. Doppelt and David Polish, *A Guide for Reform Jews* (New York: Bloch Pub. Co., 1957) p. 27, passim. Other "guides" by Reform rabbis include the following: Abraham J. Feldman, *Reform Judaism* (New York: Behrman House, 1956). Morrison D. Bial, *Liberal Judaism at Home: The Practices of Modern Reform Judaism* (Summit, N.J.: Temple Sinai, 1967). William Silverman, *Basic Reform Judaism* (New York: Philosophical Library, 1970), pp. 196–217. For evaluations of Feldman's "guide," see *American Judaism* 4, no. 3 (January 1955): 9, 12–13.

18.   *YBCCAR* 75 (1965): 189.

19.   *A Shabbat Manual* (New York, 1972), pp. 9–13. See Bernard J. Bamberger's review of the *Manual* in *Judaism* 23, no. 1 (Winter 1974): 113–16. For vigorous calls to return to *halacha* by W. Gunther Plaut and the UAHC president, Rabbi Alexander Schindler, see *Reform Judaism* 3 (October 1974): 1, 4.

20.   On the CCAR and UAHC responses to the birth of Israel, see *YBCCAR* 58 (1948): 93–95. Also *Liberal Judaism* 15, no. 1 (June–July 1948): 1–4, 37.

21.   Harry Essrig and Jack Segal, *Israel Today* (New York, 1964). *YBCCAR* 80 (1970): 39. See also *YBCCAR* 79 (1969): 141–42.

22.   On Reform Judaism in Israel, see Michael Langer, ed., *A Reform Zionist Perspective* (New York: UAHC, 1977).

23.   For two arguments against congregational democracy, see Selig Adler, "Toward a Conservative Philosophy," *United Synagogue Review* 13, no. 1 (Spring 1960): 4–5, and Samuel Z. Klausner, "Synagogues in Transition: A Planning Prospectus," *Conservative Judaism* 25, no. 1 (Fall 1970): 42–54. In the former, Adler argues that such democracy leads only to "anarchy in both belief and practice," while in the latter Klausner argues that the "allocation of synagogue power to a few is a necessary reward for maintaining loyalty, leadership and financial support."

24.   On day schools and *havurot,* see David Cohen, *American Reform Judaism and the Jewish Day School* (New York: World Union for Progressive Judaism, 1982). Lawrence Kushner, "The Post-Synagogue Synagogue," *CCAR Journal* 22, no. 2 (Spring, 1975): 45–55. Arnold Jacob Wolf, "Three *Havurot:* Our Best Hope," *CCAR Journal* 22, no. (Winter 1975): 34–36.

25.   *YBCCAR* 5651 (1890–1891): 13, 26–27.

26.   *YBCCAR* 5651 (1890–1891): 29; *YBCCAR* 5653 (1892–1893): 96–100.

27.   *Union Prayer Book,* vol. II (Cincinnati: CCAR, 1895), p. 255, or II (Cincinnati: CCAR, 1940), p. 273.

28.   *Union Prayer Book,* Vol. I (New York: CCAR, 1918), passim.

29.   *Union Prayer Book,* Vol. II (1895), pp. 33, 193, 238–39, 329.

30.   Arnold Jacob Wolf, "A More Traditional and Radical Prayer Book," in Bemporad, *Theological Foundations,* pp. 92–100. Alan S. Green, "Religious Services—How Can We Make Them More Meaningful?" *YBCCAR* 58 (1948): 239–40. Alan S. Green, interview with Marc Lee Raphael, December 1975. Joseph Baron criticized the *Union Prayer Book* in this manner in 1933; see *YBCCAR* 43 (1933): 87–88.

31.   In 1948 Rabbi Alan S. Green urged the Central Conference of American Rabbis to make

the "special services composed around different central themes by many of our men" available to the rabbinate; see *YBCCAR* 58 (1948): 244.

32. Jacob K. Shankman, "The Changing Role of the Rabbi," in Korn ed., *Retrospect and Prospect*, pp. 232–33.
33. *YBCCAR* 88 (1978): 3; 91 (1981): 295–347.
34. *YBCCAR* 32 (1922): 51, 163–77; 65 (1955): p. 14. For the opposition of some sisterhood members, see *American Judaism* 7, no. 3 (January 1958): 21.
35. Theodore I. Lenn and associates, *Rabbi and Synagogue in Reform Judaism* (New York: CCAR, 1972), pp. 51–52.
36. *YBCCAR* 13 (1903): 48.
37. Meyer, "A Centennial History," p. 324.
38. *YBCCAR* 86 (1976): 174–78.
39. For a discussion of the dimensions, and quality, of the religious revival, see Winthrop S. Hudson, "Are the Churches Really Booming?" *Christian Century* 72 (1955): 1494–96. Eugene Carson Blake, "Is the Religious Boom a Spiritual Bust?" *Look*, 20 September 1955, pp. 27–31. Editorial, "The Danger of Relying on Religious Polls," *Reconstructionist*, 21, no. 1, 18 February 1955, pp. 6–7. Arthur Hertzberg, "American Judaism: A Balance Sheet," *Judaism* 3, no. 2 (Spring 1954): 110–17. Will Herberg, "Religious Trends in American Jewry," *Judaism* 3, no. 3 (Summer 1954): 229–40. Will Herberg, "America's New Religiousness: A Way of Belonging," *Commentary* 20 (September 1955): 240–47. Will Herberg, "The 'Triple Melting Pot': The Third Generation—From Ethnic to Religious Diversity," *Commentary* 20 (August 1955): 101–08. *American Judaism* 5, no. 2 (1955): 3, 5–6, 7.
40. UAHC, *Annual Reports*. *American Judaism* 15, no. 1 (Fall 1965): 28; 6, no. 2 (1956): 17, 18. New York *Times*, 5 April 1959, p. 80; *American Jewish Year Book* 56 (1955): 231; 57 (1956): 191. For a detailed discussion of postwar synagogue growth in the UAHC, see David Abarbanel, "Liberal Synagogue Triumphant," *Liberal Judaism* 16, no. 1 (June–July 1948): 5–20; 16, no. 2 (August–September 1948): 15–26.
41. *American Judaism* 5, no. 4 (1956): 22. *American Jewish Year Book* 57 (1956): 188; 56 (1955): 247. Temple Isaiah (Los Angeles), *Bulletin*, 1955–1956. Congregation Rodef Sholem (Pittsburgh), *Bulletin*, 1956–1957. The figures on Jewish affiliation announced each year by the National Council of Churches of Christ are completely unreliable; they equated affiliation with synagogues with the number of Jews in communities! See New York *Times*, 10 September 1956, p. 1.
42. *Liberal Judaism* 18, no. 2 (September 1950): 4. *American Judaism* 7, no. 1 (1957): 3. On the UAHC move from Cincinnati to New York City, see Maurice N. Eisendrath, "Shall New York Be Home of UAHC?" *Liberal Judaism* 15, no. 10 (April–May 1948): 8–13, 41–44 (twelve reasons why the UAHC should relocate); 16, no. 3 (October 1948): 38–41.
43. New York *Times*, 14 June 1959, p. 82; 19 June 1959, p. 12.
44. *American Judaism* 6, no. 1 (1956): 20; 6, no. 2 (1956): 13; 9, no. 3 (1960): 4; 10, no. 4 (1961): 8; 15, no. 2 (1965–1966): 8. *YBCCAR* 71 (1961): 143–144. The 1959 biennial also declared its strong opposition to the testing of nuclear weapons, while the 1965 biennial in San Francisco urged an immediate withdrawal from Vietnam, an end to nuclear testing, and a "systematic, enforceable, general and complete disarmament."
45. *American Judaism* 11, no. 1 (1961): 24; 12, no. 2 (1962–1963): 8.
46. Sanford Seltzer, "The Changing Character of Reform Worship Patterns," typescript, UAHC, 838 Fifth Ave, New York, NY 10021, p. 2.
47. UAHC, 838 Fifth Ave., New York, NY 10021, Commission on Social Action of Reform Judaism, "This and That" [#1–84], passim.
48. This, and the subsequent six paragraphs, are based on Meyer, "A Centennial History," pp. 123–127, 179, 181, 218, 225, 240.
49. *YBCCAR* 91 (1981): 251–53.
50. *YBCCAR* 91 (1981): 273–93. "Report of the Committee on Patrilineal Descent on the

Status of Children of Mixed Marriages," (CCAR, 21 East 40th, New York, NY 10016) 15 March 1983.

51. *YBCCAR* 60 (1950); 80–98. *Liberal Judaism* 18, no. 3 (December 1950): 5. Roland Gittelsohn, "Wanted: The Rabbi," *Liberal Judaism* 17, no. 3 (December 1949): 34–35, 42. *YBCCAR* 71 (1961): 77–105.

52. *YBCCAR* 19 (1909): 170; 57 (1947): 161, 183; 70 (1960): 135–36, 139; 71 (1961): 11; 72 (1962): 86–87, 89, 93–105; 83 (1973): 97. See also Bernard Bamberger, "Mixed Marriages: Some Reflections on a Debate," *CCAR Journal* 11, no. 1 (April 1963): 19–22. Charles E. Schulman, "Mixed Marriage, Conversion, and Reality," *CCAR Journal* 11, no. 4 (January 1964): 27–32. "Report of the Committee on Mixed Marriages," *YBCCAR* 82 (1972): 65,91.

53. Harvey Fields, "Mixed Marriage and the CCAR," *CCAR Journal* 19, no. 2 (April 1972): 65.

54. *YBCCAR* 62 (1952): 45; 64 (1954): 22; 65 (1955): 19–22.

CHAPTER 4

1. Solomon Schechter, "The United Synagogue of America," address delivered at the 1913 convention, in United Synagogue of America, *Report* ([New York], 1913), p. 17. Louis Finkelstein, chancellor of the Jewish Theological Seminary for three decades, placed the "true roots" of Conservative Judaism two millenia earlier than did Schechter—in the era of Hillel, Yochanan ben Zakkai, and Akiba; see "The Gaze Within: The Ideals of the Founders," *Judaism* 26, no. 3 (Summer 1977): 265.

2. Gilbert Rosenthal, *Four Paths to One God: Today's Jew and His Religion* (New York: Bloch Pub. Co., 1973), p. 150.

3. *Occident* 9 (1851–1852): 212–13; 2 (1844–1845): 152. Henry Englander, "Isaac Leeser," *YBCCAR* 28 (1918): 213. Lance Jonathan Sussman, "Confidence in God: The Life and Preaching of Isaac Leeser, the Most Important Jewish Religious Leader in Antebellum America," unpublished master's thesis, Hebrew Union College, 1980, p. i.

4. Englander, "Leeser," p. 244. Sussman, "Confidence in God," p. 169. *Occident* 3 (1845–1946): 66–67f., 74–75 f., 116–117 f., 153, 486–487 f.; 1 (1843–1844): 20; 19 (1861–1862): 152. Moshe Davis,*The Emergence of Conservative Judaism: The Historical School in Nineteenth Century America* (Philadelphia: Jewish Publication Society, 1963), p. 132. Bertram W. Korn, "Isaac Leeser: Centennial Reflections," *American Jewish Archives* 19, no. 2 (November 1967): 127–41. *American Israelite,* 14 February 1968. Davis argues that the roots of twentieth-century Conservatism are in nineteenth-century Orthodoxy, and thus he makes "orthodox" leaders the forerunners of Conservative Judaism.

5. Letter, Benjamin Szold to Isaac Mayer Wise, 12 November 1859, *American Israelite* 6 (1860): 165. Kurt Wilhelm, "Benjamin Szold and the Rabbinical Post in Stockholm in 1858," *Historia Judaica* 15 (1953): 52–53.

6. Davis, *Conservative Judaism,* pp. 142–44. Minute Books, Oheb Shalom, 15 August 1879, at American Jewish Archives, 3101 Clifton Ave, Cincinnati, Oh 45220. Benjamin Szold, *Outlines of the System of Judaism, Designed as a Religious Manual for the Instruction of the Israelitish Youth,* 3rd ed. (Baltimore: Oheb Shalom, 1874), p. 10. "Congregations Comprising the UAHC, 1885–1886," UAHC, 838 Fifth Ave., New York, NY 10021, *Annual Report 1886.* Fein, *The Making of an American Jewish Community,* pp. 183–184.

7. Henry Samuel Morais, *The Jews of Philadelphia: Their History From the Earliest Settlements to the Present Time* (Philadelphia: Levytype Co., 1894), p. 76. Marcus Jastrow, *A Warning Voice: Farewell Sermon Delivered on the Occasion of his Retirement* [27 November 1892] (Philadelphia: n.p., 1892), p. 6. Henry Berkowitz, "Notes on the History of the Earliest German Jewish Congregation in America," *Publications of the American Jewish Historical Society* 9 (1901): 127. Rodef Shalom Congregation, Minutes for 27 March 1892, p. 328, American Jewish Archives, 3101 Clifton Ave., Cincinnati, OH 45220.

8. Barnett A. Elzas, "Memoir of Alexander Kohut," in Alexander Kohut, *The Ethics of*

the Fathers (New York: Publishers Printing Co., 1920), pp. ix–li. Kohut, *Ethics,* pp. 7, 9, 48. *American Hebrew,* 7 January 1887, p. 136.

9. *Jewish Messenger* 38 (12 November 1875): 5; 19 November 1876, p. 4, 26 November 1876, p. 5; 3 December 1876, p. 5; 10 December 1876, p. 5. H. Pereira Mendes, "The Beginnings of the Jewish Theological Seminary," in Cyrus Adler, ed., *The Jewish Theological Seminary of America: Semi-Centennial Volume* (New York: Jewish Theological Seminary of America, 1939), p. 37. Simon Greenberg, "The Jewish Theological Seminary: An Evaluation," in Rabbinical Assembly, *Proceedings* 24 (1960): 118.

10. Jewish Theological Seminary Association (JTSA), *Proceedings of the First Biennial Convention 1888* (New York: Jewish Theological Seminary, 1888), pp. 3–12. *American Hebrew,* 25 March 1898, p. 612. Bernard Drachman, *The Unfailing Light: Memoirs of an American Rabbi* (New York: Rabbinical Council of America, 1948), p. 181. Mordecai Waxman, "Conservative Judaism—A Survey," in Mordecai Waxman, ed., *Tradition and Change: The Development of Conservative Judaism* (New York: Burning Bush Press, 1958), p. 8. Joseph Lookstein, "The View from the Right: A Critique and a Plea," *Judaism* 26, no. 3 (Summer 1977): 326–7. Schechter, "The United Synagogue," p. 18. Hyman Solomon, "History of the Seminary," in JTS, *Students' Annual 1914* (New York: Jewish Theological Seminary, 1914), pp. 17–21. Simon Greenberg argues that Schechter himself, like Morais, only wanted the seminary to occupy a "conservative position" and embody "the spirit of Conservative Judaism," but not be transformed into a denominational school with a capital "C." See Greenberg, "The Jewish Theological Seminary," p. 121.

11. *American Hebrew,* 15 April 1892, p. 202. Davis, *Conservative Judaism,* p. 239. JTSA, *Constitution and By-Laws* (New York: Jewish Theological Seminary, 1914). Henry Speaker, a student at the early seminary, argued in 1893 that the school was founded to combat Reform Judaism and affirm "Tradition"; see *American Hebrew,* 3 February 1893, p. 460.

12. Gotthard Deutsch, "Zachariah Frankel," *The Menorah* 21 (November 1901): 329–48. Deutsch makes an interesting, but generally unsuccessful, effort to link Frankel's love of historic Judaism to his youth in "old historic Prague."

13. David Rudavsky, *Emancipation and Adjustment: Contemporary Jewish Religious Movements—Their History and Thought* (New York: Behrman House, 1967), pp. 192–213. Michael A. Meyer, "Jewish Religious Reform and Wissenschaft des Judentums: The Positions of Zunz, Geiger and Frankel," *Year Book of the Leo Baeck Institute* 16 (1971): 19–41. Louis Ginzberg, *Students, Scholars and Saints* (Philadelphia: Jewish Publication Society, 1943), pp. 195–216. Joseph L. Blau, *Modern Varieties of Judaism* (New York: Columbia University Press, 1966), pp. 91–101. Plaut, *Rise,* pp. 24–25. Zacharias Frankel, "On Changes in Judaism" (1845), in Waxman, ed., *Tradition and Change,* pp. 43–50.

14. Plaut, *Rise,* pp. 85–90, 162–163. Ginzberg, *Students,* p. 197. Ismar Schorsch, "Zacharias Frankel and the European Origins of Conservative Judaism," *Judaism* 30, no. 3 (Summer 1981): 344–54. Robert Gordis, "Reform and Conservative Judaism—Their Mutual Relationship," *YBCCAR* 61 (1951): 267–69. Frankel used the expression "positive historical" even before Frankfort; see Meyer, "Jewish Religious Reform," p. 33.

15. Plaut, *Rise,* pp. 80–90. Kaufmann Kohler, "Zacharias Frankel," *The Menorah* 21 (November 1901): 364–166.

16. Kohut's statement is from *American Hebrew,* 5 February 1886, p. 194, and is quoted in Davis, *Conservative Judaism,* p. 17, while Morais's statements are in Davis, p. 235, and in Sabato Morais, "A Jewish Theological Seminary," in Waxman, ed., *Tradition and Change,* p. 149. Cyrus Adler, *Lectures, Selected Papers and Addresses* (Philadelphia: Priv. print., 1933), pp. 257–263. *American Hebrew,* 4 July 1902, p. 184; 4 April 1902, pp. 597–601. JTSA (3080 Broadway, New York, NY 10027), *Biennial Report 1900,* p. 20. Elias Solomon, "Chief Rabbi Joseph Herman Hertz," *Conservative Judaism* 2, no. 4 (June 1946): 29–39. Bernard Drachman agreed with Adler that the seminary was established as a response to "Radical Reform"; see Drachman, *Unfailing Light,* p. 185.

17. *American Hebrew,* 2 February 1891, p. 41. Cyrus Adler, *I Have Considered the Days*

(Philadelphia: Jewish Publication Society, 1941), pp. 243–44. JTSA, *Proceedings of the Eighth Biennial Convention 1902* (New York: Jewish Theological Seminary, 1904), pp. 9–28. *American Hebrew,* 8 March 1902, p. 484. In addition to Schiff, who pledged $175,000, the included benefactors included Felix M. Warburg ($15,000), James Loeb ($15,000), Simon ($12,500) and Daniel ($12,500) Guggenheim, Emanuel Lehman ($10,-000), and Adolph Lewisohn ($10,000). See *The Jewish Theological Seminary of America: Documents, Charter and By-Laws* (New York: Jewish Theological Seminary, 1903), p. 21. Most of these men eventually gave amounts far in excess of these initial pledges.

18. Letter, Solomon Schechter to Dr. Raisin, 10 February 1905, quoted in Bernard Mandelbaum, "A Special Ingredient—The Heritage of Solomon Schechter," Rabbinical Assembly, *Proceedings* 27 (1963), p. 5.

19. Solomon Schechter, "The Assistance of the Public," in Solomon Schechter, *Seminary Addresses and Other Papers* (New York: Burning Bush Press, 1959), p. 232. Letter, Solomon Schechter to Alexander Marx, 29 July 1907, quoted in Mandelbaum, "Special Ingredient," p. 8.

20. Letter, Solomon Schechter to Cyrus Adler, 10 September 1901, quoted in Mandelbaum, "Special Ingredient," p. 9. Solomon Schechter, "The Seminary as Witness," in Schechter, *Seminary Addresses,* p. 48. Schechter, "The Building in America," in Schechter, *Seminary Addresses,* p. 85. *Yiddishes Tageblatt,* 11 July 1904 (English page). *American Hebrew,* 15 July 1904, p. 204. Aaron Rothkoff, "The American Sojourn of Ridbaz: Religious Problems within the Immigrant Community," *Publications of the American Jewish Historical Society* 57, no. 4 (June 1968): 557–72. Seymour Siegel, "Solomon Schechter: His Contribution to Modern Jewish Thought," Rabbinical Assembly, *Proceedings* 39 (1977): 44.

21. Letter, Solomon Schechter to Harry Friedenwald, 8 April 1907, quoted in Mandelbaum, "Special Ingredient," p. 11. Letter, Solomon Schechter to Harry Friedenwald, 7 November 1913, quoted in Mandelbaum, "Special Ingredient," p. 11. See also Bernard Mandelbaum, "The Maturing of the Conservative Movement," *Conservative Judaism* 21, no. 3 (Spring 1967): 54–64. Bernard Mandelbaum, "Solomon Schechter: Man and Vision," *Conservative Judaism,* 26, no. 2 (Winter 1972): 46–54.

22. Solomon Schechter, "The Charter," p. 12. Solomon Schechter, *Studies in Judaism,* 1st Series (Philadelphia: Jewish Publication Society, 1911), p. xix.

23. Solomon Schechter, "The Study of the Bible," in Solomon Schechter, *Studies in Judaism,* 2nd Series (Philadelphia: Jewish Publication Society, 1908), pp. 31–54: Solomon Schechter, "The History of Jewish Tradition," in Solomon Schechter, *Studies in Judaism: A Selection* (New York and Philadelphia: Meridian and Jewish Publication Society, 1960), p. 26. Schechter, *Studies,* 1st Series, p. xviii. Schechter, *Studies,* 2nd Series, p. 116. Herbert Parzen, "An Estimate of the Leadership of Dr. Solomon Schechter," *Conservative Judaism* 5, no. 3 (April 1949): 16–27. For an interesting attempt to reinterpret Schechter's theory of authority being vested in *klal yisrael* in practical terms, see Robert Gordis, *Judaism for the Modern Age* (New York: Farrar, Strauss and Cudahy, 1955), pp. 127–85.

24. Herman Rubenovitz, "The Birth of the United Synagogue," *Review* (United Synagogue of America, or USA) 16, no. 2 (Summer 1963): 10–11, 16, no. 3 (Autumn 1963): 8–9. Herman H. Rubenovitz and Mignon L. Rubenovitz, *The Waking Heart* (Cambridge, Mass.: N. Dame, 1967), pp. 35–47, 124–33. Cyrus Adler, "Report of the President," in USA, *Fourth Annual Report* (New York, 1917), p. 16. Adler, "Solomon Schechter," *American Jewish Year Book* 5677 (1916–1917): 61. Rabbi Solomon Goldman dated the beginning of Conservative Judaism in America to the founding of the United Synagogue of America, in *A Rabbi Takes Stock* (New York: Harper and Brothers, 1931), p. 3, as did Simon Noveck in Simon Greenberg, *The Conservative Movement in Judaism: An Introduction* (New York: United Synagogue of America, 1955), p. ii. The founding congregations, of course, were Orthodox, but they were united in their common desire to seek English-speaking rabbis trained in America.

25. *Report* (USA) (1913), p. 9. Herbert Rosenblum, "Ideology and Compromise: The Evolu-

tion of the United Synogogue Constitutional Preamble," *Jewish Social Studies* 35, no. 1 (January 1973): 18–31.

26. Schechter, "The United Synagogue," pp. 14–23.

27. Schechter, "The United Synagogue," pp. 18, 20, 23.

28. Max Drob, "President's Message," in Rabbinical Assembly, *Proceedings* 2 (1928), p. 23. Lloyd P. Gartner, *History of the Jews of Cleveland* (Cleveland: Western Reserve Historical Society, 1978), pp. 167–69.

29. *The History of Temple Adath Yeshurun of Syracuse, New York* (Syracuse: Adath Yeshurun, n.d.), p. 8. B. G. Rudolph, *From Minyan to a Community: A History of the Jews of Syracuse* (Syracuse: Syracuse University, 1970), pp. 72–74, 202–207. Mark H. Elovitz, "A History of the Jews of Birmingham 1871–1971," unpublished doctoral dissertation, New York University, 1973. *The Anshe Emeth Synagogue, 1873–1973* (Chicago: Anshe Emeth, n.d.), p. 8. Hyman L. Meites, ed., *History of the Jews of Chicago* (Chicago: Jewish Historical Society of Illinois, 1924), p. 485. Bernard Shuman, *A History of the Sioux City Jewish Community* (Sioux City: Jewish Federation, 1969), p. 47. *Bulletin* (Temple of Aaron), 29, no. 10 (18 October 1956): 1, quoted in W. Gunther Plaut, *The Jews in Minnesota: The First Seventy-Five Years* (New York: American Jewish Historical Society, 1959), p. 199. Edward Marx, "I Remember Beth El in the 1900s," in *Congregation Beth El* (Norfolk: Beth El, n.d.). *Recorder* (USA) 7, no. 1 (January 1927): 21.

30. Herman H. Rubenovitz, "My Rabbinate at Temple Mishkan Tefila," in *Temple Mishkan Tefilah: A History 1858–1958* (Newton, Mass.: Mishkan Tefilah, 1958), pp. 19–29. Rubenovitz, *The Waking Heart*, p. 34. *Ohio Jewish Chronicle*, 6 June 1922; 4 November 1922; 8 July 1924; 30 July 1926; and especially 25 June 1926 ("The Need of a Conservative Jewish Congregation in Columbus"). Temple Beth El, "Our First Fifty Years" (n.p.: Temple Beth El, n.d.). USA, *Sixth Annual Report* (New York, 1919), p. 33. *Recorder* (USA) 7, no. 4 (October 1927): 19. See also *Temple Beth Shalom, 1922–1972* (Wilmington, Delaware: Beth Shalom, n.d.), p. [13].

31. The most widely used prayer books during this period were *Song and Praise for Sabbath Eve*, ed. Israel Goldfarb and Israel Levinthal (Brooklyn: n.p. 1920, 1930, 1938, 1952); *Sabbath Prayers*, edited by Jacob Bosniak (Brooklyn: Prayer Book Publishing, 1925), and the Bloch Publishing Company's *Standard Mahzor* (New York: Bloch Pub. Co., n.d.).

    By the 1950s and 1960s, when fewer and fewer Conservative Jews worked on Saturday, there were generally successful efforts to minimize the Friday evening service and to emphasize that of Saturday morning. Typical was Adolph G. Kraus, "Back to the Sabbath," *Review* (USA) 15, no. 2 (Summer 1962): 12–13.

32. USA, *Recorder* 5, no. 3 (July 1925): 1. Louis Levitsky, "Conduct of Religious Services," in Rabbinical Assembly, *Proceedings* I (1927), pp. 77–88. *Recorder* (USA) 6, no. 1 (January 1926): 19–26, 34–35. Jakob J. Petuchowski, "Conservatism: Its Contribution to Judaism," *Judaism* 26, no. 3 (Summer 1977): 352.

33. Jacob J. Weinstein, *Solomon Goldman: A Rabbi's Rabbi* (New York: Ktav, 1973), pp. 12–16.

34. Eli Ginzberg, *Keeper of the Law: Louis Ginzberg* (Philadelphia: Jewish Publication Society, 1966), pp. 148–49. Goldman, *A Rabbi Takes Stock*, p. 4. Robert Gordis, "The Tasks Before Us," *Conservative Judaism* 1, no. 1 (January 1945): pp. 8–11. Rabbinical Assembly, *Proceedings* 12 (1948), p. 110. Morris Adler, "The Philosophy of the Conservative Movement," *Review* (USA) 16, no. 4 (Winter 1964): 25.

35. Hillel E. Silverman, "Conservative Judaism Faces the Seventies," Rabbinical Assembly, *Proceedings* 34 (1970), pp. 110–11, 113. Benjamin Z. Kreitman, "Conservative Judaism—The Next Step," *Review* (USA) 27, no. 3 (Winter 1975): 6–7, 24–25. David Lieber, "Staking Out the Conservative Position," *Conservative Judaism* 32, no. 1 (Fall 1978): 34.

    Two dedicated rabbinic leaders of the movement who scored the lack of "basic principles for our movement" and the "vagueness of the ideology" were Louis M. Epstein, in Rabbinical Assembly, *Proceedings* 12 (1948), p. 169, and Aaron H. Blumenthal, in Rabbinical Assembly, *Proceedings* 19 (1955), p. 128, while more recently a president of the United Synagogue called for the Conservative movement to "define the minimal obligations for those who will join us," in Arthur J. Levine, "Needed—A Definition," *Judaism* 26, no. 3 (Summer 1977): 295.

Harold S. Kushner, of Natick's Temple Israel, defended what some called "the ideological emptiness of our movement, in "Is the Conservative Movement Halakhic?" Rabbinical Assembly, *Proceedings* 42 (1980), pp. 365. Ben Zion Bokser defended the "diversity" of the movement, in "The American Jewish Community," *Review* (USA) 23, no. 2 (Spring [sic] 1970): 7–9, 25. Norman Salit argued that "our lack of definition" is "our greatest strength," *Recorder* (USA) 4, no. 4 (October 1924): 12. Stanley Rabinowitz has argued that Conservative Judaism's "diversity" demonstrates its "ability to embrace not contradictory, but alternative, positions," in "Where Do We Stand Now?" *Judaism* 26, no. 3 (Summer 1977): 274.

36. Mordecai M. Kaplan, "Unity in Diversity in the Conservative Movement," in Waxman, ed., *Tradition and Change*, p. 212. Adler, *Letters*, p. 261.

37. Max Arzt, "Conservative Judaism," in Theodore Friedman, comp., *What Is Conservative Judaism?* (New York: Horizon Press, [1955]?), p. 63.

38. Goldman, *A Rabbi Takes Stock*, p. 102.

39. Schechter, "The History of Jewish Tradition," p. 26. Israel Friedlander, *Past and Present* (Cincinnati: Ark Pub. Co., 1919), pp. ix–x. Louis Ginzberg, "Address of the Acting President," in USA, *Sixth Annual Report*, pp. 10–27. This tension, between change and tradition, or being both "mobile" and "static," is highlighted in Selig Adler, "Toward a Conservative Philosophy," *Review* (USA) 13, no. 1 (Spring 1960): 4.

40. USA, *Fifth Annual Report* (New York, 1918), pp. 43, 45, 49.

41. USA, *Sixth Annual Report*, p. 19. Morris S. Goodblatt, "Synagogue Ritual Survey," in Rabbinical Assembly, *Proceedings* 12 (1948), pp. 105–09. Goodblatt noted that 20 percent of the congregations used an organ during Sabbath services.

42. Greenberg, *Conservative Movement*, p. 27.

43. See, for example, the immediate rejection by Eugene Kohn and Max Kadushin of Louis Finkelstein's attempt to lay out the "basic agreement in essentials"; Rabbinical Assembly, *Proceedings* 1 (1927), pp. 54–60, 60–66. Kohn did not feel that Finkelstein proved there was agreement, while Kadushin felt that Finkelstein only stated what was "personal and valid for him," not for "us."

Several attempts, in addition to that of Finkelstein, have been made over the years to articulate a set of fundamental principles of Conservative Judaism. They include the following: Kaplan, "Unity in Diversity," pp. 214–19. Adler, "Toward a Conservative Philosophy," pp. 4–5. "The Philosophy of the Conservative Movement," *Review* (USA) 16, no. 4 (Winter 1964): 7–8, 22–24. Meyer Waxman, "A Time of Great Vision," *Review* (USA) 30, no. 2 (Fall 1977): 4–5, 22–23. Elliot Dorff, "What Does It Mean to Be a Conservative Jew," *Review* (USA) 31, no. 2 (Winter 1979): 1, 10–11. Marshall Wolke, *Review* (USA) 34, no. 1 (Spring 1982): 7. And the earliest attempt by a non-JTS graduate, Jacob Agus, is *Guideposts in Modern Judaism* (New York: Bloch, 1954), pp. 85–137.

44. Seymour Siegel, "Approaches to Halachah in the Conservative Movement," in Rabbinical Assembly, *Proceedings* 42 (1980), pp. 398–402. A convenient summary of some conservative reflections on the nature of divinity is to be found in Rosenthal, *Four Paths*, pp. 176–80.

45. Wilfred Shuchat, "Towards a Philosophy of Conservative Judaism," in Rabbinical Assembly, *Proceedings* 42 (1980), p. 80.

46. Finkelstein, "The Things That Unite Us," p. 45. William Greenfield, "Towards a Philosophy of Conservative Judaism," in Rabbinical Assembly, *Proceedings* 12 (1948), p. 127.

47. Abraham Joshua Heschel, *God in Search of Man* (New York: Harper and Row, 1955), pp. 180, 244, 245, 265. Gilbert S. Rosenthal, "The Foundations of the Conservative Approach to Jewish Law," in Rabbinical Assembly, *Proceedings* 42 (1980), p. 376. David Novak, "The Distinctiveness of Conservative Judaism," *Judaism* 26, no. 3 (Summer 1977): 307–08. Ernst Simon, "Torat Hayyim: Some Thoughts on the Teaching of the Bible," *Conservative Judaism* 12, no. 3 (Spring 1958): 3–4. Simon Greenberg, "Some

Guiding Principles for a Conservative Approach to Judaism," Rabbinical Assembly, *Proceedings* 21 (1957), p. 93. An early example of this position among Conservative thinkers comes from Jacob Kohn of New York's Anshe Chesed, "Reflections of Need of a Theory of Revelation to Establish the Authority of the Torah," in Jewish Theological Seminary, *Students' Annual 1914*, pp. 201–10.

48. Ben Zion Bokser, *Judaism: Profile of a Faith* (New York: Knopf, 1963), pp. 68–70, 273–74. Ben Zion Bokser, "The Interaction of History and Theology," *Judaism* 26, no. 3 (Summer 1977): 321. Ben Zion Bokser, "The Election of Israel," *Conservative Judaism* 3, no. 4 (July 1947): 17–25. Other examples of this position are found in Will Herberg, *Judaism and Modern Man* (New York: Farrar, Straus, and Young, 1951), p. 246 ("Revelation is *the self-disclosure of God in his dealings with the world.* Scripture is not itself revelation but a humanly mediated record of revelation"). Isaac Klein, "The Law: A Conservative View," *Review* (USA) 19, no. 3 (October 1966): 4. Elliot N. Dorff, "Revelation," *Conservative Judaism* 31, nos. 1–2 (Fall–Winter 1967): 58–69. Agus, *Guideposts,* pp. 89–90. Jacob Agus, "Torah M'Sinai—A Conservative View," *Conservative Judaism* 3, no. 2 (February 1947): 23–42; 4, no. 2 (February 1948): 2–4. In the last citation, Agus explores the idea that revelation consists of "three progressively higher levels, including "intuition" and "feeling."

49. Abraham J. Karp, "Toward a Theology for Conservative Judaism," *Conservative Judaism* 10, no. 4 (Summer 1954): 14–21. See Louis Jacobs, *A Jewish Theology* (New York: Behrman, 1973), pp. 199–210, especially p. 206.

50. Ben Zion Bokser, *Jewish Law: A Conservative Approach* (New York: Burning Bush Press, 1964), pp. 12–13.

51. Solomon Schecter, *Studies in Judaism,* 1st Series, pp. xix–xxii. Schechter, *Studies,* 2nd Series, p. 116. Greenfield, "Towards a Philosophy of Conservative Judaism," p. 123. Drob, "President's Message," p. 21. Rabbinical Assembly, *Proceedings* 12 (1948), pp. 171–72. Jacob Agus, "Halacah in the Conservative Movement," Rabbinical Assembly, *Proceedings* 38 (1975), pp. 102–17. See especially the old committee's final report in Rabbinical Assembly, *Proceedings* 11 (1947), pp. 54–63, 64–73. Each year the Rabbinical Assembly president appoints (or reappoints) five men to serve a five-year term on the Committee on Jewish Law and Standards (CJLS).

52. Kohut, *Ethics of the Fathers,* pp. 15–17. Rabbinical Assembly, *Proceedings 1933–38* (New York, 1939), pp. 432–34, and [vol.] 12 (1948), p. 152. In 1970, the expanded CJLS would face its own crisis and see sixteen members resign over the alleged power of a minority position; see "The Open Forum: Further Thoughts on the Law Committee," *Conservative Judaism* 26, no. 2 (Winter 1972): 60–84, and, especially, Robert Gordis "Toward a Revitalization of Halachah in Conservative Judaism," *Conservative Judaism* 25, no. 3 (Spring 1971): 49–55. The result was to give "official sanction" to "innovative practices" when three-fourths (family and personal status practices) or even two-thirds (personal observance) of the law committee approved, and to grant the status of "legitimate option" to liturgical and synagogue practices when only one-third approved.

53. "Responsum on the Sabbath," Rabbinical Assembly, *Proceedings* 14 (1950), pp. 112–88. *Conservative Judaism* 14, no. 3 (Spring 1960): 50.

54. Rabbinical Assembly, *Proceedings* 22 (1958), pp. 71–72. Benjamin S. Kreitman, "Updating Jewish Laws of Marriage and Divorce," *Review* (USA) 21, no. 4 (January 1969): 8–9, 28–30.

55. Robert Gordis, *Conservative Judaism: A Modern Approach to Jewish Tradition* (New York: Behrman, 1970), pp. 28–29. Benjamin Kreitman, "Toward a Creative Halachah," *Conservative Judaism* 22, no. 1 (Fall 1967): 34–41. For a striking controversy over mixed pews in Cincinnati's Adath Israel, and the impact of "sociological conditions" on *halachic* principles, see *Conservative Judaism* 11, no. 1 (Fall 1956): 1–73.

56. Kushner, "Is the Conservative Movement Halakhic?" p. 368.

57. Greenberg, *The Conservative Movement,* pp. 22–25. Gordis, *Conservative Judaism,* pp. 27–28. Greenberg, "Guiding Principles," p. 123. Bokser, "Doctrine of the Chosen People," *Contemporary Jewish Record* 4, no. 3 (June 1941): 252. Finkelstein, "The Things

That Unite Us," p. 51. For a view similar to that of Greenberg and Finkelstein, see Julius Greenstone, "The Election of Israel," *Conservative Judaism* 1, no. 2 (June 1945): 27–30.

58. USA, *Annual Reports 1913–1919*, p. 21. Marcus Jastrow, "Zionism and Its Critics," *Maccabean* 11 (October 1901): 23. Julius H. Greenstone, "Reminiscences of Old Seminary Days," *Recorder* (USA) 2, no. 1. (January 1922): 9. Robert E. Fierstien, "Solomon Schechter and the Zionist Movement," *Conservative Judaism* 29, no. 3 (Spring 1975): 3–13. *American Hebrew*, 15 October 1897, p. 712; 22 October 1897, p. 744. Herbert Parzen, "Conservative Judaism and Zionism (1896–1922)," *Jewish Social Studies* 23, no. 4 (October 1961): 237–38. *American Hebrew*, 10 March 1899, p. 653. *Students' Annual 1914*, pp. 52–57.

59. Solomon Schechter, "Zionism: A Statement," in Schechter, *Seminary Addresses*, pp. 91–104. Norman Bentwich, *Solomon Schechter: A Biography* (Philadelphia: Jewish Publication Society, 1940), p. 312. Louis Lipsky, "Early Days of American Zionism," *Palestine Yearbook* 2 (1946): 451, quoted in Simcha Kling, "Zionism in the Early Days of Conservative Judaism," in Arthur A. Chiel, ed., *Perspectives on Jews and Judaism: Essays in Honor of Wolfe Kelman* (New York: Rabbinical Assembly, 1978), *p. 263*. Evyatar Friesel, *The Zionist Movement in the United States* (Tel Aviv: Tel Aviv University, 1970), in Hebrew, pp. 77–80. An early example of the Zionist inclinations of a seminary student is the essay by Meyer Waxman, "The Importance of Palestine for the Jews of the Diaspora," *Maccabean* 23, no. 8 (August 1913): 232–36.

60. Friedlander, *Past and Present*, pp. 470–71. Finkelstein, "The Things That Unite Us," p. 51. Rabbinical Assembly, *Proceedings* 1 (1927), p. 33. Stuart E. Rosenberg, "The Conservative Movement and Zionism," *Review* (USA) 11, no. 4 (Winter 1959): 16–17. Solomon B. Freehof, "Reform Judaism and Zionism," *Menorah Journal* 32, no. 1 (April–June 1944): 26–41. For an example of one early JTS graduate's commitment to Zionism, see the essays under "Zionist" in Israel Goldstein's *Toward a Solution* (New York: G.P. Putnam's Sons, 1940), pp. 165–183.

61. Friedlander, *Past and Present*, p. 272. Mordecai M. Kaplan, "The Future of Judaism," *Menorah Journal* 2, no. 3 (June 1916): 170 ("The synagogue . . . should become a social centre where the Jews of the neighborhood may find every possible opportunity to give expression to their social and play instincts"). Mordecai M. Kaplan, "Where Does Jewry Really Stand Today?" *Menorah Journal* 4, no. 1 (February 1918), especially 36–37. And Mordecai M. Kaplan, "Judaism as a Civilization," Rabbinical Assembly, *Proceedings* 2 (1928), pp. 115–30. For the impact of Kaplan on Conservative Judaism, see Myer S. Kripke, "Judaism as a Civilization: Its Enduring Impact," *Conservative Judaism* 34, no. 4 (March–April 1981): 17–23.

62. Israel Levinthal's quote is in Rabbinical Assembly, *Proceedings* 2 (1928), p. 65. See also *Recorder* (USA) 3, no. 1 (January 1923): 18; 3, no. 4 (October 1923): 15; 4, no. 2 (April 1924): 16; 4, no. 4 (October 1924): 22–23; 5, no. 1 (January 1925): 30; 5, no. 2 (April 1925): 15–17, 22; 5, no. 3 (July 1925): 20–22, 23; 6, no. 1 (January 1926): 19, 22, 27; 7, no. 2 (April 1927): 24.

63. Samuel M. Cohen, "The Synagogue Center: Aim and Program," in Clifton Harby Levy, ed., *Problems of the Jewish Ministry* (New York: New York Board of Jewish Ministers, 1927), pp. 109–15. Israel Goldstein, "Inadequacies in the Status of the Synagogue Today," Rabbinical Assembly, *Proceedings* 2 (1928), pp. 32–40. Israel H. Levinthal, *Steering or Drifting—Which? Sermons and Discourses* (New York: Funk and Wagnalls, 1928), pp. 58–59, 63. Goldman, *A Rabbi Takes Stock*, p. 20.

64. Myer S. Kripke, "The Synagogue Center and the Jewish Center," *Conservative Judaism* 2, no. 3 (April 1946): 8–11. Aaron H. Blumenthal, "The Synagogue Center," *Conservative Judaism* 2, no. 3 (April 1946): 20–23. One of the leaders of the post–World War II revival of the synagogue-center was Simon Glustrom; see his "Some Aspects of a Surburban Jewish Community," *Conservative Judaism* 11, no. 2 (Winter 1957): 29 ("the synagogue-center [is] the hub of Jewish activity—religious, cultural, and social").

65. Kaplan, "Unity in Diversity," pp. 218–19, 221–26. See also *Conservative Judaism* 4, no. 1 (October 1947): 1–11.

66. Aaron H. Blumenthal, "An Aliyah for Women," in Rabbinical Assembly, *Proceedings* 19 (1955), pp. 168–81. Sanders A. Tofield, "Women's Place in the Rites of the Synagogue with Special Reference to Aliyah," Rabbinical Assembly, *Proceedings* 19 (1955), pp. 182–90. Bernard Mandelbaum, "Conservative Judaism: A Direction," *Conservative Judaism* 14, no. 1 (Fall 1959): 36–46. New York *Times,* 1 September 1973. *Review* (USA) 12, no. 2 (Summer 1959): 3.

67. Jordan Ofseyer, "Toward the Equality of Jewish Women," *Review* (USA) 26, no. 2 (Summer 1973): 8–9, 31. Alan Silverstein, "The Evolution of Ezrat Nashim," *Conservative Judaism* 30, no. 1 (Fall 1975): 41–51. "Women and Change in Jewish Law," *Conservative Judaism* 29, no. 1 (Fall 1974): 5–24. Jordan Ofseyer, "Why Not Women as Conservative Rabbis?" *Review* (USA) 29, no. 2 (Fall 1976): 6–7, 28, 30. "Women as Conservative Rabbis: Our Readers Respond," *Review* (USA) 29, no. 3 (April 1977): 16–17, 24, 26. Aaron H. Blumenthal, "The Status of Women in Jewish Law," *Conservative Judaism* 31, no. 3 (Spring 1977): 24–40. "The Woman's Role: A Continuing Discussion," *Conservative Judaism* 32, no. 1 (Fall 1978): 63–70. Gerson D. Cohen, "On the Ordination of Women," *Conservative Judaism* 32, no. 3 (Summer 1979): 56–62. "Final Report of the Commission for the Study of the Ordination of Women as Rabbis," *Conservative Judaism* 32, no. 3 (Summer 1979): 63–80. Los Angeles *Times,* 21 December 1979, pt. 1, p. 3. New York *Times,* 1 January 1980, p. 18; 23 March 1980, p. 40; 18 May 1980, p. 51; 9 August 1983, p. 12; 25 October 1983, p. 5.

CHAPTER 5

1. Jewish Theological Seminary of America (JTSA), *Proceedings of the Biennial Convention,* (New York: Jewish Theological Seminary) vols. 1–8 (1888–1902).
2. Drachman, *The Unfailing Light,* p. 220.
3. Rubenovitz, *The Waking Heart,* p. 7 (for a description of the interview and examination by Schechter). *American Hebrew,* 9 October 1891, p. 218; 20 April 1892, p. 84; 3 July 1892, pp. 84, 115, 155; 7 October 1898, p. 683; 3 August 1900, p. 324. For the five locations of the early seminary (1886–1903), see Drachman, *The Unfailing Light,* p. 222.
4. Letter, Solomon Schechter to Samuel Poznanski, 1902, quoted in Max Arzt, "The Legacy of Solomon Schechter," *Conservative Judaism* 11, no. 2 (Winter 1957): 8. JTS, 3080 Broadway, New York, NY 10027, *Annual Registers,* 1904–1917. Greenstone, "Reminiscences," pp. 9–10. Arthur Hertzberg, "The Conservative Rabbinate: A Sociological Study," in Joseph L. Blau [and others], *Essays on Jewish Life and Thought* (New York: Columbia University Press, 1959), pp. 309–32.
5. *Recorder* (USA) 3, no. 4 (October 1923): 4, 11–13; 4, no. 1 (January 1924): 2; 4, no. 3 (June–July 1924): 15.
6. Louis Finkelstein, "The Seminary as a Center of Jewish Learning," in *The Jewish Theological Seminary of America,* pp. 163–77. Simon Greenberg, "A Tribute to Professor Alexander Marx," *Conservative Judaism* 4, no. 2 (February 1948): 2–4. Julius H. Greenstone, "Louis Ginzberg: An Appreciation," in Milton Berger, Joel S. Geffen and M. David Hoffman, eds., *Roads to Jewish Survival: Essays, Biographies, and Articles* (New York: National Federation of Jewish Men's Clubs, 1967), pp. 26–32. "Discussion," Rabbinical Assembly, *Proceedings* 12 (1948), pp. 134–66 (especially p. 149). Arthur Cohen, "The Seminary and the Modern Rabbi," *Conservative Judaism* 13, no. 3 (Spring 1959): 1–12. Arthur Hertzberg, "Professor Louis Ginzberg," *Conservative Judaism* 20, no. 1 (Fall 1965): 19–22. Bernard Heller, "Looking Back at the Seminary," *Conservative Judaism* 23, no. 3 (Spring 1969): 42–51. Simon Greenberg, then vice-chancellor of the seminary, noted in 1960 the "widespread feeling among alumni and students that their professors have or had little respect for the American rabbinate as a profession or the American rabbi as a Jewish spiritual leader"; see Rabbinical Assembly, *Proceedings* 24 (1960), p. 135.
7. *Letters,* pp. 256–61. On Adler as a "safe" choice for president, see Ginzberg, *Keeper of the Law,* p. 133.

8. Max J. Routtenberg, "The Rabbinical Assembly of America," Rabbinical Assembly, *Proceedings* 24 (1960), p. 196.

9. Mordecai M. Kaplan, "From Strength to Strength," in *Roads to Jewish Survival,* p. 161.

10. *Recorder* (USA) 1, no. 1 (January 1921): 1.

11. *Annual Reports,* (USA) 1913–1919, passim.

12. Letter, Samuel M. Cohen to Philip C. Joslin, 8 February 1924, at Temple Emanu-El, Providence, Rhode Island, 02906.

13. Letter, Philip C. Joslin to Samuel M. Cohen, 21 February 1924, at Temple Emanu-El, Providence, Rhode Island, 02906. Louis B. Rubinstein, "Temple Emanu-El of Providence: The First Half Century," typescript, at Temple Emanu-El, Providence, Rhode Island, 02906.

14. *Recorder* (USA) 7, no. 3 (July 1927): 7. *Review* (USA) 11, no. 1 (January 1958): 18; 18, no. 3 (January 1966): 14. Silverman, "Conservative Judaism," p. 109. Wolfe Kelman, "The American Synagogue: Present and Prospects," *Conservative Judaism* 26, no. 1 (Fall 1971): 5. The United Synagogue's first period of rapid growth did not occur without serious dissension and the creation, by several rabbis and JTS faculty, of a rival organization—the Society of the Jewish Renascence; see Rubenovitz, *The Waking Heart,* pp. 57–67.

15. *Recorder* (USA) 14, no. 1 (Spring 1961): p. 1. *Conservative Judaism* 10, no. 4 (Summer 1956): p. 22–25, 74. Marc Lee Raphael, *Jews and Judaism in a Midwestern Community: Columbus, Ohio 1840–1975* (Columbus: Ohio Historical Society, 1979), p. 383 (less than 10 percent observed *kashrut* outside their home and less than 5 percent fully observed the Sabbath). Charles S. Liebman and Saul Shapiro, "A Survey of the Conservative Movement and Some of its Religious Attitudes," report submitted to the chancellor and faculty of the Jewish Theological Seminary of America (3080 Broadway, New York, NY 10027, 11 November 1979), pp. 1, 7. Rebecca Gordon, "The Religious Ideology of Conservative Jews," unpublished master's thesis, Hebrew Union College (Los Angeles), 1981. See also Marshall Sklare, "Recent Developments in Conservative Judaism," *Midstream* 18, no. 1 (January 1972): 3–19.

16. Abraham J. Heschel, "The Religious Basis of Race Equality," *Review* (USA) 16, no. 2 (Summer 1963): 5–6. Abraham J. Heschel, "What Happens to Them Happens to Me—and to You," *Review* (USA), 16, no. 4 (Winter 1964): 14, 26–27. Herbert D. Teitelbaum, "Lest We Forget," *Review* (USA), 18, no. 1 (July 1965): 8–11. Louis Levitsky, "This Is Not a War of National Defense," *Review* (USA) 20, no. 2 (July 1967): 13, 15. Joel Yor, "In the Ranks of the Marchers," *Review* (USA) 16, no. 3 (Autumn 1963): 14–17. Robert Leifert, "Tzedek Tzedek Tirdof: United Synagogue Youth and Social Action," *Review* (USA) 22, no. 1 (Spring 1969): 12–13. Lowell Bellin, "City Hall's Secret Weapon: United Synagogue Youth Peace Corps," *Review* (USA) 17, no. 4. (Winter 1965): 11–13. Kelman, "The American Synagogue," 17.

Not all the Conservative leaders, of course, agreed with every position taken by the national organizations. Professor Seymour Siegel, for example, defended the American involvement in Vietnam as late as 1967; "War Is Sometimes Tragically Necessary," *Review* (USA) 20, no. 2 (July 1967): 12, 14.

17. Walter Ackerman, "The Day School in the Conservative Movement," *Conservative Judaism* 15, no. 2 (Winter 1961): 46–57 (especially on the origins of the day school movement in the Conservative movement). Walter Ackerman, "The Story of a Conservative Day School," *Review* (USA) 12, no. 2 (Summer 1959): 8–9. *Review* (USA) 19, no. 1 (April 1966): 4; 22, no. 2 (Summer 1969): 16–17. Morton Siegel, "A Hebrew High School Grows in Brooklyn," *Review* (USA) 21, no. 4 (January 1969): 10–11. *Review* (USA) 34, no. 1 (Spring 1982): 3. Bernard Segal, "Why the Conservative Movement Is Opposed to Government Aid to Parochial Schools," *Review* (USA) 24, no. 1 (Spring 1971): 6–7. David Lieber, "The Conservative Congregational School," *Conservative Judaism* 27, no. 4 (Summer 1973): 24–34.

18. USA, *They Dared to Dream: A History of National Women's League of the United Synagogue of America* (New York: United Synagogue of America National Women's League, 1967). Women's League for Conservative Judaism, *News,* 18 November 1982.

19. *Recorder* (USA) 3, no. 1 (January 1923): 1, 22–23. *Review* (USA) 15, no. 4 (Winter 1963): 10; 17, no. 2 (Summer 1964): 22; 22, no. 4 (Winter 1970): 1–8; 34, no. 1 (Spring 1982): 1–11. Stephen C. Lerner, "Ramah and Its Critics," *Conservative Judaism* 25, no. 4 (Summer 1971): 1–28. See also the Young People's League (YPL) *Jewish Youth Journal,* especially vol. 1 (1937–38).

20. Rabbinical Assembly, *Proceedings* 24 (1960), p. 189. *Review* (USA) 11, no. 1 (January 1958): 24.

21. Routtenberg, "The Rabbinical Assembly," pp. 190–222. Aaron H. Blumenthal, "The Status of the Rabbinical Assembly in the Conservative Movement," Rabbinical Assembly, *Proceedings* 19 (1955), pp. 126–40. Simon Greenberg, "The Role of the Rabbinical Assembly: A Look Toward the Future," Rabbinical Assembly, *Proceedings* 34 (1970), pp. 96–108.

22. Joint Prayer Book Commission of the Rabbinical Assembly and the United Synagogue of America, *Sabbath and Festival Prayer Book* (New York: Rabbinical Assembly of America and United Synagogue of America, 1946). Rubenovitz, *The Waking Heart,* pp. 139–40, 148–53. Rabbinical Assembly, *Proceedings* 24 (1960), pp. 266–67, 284. Robert Gordis, "A Jewish Prayer Book for Our Times," *The Torch* (March 1947): 381–89.

CHAPTER 6

1. Hyman B. Grinstein, *The Rise of the Jewish Community of New York, 1654–1860* (Philadelphia: Jewish Publication Society, 1945). Barnett A. Elzas, *The Jews of South Carolina from the Earliest Times to the Present Day* (Philadelphia: J. B. Lippincott, 1905). Herbert T. Ezekiel and Gaston Lichtenstein, *The History of the Jews of Richmond from 1769 to 1917* (Richmond: H. T. Ezekiel, 1917), p. 239.

2. Edwin Wolf II and Maxwell Whiteman, *The History of the Jews of Philadelphia from Colonial Times to the Age of Jackson* (Philadelphia: Jewish Publication Society, 1957), pp. 116–19.

3. Minute books, Mikve Israel, 25 August 1782, in Wolf and Whiteman, *History,* p. 126. On the power of the *parnass,* see *Publications of the American Jewish Historical Society* 21 (1913): 2–3, 83–89, 95, 103–104, 112–113, 158–59.

4. *Publications of the American Jewish Historical Society* 21 (1913): 45.

5. Morris A. Gutstein, *The Story of the Jews of Newport: Two and a Half Centuries of Judaism, 1658–1908* (New York: Bloch Pub. Co., 1936), p. 131. Jacob Rader Marcus, *Early American Jewry: The Jews of Pennsylvania and the South, 1655–1790* (Philadelphia: Jewish Publication Society, 1953), p. 459.

6. Wolf and Whiteman, *History,* p. 125. *Publications of the American Jewish Historical Society* 21 (1913): 50, 73, 74. See also, in the latter, pp. 51, 66, 75, 89, 97–98, 158–59.

7. Wolf and Whiteman, *History,* pp. 225, 231. Israel Goldstein, *A Century of Judaism in New York: B'nai Jeshurun 1825–1925, New York's Oldest Ashkenazic Congregation* (New York: Cong. B'nai Jeshurun, 1930), pp. 51–52. David Philipson, "The Jewish Pioneers of the Ohio Valley," *Publications of the American Jewish Historical Society* 8 (1900): 49.

8. Goldstein, *A Century,* p. 51. Jeffrey Kaplan, "A History of Brith Shalom Beth Israel Congregation," [Charleston, South Carolina], 1975, typescript.

9. Wolf and Whiteman, *History,* p. 234. Selig Adler and Thomas E. Connolly, *From Ararat to Suburbia: The History of the Jewish Community of Buffalo* (Philadelphia: Jewish Publication Society, 1960), pp. 60, 70. Goldstein, *A Century,* pp. 81, 83. Fein, *The Making of an American Jewish Community,* pp. 50–51.

10. Israel Tabak, "Rabbi Abraham Rice of Baltimore: Pioneer of Orthodox Judaism in America," *Tradition* 7, no. 2 (Summer 1965): 100–20.

11. Nearly every Orthodox congregation whose records exist had a *mikveh* in the nineteenth century, including synagogues in Buffalo (by 1849), New York (by 1833), Syracuse (by 1851), and Rochester (by 1858). This fact contradicts the conclusion of Charles Liebman in "Orthodoxy in American Jewish Life," *American Jewish Year Book* 66 (1965): 28.

12. Stuart E. Rosenberg, *The Jewish Community in Rochester, 1843–1925* (New York: American Jewish Historical Society, 1954), pp. 21–22.

13. Wise, *Reminiscences,* p. 45.

14. Abraham J. Karp, "New York Chooses a Rabbi," *Publications of the American Jewish Historical Society* 44 (1955): 129–98. David De Sola Pool and Tamar De Sola Pool, *An Old Faith in the New World: Portrait of Shearith Israel, 1654–1954* (New York: Columbia University Press, 1955), p. 385.

15. Karp, "New York," p. 136. Erich Rosenthal, "The Jews of Boro Park," *Journal of Jewish Sociology* 22, no. 2 (December 1980): 190–91.

16. Nathan Glazer, *American Judaism* (Chicago: University of Chicago, 1957), p. 38. Edward Steiner, *The Immigrant Tide* (New York: F. H. Revell, 1909), p. 176.

17. Karp, "New York," pp. 130–31. *Jewish Messenger,* 7 July 1882, quoted in Jeremiah J. Berman, "The Trend in Jewish Religious Observance in Mid-Nineteenth-Century America," *Publications of the American Jewish Historical Society* 37 (1947): 44.

18. Moses Weinberger, *People Walk on Their Heads,* trans. by Jonathan D. Sarna (New York: Holmes and Meier, 1887, 1981), p. 22. Leibman, "Orthodoxy," p. 28.

19. Liebman, "Orthodoxy," pp. 27–28. Liebman's suggestion finds documentation in an early twentieth-century description of New York City Orthodoxy; see Edmund L. James, *The Immigrant Jew in America* (New York: B. F. Buck and Co., 1906), pp. 150–51, 174.

20. Karp, "New York." For a description of Jacob Joseph's activities in New York, see Benjamin L. Gordon, *Between Two Worlds: The Memoirs of a Physician* (New York: Bookman Associates, 1952), pp. 142–43.

21. *American Israelite,* 23 December 1887, quoted in Karp, "New York," p. 152. *American Israelite,* 30 March 1888, quoted in Karp, p. 184. Judah D. Eisenstein, *Otsar Zichronotai,* in Hebrew (New York: By the author, 1929), p. 268.

22. James, *Immigrant Jew,* p. 165. Joseph Lookstein, "Rabbi Moses Margolies: High Priest of Kehilath Jeshurun," in *Congregation Kehilath Jeshurun Diamond Jubilee Year Book* (New York: Kehilath Jeshurun, 1946), pp. 48–51. Each of the men listed has been called a communal "chief rabbi" by one or more historians; see, for example, Louis J. Swichkow and Lloyd P. Gartner, *The History of the Jews of Milwaukee* (Philadelphia: Jewish Publication Society, 1963), p. 483 ("Scheinfeld was the recognized rabbinical head of all the orthodox congregations . . .").

23. Eugene Markovitz, "Henry Pereira Mendes: Architect of the Union of Orthodox Jewish Congregations of America," *American Jewish Historical Quarterly* 55 (1966): 390.

24. De Sola Pool, *An Old Faith,* pp. 193–95.

25. Judah Isaacs, "Abraham J. G. Lesser," in Leo Jung, ed., *Guardians of Our Heritage* (New York: Bloch, 1958), p. 352. Moshe Davis, "Jewish Religious Life and Institutions in America," in *The Jews: Their History, Culture, and Religion,* Louis Finkelstein, ed., 3rd ed., vol. 1 (Philadelphia: Jewish Publication Society, 1960), p. 539.

CHAPTER 7

1. *Jewish Gazette,* 17 June 1898, English Supplement, pp. 1–2. *American Hebrew,* 4 January 1901.

2. Union of Orthodox Jewish Congregations of America (UOJCA), 45 West 36 Street, New York, NY 10018, *Second Biennial Convention* (21 June 1903), (Philadelphia: UOJCA, 1903), p. 34.

3. UOJCA, *Second Biennial Convention,* p. 158. *American Jewish Year Book* 5663 (1902–1903). *American Hebrew* 4 January 1901; 27 January 1903.

4. Salo Wittmayer Baron, *Steeled by Adversity: Essays and Addresses on American Jewish Life* (Philadelphia: Jewish Publication Society, 1971), p. 182. Herman H. Rubenovitz and Mignon L. Rubenovitz, *The Waking Heart,* p. 28.

5. See, for example, James, *Immigrant Jew,* p. 174.

6. Congregation Tifereth Israel, *A Record of the Early Years* [1902–1930] (Greenport [Long Island], N.Y., 1978), courtesy Oscar Goldin of Greenport. Not all Orthodox congrega-

tions, of course, were poor; Chicago's Anshe Kenesseth Israel, early in the twentieth century, had 200 members, twenty Torah scrolls, and a building valued at $35,000; see James, *Immigrant Jew*, p. 174.

7. *The Orthodox Union* 1, no. 3 (October 1933): 1; 2, no. 5 (February 1935): 1. "Membership," UOJCA (New York), courtesy Bracha Osofsky. UOJCA, *Jewish Action*, passim. The figure 3,000, announced by the UOJCA in 1969, was for the first time qualified by the explanation that this was actually the estimated number of Orthodox synagogues in America, and that the "overwhelming majority affiliated with the Union." See *New York Times*, 1 December 1969, p. 36.

8. UOJCA, *1947 Year Book*, pp. 14–22.

9. *New York Times*, 17 July 1966, p. 59; 19 March 1967, p. 61. UOJCA, *70th Annual Convention*, November 1970 (Washington, D.C.), p. 31. Jack Simcha Cohen, "The Orthodox Synagogue: Challenges of the Inner City and Suburbia," *Jewish Life* 2: 2–3 (Fall–Winter 1977–1978): 67–72. Although the UOJCA meets biennially, it often refers to its conventions as "annual" and numbers them as if they took place every year.

10. UOJCA, *33rd Annual Convention*, July 1933 (New York), p. 17. UOJCA, *40th Annual Convention*, May 1938 (Atlantic City), p. 18. UOJCA. *56th Biennial Convention*, 25–28, October 1956 (Atlantic City), p. 21.

11. UOJCA, *Second Biennial Convention*, p. 37.

12. Herbert S. Goldstein, "Kashrut and Union Supervision," *The Orthodox Union* 1: no. 1 (August 1933): 4. UOJCA, *27th Annual Convention*, 24–26 October 1925 (New York City), p. 8. UOJCA, *Jewish Life*, passim. Harold P. Gastwirth, *Fraud, Corruption and Holiness: The Controversy over the Supervision of the Jewish Dietary Practices in New York, 1881–1940* (Port Washington, N.Y.: Kennikat Press, 1974).

13. UOJCA, *38th Annual Convention*, April 1936 (New York City), p. 13. UOJCA. *62nd Annual Convention*, November 1960 (Atlantic City), p. 20. UOJCA, *65th Annual Convention*, June 1963. See, for example, the twenty-one resolutions unanimously ratified on 26 November 1982, in the *84th Annual Convention* (Vernon Valley, New Jersey), or the substantive effort to save the "deteriorating religious life" in Latin America at the Washington, D.C., 1968 "biennial" convention. All these reports are in the UOJCA archives.

14. UOJCA, *Jewish Action* (Fall 1982, Winter 1983).

15. Weinberger, *Jews and Judaism in New York*, pp. 33–39, 53–56. Agudath Israel of America, *The Struggle and the Splendor* (New York: Agudath Israel, 1982), p. 35.

16. Gilbert Klaperman, *The Story of Yeshiva University* (Toronto: Macmillan, 1969), chap. 1.

17. Klaperman, *Story*, chap. 2, p. 237.

18. Klaperman, *Story*, chaps. 4, 5. William B. Helmreich, "Old Wine in New Bottles: Advanced Yeshivot in the United States," *American Jewish History* 69, no. 2 (December 1979): 235. RIETS's oldest student ever may have been Abraham L. Raich, who at age fifty-eight left the CF&I Steel Corporation in Pueblo, Colorado, to enter RIETS and begin four years of study for the rabbinate. See *New York Times*, 30 October 1980, Part 4, p. 6.

19. Klaperman, *Story*, chaps. 6, 7.

20. *Union of Orthodox Rabbis of the United States and Canada Jubilee Volume* (1902–1927), in Hebrew (New York: Union of Orthodox Rabbis, 1928), p. 24.

21. Aaron Rothkoff, *Bernard Revel: Builder of American Jewish Orthodoxy* (Philadelphia: Jewish Publication Society, 1972).

22. These figures come from scattered pamphlets in the Yeshiva University Library, 500 West 185 Street, New York, N.Y. 10033.

23. Leo Levi, "The Torah and Secular Studies," *Jewish Life*, 4, no. 1 (Spring 1980): 41–44. On the aborted merger, see Rothkoff, *Bernard Revel*, pp. 94–114.

24. Rothkoff, *Bernard Revel*, pp. 115–23, 135–57. Louis Bernstein, "Generational Conflict in American Orthodoxy: The Early Years of Rabbinical Council of America," *American Jewish History* 69, no. 2 (December 1979): 228. Aaron Rakeffet-Rothkoff, *The Silver*

Years in American Orthodoxy: Rabbi Eliezer Silver and His Generation (Jerusalem and New York: Yeshiva University Press, 1981), pp. 264–71.

25. Rothkoff, *Bernard Revel,* pp. 111, 164–66, 175. Ira Robinson, "Cyrus Adler, Bernard Revel, and the Prehistory of Organized Jewish Scholarship in the United States," *American Jewish History* 69, no. 4 (June 1980): 497–505. New York *Times,* 7 November, 1966, p. 4; 15 November 1966, p. 26; 27 November 1966, p. 70.

26. Jewish Telegraphic Agency *Bulletin,* 23 September 1973. Klaperman, *Story,* p. 183.

27. *Catalogues* (1956, 1957, 1958) in the Yeshiva University Library.

28. Klaperman, *Story,* chap. 11. New York *Times,* 19 September 1962, p. 59; 16 February 1969, Part 8, p. 1; 11 June 1982, Part 2, p. 3.

29. New York *Times,* 30 April 1970, p. 30; 14 December 1970, p. 16; 6 March 1980, Part 2, p. 5; 15 November 1981, p. 58.

30. Saul Adelson, "Chicago's Hebrew Theological College," in UOJCA, *1947 Year Book,* pp. 160–68.

31. On Abraham Jacob Gershon Lesser, see Judah M. Issac's essay in Leo Jung, ed., *Guardians of Our Heritage* (New York: Bloch, 1958), pp. 347–59.

32. Rothkoff, *Bernard Revel,* p. 14. Union of Orthodox Rabbis (UOR), *Union of Orthodox Rabbis Jubilee Volume,* pp. 19–21. M. S. Margolies, "The Union of Orthodox Rabbis of the United States and Canada," in *The Jewish Communal Register of New York City 1917–18,* 2nd ed. (New York, 1918), pp. 1180–88. *Union of Orthodox Rabbis Jubilee Volume,* pp. 19–24.

33. UOR, *Union of Orthodox Rabbis Jubilee Volume,* passim.

34. UOR, *Union of Orthodox Rabbis Jubilee Volume,* pp. 21–23. For a summary, in English, of the first fifteen years of UOR activity, under the headings foreign affairs, home affairs, and religious education, see UOJCA, *Reports, Etc. of the Sixth Convention,* 29 June 1913 (New York, 1913).

35. *Brooklyn Jewish Center Review* (October 1955). UOR, *Union of Orthodox Rabbis Jubilee Volume,* pp. 2–24. At the 1922 convention in Lakewood, New Jersey, for example, the rabbis cabled the political leaders gathered at San Remo and urged them to help Jews attain the goals of the Balfour Declaration.

36. Letter, Union of Orthodox Rabbis to Henry Pereira Mendes, in *American Hebrew,* 30 July 1904, p. 282.

37. Court suits over mixed seating included those heard in Hamilton County, Ohio, Probate Court (1954), Macomb County, Michigan, Circuit Court (1955), and New Orleans Civil District Court (1957, 1961); see typescript summaries in the UOR archives 235 East Broadway, New York, NY, 10002 and Baruch Litvin, ed., *The Sanctity of the Synagogue* (New York: Spero Foundation, 1959), pp. 53–77, 345–419.

38. In 1937 the UOR issued a Hebrew booklet, *Unto the Last Generation,* listing 1,500 rabbis who favored making no changes in the laws affecting the *agunah.* These laws sustained perpetual widowhood for women whose husbands deserted them or disappeared from view, and left the woman without a legal Jewish divorce and hence unable to marry again.

39. See the scattered, typescript proceedings in the UOR archives (New York City).

40. Bernstein, "Generational Conflict," *The Orthodox Union* 3, no. 11 (July–August, 1936).

41. Louis Bernstein, *Challenge and Mission* (New York: Shengold, 1982), passim.

42. Compiled from typescript proceedings of the Rabbinical Council of America (RCA) annual conventions at the RCA in New York.

43. Compiled from typescript proceedings of the RCA, 1250 Broadway, New York, NY 10001. New York *Times,* 6 July 1969, p. 35. *Rabbinical Council Record* 24, no. 6 (May 1979). In 1982 the RCA published a pharmaceutical guide to more than 1,400 medications in order to make available, to doctors whose patients observed Passover strictly, the necessary technical information about starch, alcohol, yeast, and other grain derivatives. See David Hurwitz and John D. Loike, comps., *Passover Medication: A Guide for Physicians and Rabbis* (New York: Rabbinical Council of America, 1982).

44. Jewish Telegraphic Agency (JTA), *Bulletin,* 29 December 1954. A few months earlier

the National Council of Young Israel had urged Orthodox Jews never to attend Conservative worship or religious services; see JTA, *Bulletin*, 14 September 1954. See also *New York Times*, 9 March 1956, p. 20, and RCA *Proceedings, 20th Annual Convention, Fallsburg, New York* [June 1956]. For other antagonistic actions of the RAA toward Reform and Conservative Judaism, see JTA, *Bulletin*, 1 June 1956, and *American Jewish Year Book* 60 (1959): 59.

45. RCA, *Proceedings, 20th Annual Convention* [1956]. RCA, *Proceedings, 22nd Annual Convention, Miami Beach, Florida* [July 1958]. Rabbi Hollander's fierce opposition to Orthodox rabbinical participation with non-Orthodox rabbis remained as strong two decades later; see *Rabbinical Council Record* 24, no. 2 (March 1977) pp. 1–2.

46. RCA, *Proceedings, 25th Annual Convention, Atlantic City, N.J.* [April 1961]. *Rabbinical Council Record* 26, no. 6 (May 1981); 27, no. 3 (April 1982). This issue did not die easily. At Agudath Israel's forty-fifth annual dinner (1967), its most revered rabbinical sage, Moshe Feinstein, condemned Orthodox rabbis and laypeople who engaged in "dangerous exercises" such as interfaith dialogue or who participated in "mixed" Jewish bodies such as the Synagogue Council; see *Struggle and Splendor*, pp. 118–19.

47. See especially Rabbi Fabian Schonfeld's address at the thirty-ninth annual convention, June 1975, in the *Proceedings, 39th Annual Convention* [1975].

48. *Rabbinical Council Record*, passim.

49. Moses H. Hoenig, "In Retrospect: Twenty Years of Young Israel," in Council of Young Israel, *Convention Annual 5692 (New York, 1932), 20th Anniversary*, pp. 20–21.

50. Of the fifty-nine Young Israel synagogues in 1945, thirty were in New York City, Bronx, Queens, and Brooklyn, two in Canada, and twenty-seven in other American cities. See *Young Israel Viewpoint* 11 Nisan 5705 (25 March 1945).

CHAPTER 8

1. *Tradition* 20, no. 1 (Spring 1982): 58. Nearly forty years earlier Robert Gordis noted that the term "orthodoxy" applies "not to *one* but to *three* groups in Jewish life"; see *The Young Israel Viewpoint*, Tammuz 5705 (June 1945), p. 4.

2. The Jewish Statistical Bureau, in a January 1952 survey, found that only 2,577 of 3,876 synagogues in the United States and Canada even had rabbis; see *American Jewish Year Book* 54 (1953): 98.

3. Liebman, "Orthodoxy," pp. 24–25, 55. Bernard Drachman, "The Task of the Jewish Congregation in America," in *The First Hungarian Congregation Oheb Zedek, 1873–1923, Golden Jubilee Volume* ([New York], 1923).

4. On advanced *yeshivot* or Talmudic academies, see William Helmreich, *The World of the Yeshiva: An Intimate Portrait of Orthodox Jewry* (New York: Free Press, 1982). *Tradition* 20, no. 1 (Spring 1982): 11, 22.

5. For the platform, see UOJCA, *Second Biennial Convention*, 21 June 1903 (Philadelphia, 1903).

6. *Tradition* 20, no. 1 (Spring 1982): 7.

7. Leo Jung, ed., *The Jewish Library*, vol. 1: *Faith* (London: Soncino Press, 1968), p. 5. Samuel Belkin, *Essays in Traditional Jewish Thought* (New York: Philosophical Library, 1956), p. 36. Editors of *Commentary* [Magazine], *The Condition of Jewish Belief* (New York: Macmillan, 1966), pp. 23, 59, 124, 236. Emanuel Rackman, "American Orthodoxy: Retrospect and Prospect," in Theodore Friedman and Robert Gordis, eds., *Jewish Life in America* (New York: Horizon Press, 1955), p. 34.

8. See B. Barry Levy, "Artscroll: An Overview," in Marc Lee Raphael, ed., *Approaches to Modern Judaism* (Chico, Calif.: Scholars Press, 1983), pp. 111–40.

9. *Condition of Jewish Belief*, pp. 125, 180. See also Belkin, *Essays*, p. 117.

10. *Condition of Jewish Belief*, p. 61.

11. *Condition of Jewish Belief*, p. 237. *Jewish Life in America*, p. 33.

12. Eliezer Berkovits, "Authentic Judaism and Halakhah," *Judaism* 19, no. 1 (Winter 1970): 66, 72.

13. Rackman, *One Man's Judaism* (New York: Philosophical Library, 1970), p. 3. Berkovits, "Conversion 'According to Halakhah'—What is it?" *Judaism* 23, no. 4 (Fall 1974): 467–74.
14. Leon D. Stitskin, ed., *Studies in Torah Judaism* (New York: Yeshiva University Press, 1969), p. 8.
15. A sea of *halachic* literature on electricity appeared in the 1970s.
16. *Tradition* 7, no. 2 (Summer 1965): 52. Abraham R. Besdin, *Reflections of the Rav: Lessons in Jewish Thought* (Jerusalem: World Zionist Organization, 1979). J. David Bleich, in *Contemporary Halachic Problems* (New York: Ktav, 1977), also demonstrates the Orthodox concern for extending Torah and *halachah* into every corner of the world—and the moon.
17. Berkovits, "Conversion"; Rackman, *One Man's Judaism.*
18. Samuel Halperin, *The Political World of American Zionism* (Detroit: Wayne State University Press, 1961), p. 8. Hyman B. Grinstein, "Orthodox Judaism and Early Zionism in America," in Isidore S. Meyer, ed., *Early History of Zionism in America* (New York: Arno Press, 1977), pp. 219–27.
19. Samuel Rosenblatt, *The History of the Mizrachi Movement* (New York: Mizrachi Organization of America, 1951), pp. 28–33.
20. Agudath Israel of America, *The Struggle and the Splendor.* The 1940 convention proposed the transfer of Agudath's world headquarters to New York, and this shift took place in 1941. See *Contemporary Jewish Record* 3, no. 5 (September–October 1940): 532.

CHAPTER 9

1. David Singer, "The *Yeshiva* World," *Commentary* 62, no. 4 (October 1976): 70–74. *Tradition* 20, no. 1 (Spring 1982): 47.
2. *Tradition* 20, no. 1 (Spring 1982): 53, 65. Liebman, "Orthodoxy," p. 69.
3. In addition to Torah Umesorah press releases, collected at the Blaustein Library of the American Jewish Committee, 165 East 56 Street, New York, NY 10023, see Alvin I. Schiff, *The Jewish Day School Movement in America* (New York, 1966), pp. 49, 245–46. New York *Times,* 25 May 1964, p. 67.
4. New York *Times,* 4 February 1971, p. 8; 27 November 1971, p. 20; 27 January 1972, p. 11; 17 November 1972, p. 9.
5. Agudath Israel of America, The *Struggle and the Splendor,* (New York, 1982) p. 172.
6. Agudath Israel, *Struggle and Splendor,* pp. 123–40. *Jewish Press,* 15 July 1983, p. 37.
7. For an interesting attempt to distinguish "modern" from "traditional" Orthodox, see Samuel C. Heilman, "Inner and Outer Identities: Sociological Ambivalence Among Orthodox Jews," *Jewish Social Studies* 39, no. 3 (Summer 1977): 227–40. And for provocative reflections on the "modernity" of Orthodoxy, see Shlomo Riskin, "Where Modern Orthodoxy Is At—And Where It Is Going," *Jewish Life* 1 (Spring 1976): 27–31.
8. New York *Times,* 17 December 1978, Part 11, p. 22; 14 February 1982, Part 21, p. 3. Los Angeles *Times,* 2 July 1978, Part 8, p. 12. New York *Times,* 15 March 1976, p. 35.
9. Recent discussions of *baale teshuvot* include Yaakov Jacobs, "Teshuva: The Jew's Return to His Origins—The State of the Art in 5740/1980," *Jewish Life* 3, no. 4 (Winter 1979–1980): 3–9. Harold Fisch, "Alienation: An Ideological Basis for Return," *Jewish Life* 3, no. 4 (Winter 1979–1980): 11–23. Barbara Soferr, "Return: A Case History," *Jewish Life* 3, no. 4 (Winter 1979–1980): 37–43. Ralph Pelcovitz, "The Teshuva Phenomenon: The Other Side of the Coin," *Jewish Life* 4, no. 3 (Fall 1980): 15–21. "The Teshuva Phenomenon: Responses from Our Readers," *Jewish Life* 4, no. 4 (Winter 1980–1981): 23–29. Abby Mendelson, "The Long Journey Back," *Pittsburgh* (December 1980): 45–49. Typical praise for a successful ministry among "repenters" is found in *Jewish Life* 3, no. 3 (Fall 1979): 49—"one of the most renowned and successful leaders of the American orthodox community, having brought large numbers of Jewish youth back to the fold of Torah."

10. Marvin Schick, "Borough Park: A Jewish Settlement," *Jewish Life* 3, no. 2 (Winter 1979): 23–35. Bernard Weinberger, "Confessions of an Orthodox Rabbi or A Tale of Three Bridges," *Jewish Life* 1 (1975–1976): 15–27. New York *Times,* 22 June 1983, p. 18.

11. New York *Times,* 27 June 1959, p. 25; 7 June 1962, p. 28; 25 September 1963, p. 36; 31 October 1976, p. 56.

12. Harry Steinberg, "New Square," *The Times of Israel* (March 1974): 3–8. New York *Times,* 14 July 1961, p. 20; 18 July 1971, p. 48.

13. New York *Times* 18 July 1975, p. 33.

14. *Jewish Telegraphic Agency (JTA) Daily News Bulletin,* 24 December 1976. Elaine Starkman, "Habad House: A Pad for Torah Rapping," *Hadassah Magazine* (March 1973): 12–13 (the Habad House at the University of California at Berkeley). Elaine Starkman, "Glimpsing Another World," *Present Tense* 7, no. 1. (Autumn 1979): 14–16 (a Habad week for Jewish women at Lake Tahoe). J. Immanuel Schochet, "The Philosophy of Lubavitch Activism," *Tradition* 13, no. 1 (Summer 1972): 18–35. Isidore Haiblum, "The Mitzvah Mobiles of Manhattan," *Moment* 1 (Spring 1975): 62–66. *The Lubavitcher Rebbe: A Brief Biography* (Brooklyn: Merkes L'inyonei Chinuch, 1979), pp. 12–20.

15. New York *Times,* 8 October 1972, p. 135.

16. For accounts of hostilities between Hasidic Jews, hispanics, and blacks in Brooklyn, see New York *Times,* 27 May 1964, p. 1; 22 November 1967, p. 7; 31 October 1971, Part 15, p. 9; 3 June 1973, p. 21; 5 June 1973, p. 19; 12 June 1973, p. 13; 12 November 1975, p. 47; 3 December 1978, p. 1; 10 December 1978, Part 4, p. 1; 18 June 1979, Part 2, p. 6; 26 October 1979, Part 2, p. 1; 27 October 1979, p. 23. "New Maccabees," *Reconstructionist* 30, no. 9 (12 June 1964): 4–5. Dorothy Rabinowitz, "Blacks, Jews and New York Politics," *Commentary* 66 no. 5 (November 1978): 42–47.

17. New York *Times,* 17 May 1963, p. 66; 16 June 1974, p. 86; 26 March 1982, Part 2, p. 6. Jewish Observer and Middle East Review 25, no. 42 (15 October 1976): 8.

18. New York *Times,* 1 June 1977, Part 2, p. 1; 29 October 1979, Part 2, p. 3. Bernard Weinberger, "Satmar and Lubavitch: The Dynamics of Disagreement," *Jewish Life,* Part 2, no. 2–3 (Fall–Winter 1977–1978): 55–65.

19. New York *Times,* 8 March 1981, Part 4, p. 6.

CHAPTER 10

1. Mordecai Kaplan, *Judaism as a Civilization* (New York: The Macmillan Co., 1934), p. xii. Kaplan, "The Way I Have Come," in Ira Eisenstein and Eugene Kohn, eds., *Mordecai M. Kaplan: An Evaluation* (New York: Jewish Reconstructionist Foundation, 1952), pp. 283–98. Mortimer J. Cohen, "Mordecai M. Kaplan as Teacher," in Ira Eisenstein and Eugene Kohn, eds., *Mordecai M. Kaplan: An Evaluation* (New York, 1952), pp. 3–14. Judah Cahn, "Mordecai Kaplan and Stephen S. Wise as Teachers," *Reconstructionist* 47, no. 5 (July–August 1981): 32–35. Harold S. Kushner, "Mordecai M. Kaplan: A Student Remembers His Teacher," *Conservative Judaism* 34, no. 4 (March–April 1981): 8. Israel B. Levinthal, "Professor Mordecai M. Kaplan: A Tribute on his Ninetieth Birthday," *Conservative Judaism* 25, no. 4 (Summer 1971): 29–32.

2. Kaplan, "The Way I Have Come," pp. 311–13. Kaplan, "A Program for the Reconstruction of Judaism," *Menorah Journal* (August 1920). Conversations at the Jewish Center and the Society for the Advancement of Judaism, 1 August 1983.

3. Herbert Rosenblum, "The Emergence of the Reconstructionist Movement," *Reconstructionist* 41, no. 4 (May 1975): 7–20. *Reconstructionist* 6, no. 1 (16 February 1940): 1. Kaplan, *Judaism as a Civilization,* p. xiii.

4. Kaplan, *Judaism as a Civilization,* pp. 91–169.

5. Kaplan, *Judaism as a Civilization.* See also Kaplan, *The Meaning of God in Modern Jewish Religion* (New York: Jewish Reconstructionist Foundation, 1947, 1962), pp. 57–61, 104–87.

6. Kaplan, *Judaism as a Civilization,* p. 399.

7. Kaplan, *Judaism as a Civilization,* p. 515. Samuel Dinin, "Mordecai M. Kaplan's Con-

cept of Organic Jewish Community," in Eisenstein and Kohn, eds., *Mordecai M. Kaplan: An Evaluation,* pp. 45–64.

8. On the rationale, function, and justification of ritual observances, see Mordecai M. Kaplan, "A Reply," *Reconstructionist* 7, no. 18 (9 January 1972): 12–19.

9. Kaplan, *Judaism as a Civilization,* p. 335. William E. Kaufman, "The Contemporary Relevance of Mordecai M. Kaplan's Philosophy," *Conservative Judaism* 34, no. 4 (March–April 1981): 12 ("Durkheim's influence was most decisive").

10. Kaplan, *Judaism as a Civilization,* pp. 511–22. Kaplan, "The Way I Have Come," p. 298.

11. Kaplan, *Meaning of God,* 25–30, 242–264, 294, 323–324, 330–368. Harold C. Weisberg, "Mordecai M. Kaplan's Theory of Religion," in Ira Eisenstein and Eugene Kohn, eds., *Mordecai M. Kaplan: An Evaluation* (New York, 1952), pp. 155–62. Henry N. Wieman, "Mordecai M. Kaplan's Idea of God", pp. 193–210. Kaplan, "The God Idea in Judaism," in Mordecai M. Kaplan, ed., *The Jewish Reconstructionist Papers* (New York: Behrman, 1936), p. 95.

12. Kaplan, *Judaism as a Civilization,* pp. 303–405. For a critique and a defense of Kaplan's attempt at "process" philosophy, see Eliezer Berkovits, "Reconstructionist Theology: A Critical Evaluation," in his *Major Themes in Modern Philosophies of Judaism* (New York: Ktav, 1974), pp. 149–91, and William E. Kaufman, "Mordecai M. Kaplan, Process Philosophy and the Problem of Evil," *Reconstructionist* 47, no. 5 (July–August 1981): 26–31.

13. Mordecai M. Kaplan, "The *New Haggadah,*" *Reconstructionist* 7, no. 5 (18 April 1941): 17–18. Editorial, *Reconstructionist* 7, no. 7 (16 May 1941): 5. Kaplan, *Meaning of God,* pp. 265–96.

14. *Reconstructionist* 11, no. 6 (11 May 1945): 8. "Introduction," *Sabbath Prayer Book* (New York: Jewish Reconstructionist Foundation, 1945), p. xvii.

15. For perceptive reflections on the *New Haggadah* and *Sabbath Prayer Book,* see David Polish, "Mordecai M. Kaplan and Jewish Liturgy," in Ira Eisenstein and Eugene Kohn, eds., *Mordecai M. Kaplan: An Evaluation* (New York, 1952), pp. 211–21.

16. New York *Times,* 15 June, p. 11; 6 September 1945, p. 12. *Time,* 25 June 1945. This particular reception of the Reconstructionist *Sabbath Prayer Book* by the Orthodox rabbinate was predicted by one Reconstructionist supporter, Ario S. Hyams, in the *Reconstructionist* 11, no. 15 (14 December 1945): 23–24.

17. Kaplan, "Introduction to 'Sabbath Services for the Modern Synagogue,' " *Reconstructionist* 10, no. 11 (6 October 1944): 9–15.

18. Kaplan, *Journals* 13–146. *Reconstructionist* 11, no. 13 (16 November 1945): 20.

19. *Reconstructionist* 2, no. 15 (27 November 1936): 3–4.

20. *Reconstructionist* 11, no. 6 (11 May 1945): 8. Mordecai Kaplan, "Reconstructionism as Both a Challenging and Unifying Influence," *Reconstructionist,* 10, no. 11 (6 October 1944): 16–21. See also *Reconstructionist* 7, no. 20 (6 February 1942): 17.

21. Kaplan, *The Reconstructionist Papers,* p. v.

22. Federation of Reconstructionist Congregations and Havurot, 2521 Broadway, New York, NY 10025 (FRCH), *Newsletter* (Fall 1981). FRCH, "23rd Annual Convention Program," 2–5 June 1983.

23. Jewish Reconstructionist Foundation (JRF), 2521 Broadway, New York, NY 10025, "By-Laws of the JRF, Inc.," June 1983.

24. Reconstructionist Rabbinical Association (RRA), Church Road and Greenwood Avenue, Wycote, PA 19095, "Guidelines on Religious Standards" (Philadelphia, 1980).

25. RRA, "Guidelines on Intermarriage," 16 March 1983.

CHAPTER 11

1. The founders of the Society for the Advancement of Judaism (SAJ) included Israel Unterberg (1863–1934), an immigrant shirt manufacturer, Bennett E. Siegelstein (1880–1974), an attorney and former state legislator, and Samuel C. Lamport (1880–1941), an

immigrant investment banker who served on the board of directors of numerous Jewish organizations.

2. *SAJ Review* 1–8 (1922–1928): passim. Ira Eisenstein, "Life and the Synagogue," *SAJ Review* 7, no. 35 (11 May 1928): 15–23.
3. *SAJ Review,* 1–8 (1922–1928).
4. Kaplan, "The Way I Have Come," p. 305.
5. *SAJ Review* 5, no. 4 (9 October 1925). Branches were also established in Scranton (1925), Wilkes-Barre (1926), and Hartford (1926).
6. *Reconstructionist* 6, no. 1 (16 February 1940): 1.
7. For early discussions of fellowships, see *Reconstructionist* 8, no. 17 (20 October 1942): 17. Nathan A. Barack, "The Role of the Religious Fellowship," *Reconstructionist* 11, no. 11 (19 October 1945): 8–12. *Reconstructionist* 11, no. 13 (16 November 1945): 20–23.
8. *Reconstructionist* 9, no. 1 (19 February 1943); 9, no. 18 (7 January 1944).
9. "A Step Forward for Reconstructionism," *Reconstructionist* 21, no. 9 (10 June 1955): 3; 26, no. 14 (18 November 1960): 3.
10. Federation of Reconstructionist Congregations and Havurot, *A History of Congregations and Havurot,* (New York: FRCH) May 1983.
11. Ira Eisenstein, "Whither Reconstructionism?" *Reconstructionist* 33, no. 11 (6 October 1967): 25–29; 33, no. 20 (9 February 1968): 3–5; 34, no. 4 (5 April 1968): 5–6.
12. Bernard Phillips, "When Religions Meet in Scholarly Dialogue," *Reconstructionist* 34, no. 1 (11 October 1968): 7–9. Ira Eisenstein, "The Reconstructionist Rabbinical College Is Dedicated," *Reconstructionist* 34, no. 13 (8 November 1968): 28–31.
13. "A Statement of Objectives of the Reconstructionist Rabbinical Fellowship," *Reconstructionist* 16, no. 19 (26 January 1951): 24–25.
14. See the exchange between Robert Gordis and Ira Eisenstein in *Conservative Judaism* 2, no. 4 (June 1946): 17–28; *Conservative Judaism* 3, no. 1 (November 1946): 21–25.
15. Alexander Burnstein, "Mordecai M. Kaplan's Contribution to Conservative Judaism," in Eisenstein and Kohn, eds., *Mordecai M. Kaplan: An Evaluation,* pp. 223–32. Roland B. Gittelsohn, "Mordecai M. Kaplan and Reform Judaism: A Study in Reciprocity," in Eisenstein and Kohn, eds., *Kaplan: An Evaluation,* pp. 233–42.
16. Charles Silberman, "Myth, Metaphor and Prayer," *Raayonot* 3, no. 2 (Spring 1983): 4–11. Jewish Reconstructionist Foundation Prayer Commission, "Prayer book: Tentative Principles," *Raayonot* 3, no. 2 (Spring 1983): 19–22.

Index